POETRY AND LAN

Michael Ferber's accessible introduction to poetry's unusual uses of language tackles a wide range of subjects from a linguistic point of view. Written with the non-expert in mind, the book explores current linguistic concepts and theories and applies them to a variety of major poetic features. Equally appealing to linguists who feel that poetry has been unjustly neglected, the broad field of investigation touches on meter, rhyme (and other sound-effects), onomatopoeia, syntax, meaning, metaphor, style, and translation, among other topics. The poetic examples are mainly in English, but the book also focuses on several French, Latin, Greek, German, and Japanese examples, to show what is different and far from inevitable in English. This original and unusually wide-ranging study delivers an engaging and often witty summary of how we define what poetry is.

MICHAEL FERBER is Professor Emeritus at the University of New Hampshire. His previous publications include *Romanticism: A Very Short Introduction* (2010), *The Cambridge Introduction to British Romantic Poetry* (Cambridge, 2012), and *A Dictionary of Literary Symbols, Third Edition* (Cambridge, 2017).

POETRY AND LANGUAGE

The Linguistics of Verse

MICHAEL FERBER

CAMBRIDGE
UNIVERSITY PRESS

CAMBRIDGE
UNIVERSITY PRESS

University Printing House, Cambridge CB2 8BS, United Kingdom

One Liberty Plaza, 20th Floor, New York, NY 10006, USA

477 Williamstown Road, Port Melbourne, VIC 3207, Australia

314–321, 3rd Floor, Plot 3, Splendor Forum, Jasola District Centre, New Delhi – 110025, India

79 Anson Road, #06–04/06, Singapore 079906

Cambridge University Press is part of the University of Cambridge.

It furthers the University's mission by disseminating knowledge in the pursuit of education, learning, and research at the highest international levels of excellence.

www.cambridge.org
Information on this title: www.cambridge.org/9781108429122
DOI: 10.1017/9781108554152

© Michael Ferber 2019

First published 2019

Printed and bound in Great Britain by Clays Ltd, Elcograf S.p.A.

A catalog record for this publication is available from the British Library.

Library of Congress Cataloging-in-Publication Data
NAMES: Ferber, Michael, author.
TITLE: Poetry and language : the linguistics of verse / Michael Ferber.
DESCRIPTION: New York, NY : Cambridge University Press, 2019. | Includes bibliographical references and index.
IDENTIFIERS: LCCN 2019008520 | ISBN 9781108429122 (hardback)
SUBJECTS: LCSH: Poetics. | Language and languages – Poetry. | BISAC: LITERARY CRITICISM / European / English, Irish, Scottish, Welsh.
CLASSIFICATION: LCC P311 .F47 2019 | DDC 808.1–dc23
LC record available at https://lccn.loc.gov/2019008520

ISBN 978-1-108-42912-2 Hardback
ISBN 978-1-108-45306-6 Paperback

To Charles and Helen Simic

Contents

Illustrations

Acknowledgments

I must first thank Rochelle Lieber, a distinguished linguist, for helping to inspire this book in the first place while we jointly taught two courses in linguistics and literature, and above all for carefully reading the typescript of this book at several stages. She saved me from quite a few technical mistakes and made good suggestions for improvements of many kinds. For her patience in the face of my sometimes stubborn idiosyncrasies and for her encouragement throughout, I am deeply grateful. I have been lucky to have her as a colleague at the University of New Hampshire.

Though I had been interested in foreign languages since high school, it was the theoretical work of Noam Chomsky in the 1960s that drew me to linguistics as a field. Other than a famous sentence that poets have seized on, he has written nothing, as far as I know, about poetry, but this book would never have come about without him. I am grateful too for his personal encouragement.

Lucy Arnold, Susan Arnold, Chase Ebert, Midge Goldberg, Martin McKinsey, and Paul Rowe have helped in various ways – Chase especially for commenting on an early version. I owe much to Ann Berthoff for ongoing conversations about metaphor.

And for many evenings of good food, wine, and talk, often about poetry, I am more indebted than I can say to Charles and Helen Simic.

Portions of Chapter 8 were published as "Causley's Version of Rimbaud: *Sleeper in a Valley,*" in Michael Hanke, ed., *Through the Granite Kingdom: Critical Essays on Charles Causley* (Trier: Wissenschaftlicher Verlag, 2011); and as "The the," in *Pusteblume* 9:1 (Spring 2018).

CHAPTER ONE

Introduction

This book is intended for readers who care about poetry, or who need to study it in university courses, but who know little about linguistics, and would like to know what, if anything, linguistics has to say about it. I hope the book also appeals to linguists who have paid little attention to poetry, but it is the first group that I have kept in mind. It arose out of lecture notes and class handouts for a course that drew mainly students of literature but also a few students of linguistics, as I was unable to find a textbook that covered even half the topics I wanted to deal with. Not surprisingly, it was the literature students who had the steeper learning curve, at least at first. Nonetheless, I will begin by talking about what poetry is, not what linguistics is. As it turned out, neither group of students found poetry easy to define.

What is poetry? What is a poem? To find agreement on brief and useful definitions of these words today, and of their kindred words "poet," "poetic," and the old-fashioned "poesy," is a difficult task, and maybe impossible, because these terms have been applied to widely different kinds of writing or oral speech in recent years, and even to things that are not composed of words at all; they have been applied by those who make such things, by publishers who put labels on them, and by consumers who read, hear, or contemplate them. If someone calls something a poem these days, it's a poem.

It's not just these days: the confusions and ambiguities are not new. People have been casually tossing these terms around for centuries, as well as the equivalent terms in other languages. "Poem," "poetry," and their kin were sometimes applied to prose, the kind of writing usually thought to be their opposite, as early as the sixteenth century, and to the other arts since at least the nineteenth – earlier than that in French – mainly as honorific terms, used to praise a work of whatever kind. John Denham in 1662, the *Oxford English Dictionary* (*OED*) tells us, spoke of "Poems in prose," two centuries before Baudelaire's influential example of *Petits poèmes en prose*

I

(1869). John Dryden in 1664 described dancing as "the Poetry of the Foot" (*Rival Ladies* 3.1.32), perhaps punning on "foot" as the unit of meter. The French writer Denis Diderot in the eighteenth century called certain paintings "poétique." The English painter John Constable wrote that an artist's purpose is "to make something out of nothing, in attempting which he must almost of necessity become poetical."[1] A German critic in 1804 called Beethoven's *Eroica* a "symphony-poem" (*Simphonie-Dichtung*).[2] Franz Liszt in the mid nineteenth century composed twelve "symphonic poems." And so it went: by the nineteenth century, it seemed almost any work of art could in all seriousness be called a poem.

Even when they confined "poem" and "poetry" to things made of words, some of the Romantics – and it was the Romantics who particularly went in for this – extended the terms to refer to language itself, at least in its creative or generative aspect. Language, A. W. Schlegel wrote, is "the most miraculous creation of the human poetic power," the "great, never accomplished poem in which human nature represents itself."[3] In his essay "The Poet," Emerson wrote: "Every word was once a poem" and "Language is fossil poetry." These writers might say that this book's subject, poetry and language, is redundant, for to study one is to study the other.

Sometimes Romantic writers used the words to refer to something as basic as the creative power residing not only in human beings but in all living things, even in all of nature. The German philosopher Friedrich Schelling used "Poesie" this way. His friend Friedrich Schlegel wrote about "the unconscious poetry" that "moves in the plant, that streams forth in light, that laughs out in the child, that shimmers in the bud of youth, that glows in the loving breasts of women."[4] Wordsworth, describing the growth of a baby's creative power, concludes, "Such, verily, is the first / Poetic spirit of our human life" (1805 *Prelude* 2.260–61).

Such expansive applications as these, evocative though they are, take us well beyond the scope of this book, which must keep in mind a more down-to-earth concept of poetry if it is to be useful to those who want to understand how "poetry," as we usually understand it, works. That so many poets, artists, composers, and philosophers have given such grand definitions of it nonetheless testifies to the prestige of poetry in this narrower sense, and to the charm or rapture it has induced in its audience for as far back as we have record. Later, as we look at the sometimes technical details of sound-effects, meter, syntax, and figurative language, we should remember this strange power that poetry seems to have – or once had – in all cultures.

Figure 1.1 The six factors of a speech event

Can linguistics help us define poetry? One of the most influential linguists of the twentieth century, Roman Jakobson, made a famous attempt at it.[5] He identified six "constitutive factors in any speech event, in any act of verbal communication," and arranged them in a simple diagram (see Figure 1.1).

"The ADDRESSER," he writes, "sends a MESSAGE to the ADDRESSEE. To be operative the message requires a CONTEXT referred to," which might also be called the "referent"; "a CODE fully, or at least partially, common to the addresser and addressee"; and "a CONTACT, a physical channel and psychological connection between the addresser and the addressee."

Each of these factors defines a different "function" of language, and in different kinds of communicative acts one or another function will be dominant. An emphasis on the context is the REFERENTIAL function, "the leading task of numerous messages"; it is perhaps the normative or default function of language and the main purpose of communication, but the other functions are tacitly in play. The EMOTIVE or "expressive" function focuses on the addresser; at its simplest it might be embodied in just an interjection that expresses his or her feelings. The function that Jakobson obscurely calls the CONATIVE (from a Latin verb meaning "endeavor" or "strive") focuses on the addressee, and might consist of imperatives ("Drink!") or other modes of direct address. The function that focuses on the contact is the PHATIC (from Greek *phatis*, meaning "speech" or "saying"); it consists of speech-acts that try to keep the channel open, or reassure the addresser, as when we say "uh-huh" periodically to let the speaker know we are still listening, or when we exchange remarks about the weather with someone we meet on the street. Small talk and gossip are mainly phatic. The METALINGUAL function deals with the code, the language the message is in, as when we say "I don't understand that" or ask what a word means. Finally, when we focus on the message for its own sake, and not for what it tells us about the world, the speaker, or the hearer, we activate the POETIC function.

When the message is foregrounded in this way, the other functions of a speech-act are suspended, and such features as its sound patterns, balance of clauses, and figurative language emerge as objects of interest in their own right. To restate and elaborate on Jakobson's brief account, we might say that, by a kind of psychic withdrawal or distancing, we can take any utterance or text as a thing in itself and contemplate it apart from the information it conveys, its demands on us, and however else it is embedded in the "real" world. Coleridge came near to describing this attitude with his famous phrase "the willing suspension of disbelief," for in this mode we are not concerned with the truth of a statement or with its practical bearing. But there is more to it than that. Under this suspension, texts seem to "thicken" or grow opaque; they are no longer transparent windows onto the world or the intentions of the speaker. There was once, allegedly, a notice posted in railroad passenger cars that read: "Passengers will please refrain from flushing toilets while the train is standing in the station." With its rhymed trochaic tetrameter opening and its alliteration throughout, the sign delighted many passengers, and soon it was set to Dvořák's seventh *Humoresque* and performed on stage.[6] In a similar spirit, W. K. Wimsatt has written, "Of a garden image ... we ask: What is it? Of a road sign giving the name of a town, we ask: What does it tell us? A poem is a road sign which through the complexity and fullness of its told message approximates the status of the garden image."[7] Texts that we call "literary," then, would be those which lend themselves best to this distancing process; they are meant to be withdrawn from the real world and experienced aesthetically.

Jakobson admits that the "poetic" function, despite its name, is too broad to distinguish poetry from other kinds of literary texts, and even from non-literary texts such as railroad signs that afford a "poetic" perspective, so he adds another clause, baffling at first sight: "The poetic function projects the principle of equivalence from the axis of selection into the axis of combination." A statement like this, so unpoetic itself, is enough to drive poetry readers to the exits, but it can be unpacked fairly readily. The "axis of combination," which we might take as horizontal, is the chain or string of words in a sentence or phrase, one after the other, and ordered by the combinatory rules of syntax. So "the young child is sleeping" combines a singular noun phrase ("the young child") with a singular verb phrase ("is sleeping"); the verb phrase must agree with the noun phrase in number (singular here), so it is "is sleeping" and not "are sleeping." Within the noun phrase, the definite article must precede the adjective, and they must both precede the noun. These are a few of the

English syntactic (or grammatical) rules that combine words into phrases, clauses, and sentences.

The "axis of selection," which we might imagine as vertical, is the way into the storehouse of "equivalences" for each word. The speaker might have chosen "kid" for "child," for example, and "is napping" for "is sleeping." (When we take up metaphor later in this book we will return to these two axes.) The "principle of equivalence," I think, means the *concept* or *category* of equivalence, and to "project" it from the vertical selective axis into the horizontal combinatory axis is to organize the chain of words in an utterance into equivalent units of some kind. The examples Jakobson gives for this projection all have to do with sounds, however, not words and their meanings; it is hard to imagine what a string of equivalent words would be like – perhaps a list of nouns or adjectives from the same semantic realm – but in any case it would not resemble a poem, or any sentence. So he discusses sound patterns, and we are back to familiar ground: "In poetry one syllable is equalized with any other syllable of the same sequence; word stress is assumed to equal word stress, as unstress equals unstress; prosodic long is matched with long, and short with short," and so on. ("Prosodic" here, as we will see in the next chapter, refers to metrical patterns.) In fact, Jakobson is defining *verse*, which is based on a binary pattern of stresses or lengths or some other salient sound-feature; these features recur or repeat in regular patterns we call meters. Elsewhere, he includes other patterns of sound-equivalences, such as rhyme, alliteration, assonance, and consonance as characteristic of the poetic.

We should add that Jakobson's "poetic function," and Wimsatt's road sign taken as a garden image, are products of modern cultural practices that seem not to have been shared, or fully shared, by earlier cultures, even in the west. While there is evidence that the Greeks felt the "charm" or "enchantment" of Homer, they also took his epics seriously as history and as compendia of useful knowledge. Hesiod's *Works and Days* and Virgil's *Georgics* are versified advice on farming and beekeeping, while Lucretius' *On the Nature of Things* explains Epicurean physics in dactylic hexameters. It is not obvious that the poetic function was dominant in the minds of those who first heard or read these didactic works; their referential function may have been uppermost. Today, we (or those of us with the leisure) are used to taking a detached stance toward poetry, like the attitude we assume when we enter an art gallery or concert hall, but that is a habit people have widely cultivated only in recent centuries.

The other problem with Jakobson's formula is that, while it defines metrical verse in an interesting way, it does not include everything that has been called poetry, such as so-called "free verse," at least when it abandons meter.

There may be no formula or brief definition that can capture our intuition into what poetry is. Nothing else, at any rate, has come forth from theoretical linguistics, as far as I know. The best they can do is to define "verse." So we might turn to another branch of linguistics for help.

Throughout the nineteenth century, most serious linguistic research was historical: dedicated mainly to reconstructing the ancestor of most of the languages of Europe and India, and secondarily to the ancestors of other families such as Semitic. Various laws of sound-change were derived from regular patterns, such as Grimm's Law, which describes a regular corre-spondence between certain consonants in the Germanic languages (German, English, Danish, and so on) and others in the larger family. The sound [p] in Greek, Latin, Sanskrit, and Slavic, for example, corre-sponds to [f] in Germanic: Greek *pous*, Latin *pes*, Sanskrit *pada*, Russian *pod*, as opposed to English *foot*, German *fuß* (= *fuss*), Danish *fot*. More and more laws were discovered and now, nearly two centuries later, the devel-opment of the Indo-European family into its many branches is pretty well understood, and the ancestor, spoken about 5,000 years ago, has been reconstructed in rich detail – entirely by inference, since its speakers had no writing.

When a word is hard to define, as "poem" is, it is worth the effort to find out its etymology, and make use of the labors of the historical linguists. The etymology of a word is the history of its form or sound, which changes gradually over the centuries, and the history of its mean-ing, which may also change, sometimes abruptly. "Etymology" itself, of course, has an etymology. It was taken into English from French during the Middle Ages, and perhaps at the same time from Latin *etymologia*, which in turn was taken unchanged from Greek ἐτυμολογία, which is an abstract compound of ἔτυμος (*etymos*), which meant "true" – and, in particular, the "true" or "literal" sense of a word according to its origin – and of λόγος (*logos*), which meant "word" or "speech." The assumption among ancient Greek scholars who studied their own language was that the "original" meaning of a word is the true one, and later deviations from it are false or errant. Some major thinkers have held this belief even in recent years, such as the German philosopher Martin Heidegger, who traced everything back to the pre-Socratic Greek philosophers, but linguists do not. Linguists maintain that, while we may deplore a change in a meaning of a word (such as "awesome," which until about 1980 meant "awe-inspiring" but now means "good"), the new meaning is not less "true" than the old. There is no such thing, too, as an "original" meaning of a word, only its first attested (or recorded) meaning, or, farther back, an unattested one that we can infer from its various descendants. As we trace "poem" and its family back to Greek and even earlier, then, we will not claim that the earliest meanings are truer or better than the later ones. But they are interesting to know about, and they might help us understand what the word has come to mean in English.

"Poet," "poem," "poetry," "poetic," and "poesy" (or "poesie") all passed from Greek through Latin and then through Old French into English, though English writers sometimes absorbed the forms directly from Greek. The Greek words were based on the root *poi-*, which meant "make": a ποίημα (*poiēma*) or πόημα (*poēma*) is "something made" or a "made thing," and a *poiētēs* or *poētēs* is a "maker." The root *poi-* comes from the Proto-Indo-European (PIE) root **kwoi-*, the o-variant of the root **kwei-*, which meant "pile up, build up, make." A poem is a made thing, then, made by a maker: not a very exciting etymology, and not very specific, but there you are.

We had better stop here for a moment. "Proto-Indo-European" is the name given by English-speaking linguists (German linguists call it *Indogermanisch*, of course) to the ancestral language we have been speaking of, with descendants from Ireland in the west to northern India in the east and, since the age of discovery, also in the Americas, Australia, the Philippines, Oceania, and many other places. There is some dispute as to where to locate the homeland of the Proto-Indo-Europeans, which may have been unstable, as we think the people who spoke it were semi-nomadic pastoralists, but most historical linguists and archeologists place them somewhere north of the Black Sea and east toward the Caspian. They were illiterate: there are no written texts of this language. Besides Greek, Latin, Sanskrit (in India), Slavic, and Germanic, the daughter subfamilies include Celtic (Irish, Welsh), Baltic (Lithuanian, Latvian), Armenian, and several extinct groups, such as Anatolian (which probably included the language spoken by Homer's Trojans). These all go back to this language, once spoken by perhaps a few thousand people. Some clans that spoke it moved away at various times from about 5000 to 2000 BCE, so the time-depth of the reconstructed language is quite long, but we know a great deal about it. We even have some idea of what PIE poetry was like. Sometime around 3000 BCE, these people seem to have mastered horseback riding, and figured out how to attach a workable chariot to horses; soon they invaded Europe, Iran, and India, and prevailed virtually everywhere they went. Or at least their language prevailed: in western Europe, for example, only Basque remains of the old languages spoken before the invasions.

Proto-Indo-European, then, refers to this hypothetical language, and when they cite a word or root from this language linguists put an asterisk in front of it to indicate that it is indeed hypothetical. They say the Greek root *poi-* descends from PIE root *kwoi-*. How do they know this? And what happened to the kw- sound to yield p- in Greek 2 or 3,000 years later? We mentioned Grimm's Law. All the "laws" are assumed to be exceptionless: an apparent exception will be governed by another law. If an s- sound at the beginning of one word changes to an h- sound, for instance, then all words that begin with s- will change to h-, unless there is a feature in some words that interferes, but then that feature will also induce a different pattern common to all words that have it. The differences among daughter languages will then appear systematic. The Latin word for "six" is *sex*, while the Greek word is ἕξ (*hex*). If we didn't know the Greek word for "seven" but knew that the Latin word for it is *septem*, we could predict that the Greek word must be something like *heptem*; it is in fact ἑπτά (*hepta*).

One of the patterns linguists have discovered has to do with a peculiar PIE consonant, called the labio-velar stop, the contact of the back of the tongue with the velum, in the back of the throat (which we bring about when we make the k- sound), at the same time as a semi-closure of the lips (as with English w). We could write it kw- but it is better to write it k^w-, with a superscript w, to indicate that it is one double sound and not a succession of sounds. This k^w- sound shows up in many Latin words beginning with *qu-*, not much changed from PIE, such as *quis, qua, quod*, and other interrogative and relative pronouns or adverbs (meaning "who," "what," "where," "whether," and so on), but in Greek we find words with similar meanings beginning with p-, such as *pou* ("where"), *poios* ("of what sort"), *posos* ("how much"), and *poteros* ("whether"), all of them with a back vowel (o or ou) after the initial p-. That pattern alone suggests a common ancestor for those initial consonants. Then there is the Latin word *equus* ("horse"), earlier *equos*, corresponding to Greek *hippos*. In the earliest recorded Greek, called Mycenaean (found in the Linear B script), the Greek spoken at about 1400 BCE, the word for "horse" is transliterated into syllabic symbols equivalent to *i-qo*, where the q was probably pronounced like k^w. And there are other examples; they add up to a law: before a rear vowel, k^w- became p- in most dialects of ancient Greek. In the Germanic branch of the family, the PIE k^w- became a fricative or voiceless gurgle, like the sound in German *ach*, but still with the labial w (linguists write it χ^w-), and then it weakened to h^w-, which in Old English is spelled hw- (as in *hwæt*, the first word of *Beowulf*) and in modern English is spelled wh-; thus PIE *k^wod* became *quod* in Latin and "what" in English. In other languages, such as Sanskrit and Old Church Slavonic, we find verbs that mean "make" or "pile up" that begin with a sound that is traceable back to initial k^w- in PIE, and in particular to the hypothetical root *k^wei-*.

Another feature of PIE, now well established with abundant examples, is that the roots of verbs usually came in three forms, depending on the vowel, a pattern English inherits from PIE with its sets of irregular verbs like "sing, sang, sung" or "drink, drank, drunk." The o-form of *k^wei-* was *k^woi-*, and that seems to be the source of Greek *poi-*, which meant "make." And there you have it.

In Homer, the oldest recorded Greek poet, the verb ποιεῖν (*poiein*) meant "to make, form, bring about, do," and the adjective ποιητός (*poiētos*) meant "made" or "well-made"; neither of them bore any suggestion of "poetry" as verse or song. The word for "poet" or "bard" in Homer was ἀοιδός (*aoidos*, "singer"); the related word for "song," *aoidē*, was inherited by English as "ode." By Plato's time, however, several centuries later, ποιητής (*poiētēs*, "poet") had already narrowed to its modern sense, but Plato is, of course, aware of the older and broader meaning. In Plato's *Symposium*, Diotima tells Socrates:

> you know, for example, that "poetry" (ποίησις, *poiēsis*) has a very wide range. After all, everything that is responsible for creating something out of nothing is a kind of poetry, and so all the creations of all the crafts are themselves a kind of poetry and the practitioners of these are all poets ... Nevertheless, as you also know, these craftsmen are not called "poets." We have other words for them, and out of the whole of poetry [in the broad sense] we have marked off one part, the part the Muses gave us with melody and rhythm, and we refer to this by the word that means the whole. For this alone is called "poetry," and those who practice this part of poetry are called "poets" (ποιηταί). (205b–c; trans. Nehamas and Woodruff, modified)

Aristotle's *Poetics* (*Peri poiētikēs*) has the word *poiēma* (plural *poiēmata*) several times in more or less its English sense. Once, it has the phrase *poiēmata pepoiēkasin* ("they made poems"), as if to signal the etymology of "poem" through a kind of pun: they "poemized" poems (1451a21).

In English from the fourteenth century, poets were sometimes called "makers," as in the Scottish poet William Dunbar's *Lament for the Makars* (c. 1505). Sir Phillip Sidney, in *A Defence of Poetry* (1595), writes, "The Greeks called him a 'poet,' which name hath, as the most excellent, gone through other languages. It cometh of this word ποιεῖν, which is, to make:

wherein, I know not whether by luck or wisdom, we Englishmen have met with the Greeks in calling him a maker."

As for "poem," the *OED* tells us it was apparently not in use in English until the sixteenth century; before then, "poesy" was sometimes used for an individual poem, as *poésie* still is in French, as well as for poetry in general.

If "maker" and "made thing" seem disappointing as the oldest known meanings of these words, we should ask what we might have expected. "Heavenly harmony"? "Spontaneous overflow of powerful feelings"? These might have been more satisfying to us if we love poetry, but they are very unlikely meanings of ancient verbal roots. Besides, "to make" carries considerable dignity. Poets themselves, even now, often lay weight on the skill at "making" that the craft of poetry requires. Sidney, a master of the craft, called the Greek word "most excellent," after all. The Greek poet Pindar likened himself to an archer, a carpenter, and a weaver, among other skilled workers. When Dante meets the poet Guido Guinizzelli in Purgatory, the latter refers to another poet, Arnaut Daniel, as *miglior fabbro* ("a better craftsman"; *Purgatorio* 26.117); T. S. Eliot quoted the phrase to pay a compliment to a poet who had taught him a great deal, Ezra Pound. (Italian *fabbro*, by the way, comes from Latin *faber* ["worker, craftsman"], from a root meaning "fit together," as in our word "fabricate.") And some poets noticed that they share something with God: they both make worlds. Shelley, who ends his *Defence of Poetry* with the claim that poets are the unacknowledged legislators of the world, also quotes a line in Italian that he attributes to the poet Tasso: *Non merita nome di creatore, se non Iddio ed il Poeta* ("None deserves the name of creator except God and the Poet"). The French poet Lammenais wrote, "the universe is a great poem, God's poem, which we endeavor to reproduce in ours."[8]

"Poet" entered the vernacular languages in the Middle Ages, and for some time it referred only to classical (Greek and Latin) poets. Dante uses *poeta* twenty-five times in *The Divine Comedy*: twenty-one times of the great Roman poet Virgil, his guide through Hell and Purgatory; once of Homer; once of the Roman poet Statius; once of a generic poet; and finally once of himself, as he imagines returning to Florence from his exile and receiving the laurel crown (*Paradiso* 25.8–9). That may be the first time a writer in the vernacular language (here Italian, as opposed to Latin) used the word "poet" for himself or for any other vernacular writer.

My patient reader will have noticed that one thing leads to another in the pursuit of etymologies, and it is time to cut off this particular thread. We will look at quite a few more etymologies in this book, though not at such length, and we will do so for three good reasons. Certain terms used in the discussion of poetry, many of them ancient, have interesting histories that will help us understand them. More importantly, the words *of* poetry, the words found *in* poetry, are often odd and old, and often evoke earlier poetry, so the best way to get to know them, and take pleasure in them, is to learn their genealogy. Finally, when we take up the subject of metaphor, which some would call the essence of poetry, etymology will emerge as a key tool for understanding how deep metaphor goes in any language – perhaps all the way down. The *Oxford English Dictionary*, based on historical principles, is the indispensable guide; daunting at first, your admiration for it will mount as you get to know it, while you get to know the words you look up in it.

Has the etymology of "poem" helped us define it? Well, it does remind us that poetry was seen as a craft – it was made – and not as a spontaneous overflow of powerful feelings or the like. It was more like carpentry or weaving than whistling a tune. Poets worked hard at being poets, and before the alphabet they had to develop prodigious memories as well. When we look at some of the most ancient poems of Europe and India we find very intricate forms of the sort you don't just pick up the way you might work out a melody on your guitar. The dactylic hexameter of Homer, for example, is very demanding: it is not natural to spoken everyday Greek. In fact, Homer's Greek was never spoken by anyone, even apart from its meter; its vocabulary is an artificial composite of many dialects of Greek, and it must have taken a good deal of time to master. In Sanskrit, the ancient Indian language, there was a rigorous verse form called *mandākrāntā*, which began with four long syllables, followed by five short ones, then a pair of what we would call anapests (short-short-long), and then two shorts. Medieval Welsh poets developed a complicated system called *cynghanedd*, which stipulated numbers of syllables, rhymes, alliteration, and other sound-effects that beggar description. Traditional poetry, then, was an artifice, a construction, a skill, and there were professional poets or bards who had spent years mastering it.

It was *verse*, above all. As the meaning of "poetry" has inflated into nearly meaningless clouds of connotations, we have relied on the word "verse" to distinguish the main tradition of poetry from prose. Verse, we usually say, is metered, and is organized into lines. The word (here we go again) comes from Old French *vers*, which descends from Latin *versus*, which meant "turning," in particular "the turning of a plow" or "furrow," and thence "line" and "line of verse." *Versus* is the participle of the verb *vertere* ("turn"), from PIE **wert-* (also "turn"). The Latin root gave English a large number of words, such as "avert," "convert," "divert," "invert," "pervert," and the like, as well as "anniversary" ("turning of the year"), "universe," "version," and "vertebra"; while, through the Germanic branch of the family, English inherits the "-ward" suffix, as in "backward," "forward," "inward," etc., as well as "weird," from Old English *wyrd*, meaning "fate" or "turn of events." The *OED* states that Latin *versus* is "so named from turning to begin another line." Wordsworth plays on this etymology when he speaks of "the turnings intricate of verse" (1805 *Prelude* 5.627).

The idea of plowing a line of verse remained alive in the word. The Greek poet Pindar had already called poets the "plowmen of the Muses" (*Nemean* 10). The Latin verbs *aro* and *exaro* ("plow up") were used to mean "write." Isidore of Seville quotes a lost Roman play by Atta: "Let us turn the plowshare (*Vertamus vomerem*) in the wax and plow with a point of bone." The Italian poet Petrarch uses the phrase *vomer di penna* ("plowshare of a pen") (*Rime* 228), and Spenser uses "furrow" once to mean "line of verse" (*Faerie Queene* 6.9.1). William Blake, who normally engraved his lines with a burin into copper plate, much like a bone stylus into a waxed tablet, told his readers to "Follow me with my Plow" (*Milton* 8.20). And Seamus Heaney gives us a collateral descendant of this metaphor when he likens his pen to a spade: "Between my finger and my thumb / The squat pen rests. / I'll dig with it" ("Digging").

So "verse" implies "line," and lines are the units of verse. "Verse" used to imply "meter" as well, since lines used to be metered – that is, they were parceled out in equal measures of one sort or another (iambic, say, or dactylic). But in the late nineteenth century something called "free verse" took hold of young avant-garde poets, first in France and then, with the help of Walt Whitman, in America and Britain. The French poet Laforgue wrote, "I forget to rhyme, I forget about the number of syllables [crucial in French poetic meter for centuries], I forget about stanzaic structure." With all these things forgotten, what was left? Well, perhaps "verse," the line itself. With prose, it does not matter how the words are disposed on the page as long as they are in the right order, whereas a poem, as Terry Eagleton defines it, is a literary work "in which it is the author, rather than the printer or word processor, who decides where the lines should end."[9] The poet is in charge of the hard returns. Hence, in another definition, a poem is a text with a ragged right-hand margin, though this is not always true these days, as some publishers like to turn off the right-hand justification even for prose works. Nigel Fabb and Morris Halle, who have worked out a rigorous theory of meter and traced it through many languages, write: "What distinguishes all poetry from prose is that poetry is made up of lines (verses). Syllables, words, phrases, clauses and sentences are found in both prose and poetry, but only poetry has lines."[10] By "poetry" they mean "verse," of course, because there are those "prose poems," where even the line has evaporated. A prose poem is a poem by virtue of something else: its brevity, its metaphorical density, its elusive meaning, its dreamlike logic – some poetic something or other that its author believes licenses the name.

With even the line doubtful as a criterion, if we still want to tidy up this messy state of affairs, we might fall back on Ludwig Wittgenstein's idea of "family resemblances," from his *Philosophical Investigations* (1953). Among ten members of the same family, it might turn out that there is no single distinctive trait they all share, but you can still tell they belong to the same family because there are half a dozen such traits or "strands of similarity" that run through them. Member X might have three of those traits and member Y three different ones; if we compared only these two side by side we might assign them to different families, but when we see that member Z has two traits that X has and two that Y has we recognize all three as siblings. With "poem," we might concede there is no single common denominator – not even words, it would seem – but we might still agree to call certain works poems if they had either (1) at least one feature of a small "definitive" set (meter, line, stanza), or (2) several features of a larger "optional" set (rhyme, rhythm, brevity, figurative language, dreamlike imagery and transitions, a "lyric" personal voice, and other possible traits). (Rhyme might seem to belong to the first set, but there is such a thing as rhyming prose, while rhythm is a looser thing than meter, and is found in prose as well.) There would still be room for debate over how many of the second set would be necessary, and over the relative importance of each of them, but at least we would have a framework for the debate.

In the end, it may not matter much whether or not we have a reliable definition or "poem" and "poetry," or even "verse," once we recognize the lengths to which we are driven to contain these slippery words even minimally. This book, happily, is not bound by such minimalism, nor by any definition at all. It will devote several sections to features once considered requirements, such as meter, and others that were widespread in certain times and places, such as rhyme. Other aspects, such as metaphor, are also found in prose, of course, but will get attention here because they are at home in poetry.

There are many fine books that describe and illustrate these aspects of poetry, and I have drawn ideas from several of them. What makes the present book different is its attempt to bring to bear what modern linguistics can show us about many of poetry's distinctive characteristics. Even a slight acquaintance with modern linguistics, of course, with its often forbidding technical vocabulary, acoustic graphs, and syntactic tree-diagrams, might send anyone who cares about poetry fleeing in the opposite direction. Since deep appreciation of poetry has been possible for centuries without any of this scientific stuff, it might seem that knowledge of linguistics is about as useful for understanding poetry as mastery of papermaking and bookbinding. That seems mistaken to me, not because you cannot experience poetry deeply and intelligently without linguistics, but because there are different kinds and degrees of understanding of any subject, and certainly of any work of art, and linguistics has many contributions to make at several levels. Linguistics is the study of how language works, and one of the ways it works is to make poems. The more you know about language, it seems obvious, the more you will know about – and the better you will experience – poetry. That said, I think poetry also has something to teach linguistics, or at least linguistics will be a richer and more cogent field if it can think clearly about what goes on in poetry, which is not as marginal a practice as some linguists have thought.

This book's three main divisions correspond to the three main branches of linguistics: (1) phonology, or the sounds of a language; (2) syntax, or grammatical structure; and (3) semantics, or meaning. These three threads are tightly interwoven in any language, and no language is possible without all three. (Sign languages for the deaf dispense with sound, of course, but they have a visual equivalent of phonology.) In poetry, the special dimensions of sound, such as meter and rhyme, interact in subtle ways with both syntax and meaning, while syntax affects the way we recite a poem, altering the metrical pattern here and there to produce a unique rhythm.

There are other branches of linguistics, such as pragmatics – which is the study of what people do with language (assert, question, gossip, pray, joke, praise, swear, ridicule, lie, promise, baptize, confer knighthood, and write poems) – and sociolinguistics, which studies a broad range of topics such as registers or levels of formality, interaction between languages, and bilingualism. Except for a page or two about pragmatics, neither of these branches will occupy us much in this book, which must be kept reasonably short – though they have much to do with semantics especially; a good grasp of a poem, for instance, may rely on what kind of pragmatic speech-act in "real life" the poem represents. Another branch, historical linguistics, which studies language change and the reconstruction of dead and even lost languages, we have already drawn on for what it can tell us about "poetry" and "verse," and it will be a constant point of reference throughout. Finally, there is the theory and practice of translation, which we will take up at the end; they deal with how much of a poem we can preserve when we put it into another language. In a backhanded way, this last subject also offers us the brief definition that we just gave up searching for: "Poetry is what gets lost in translation." We shall see.

Notes

1. Letter to Archdeacon Fisher, August 29, 1824 (*Correspondence*, Vol. vi, ed. Beckett, p. 172), quoted in Rosen, *Romantic Generation*, 173.
2. Quoted in Sipe, *Beethoven: Eroica Symphony*, 54.
3. Quoted in Behler, *German Romantic Literary Theory*, 269.
4. *Gespräch über die Poesie*, quoted in Robert J. Richards, *Romantic Conception of Life*, 111.
5. "Linguistics and Poetics" (1960), partly reprinted in Jakobson, *On Language*. For comments on the essay, see Ricoeur, *Rule of Metaphor*, 222–24, and Culler, *Structuralist Poetics*, 55–57.
6. It is quite possible that the "sign" was invented to fit the well-known tune, but the point remains.
7. Wimsatt, *Verbal Icon*, 232.
8. *Esquisse d'une philosophie* (1840–46), quoted in Gilman, *Idea of Poetry in France*, 148.
9. Eagleton, *How to Read a Poem*, 25.
10. Fabb and Halle, *Meter in Poetry*, 1. See Fabb, *Linguistics and Literature*, 2. In his most recent book, *What is Poetry?* (2015), Fabb posits "poetry" as a term more clearly definable than the ambiguous "verse" (14). It is true that "verse" has several meanings in English, but I think it is much less ambiguous than "poetry." Fabb even excludes "free verse" as poetry even though it is arranged as lines.

CHAPTER TWO

Meter and the Syllable

Before writing systems were invented, starting around 5,000 years ago, all poetry was oral, and some poetry today, even in societies with universal literacy, is still composed and performed without the aid of writing. When poets learned to write, poetry changed. Thanks to the work of Milman Parry (1902–35), we are now almost certain that the *Iliad* and the *Odyssey*, for example, were largely composed orally by an illiterate bard, or more likely by a long series of illiterate bards who recomposed and elaborated the stories they inherited. Homer and his predecessors, it seems, did not so much memorize their long poems as reconstruct them each time they performed them, rather as a jazz musician may improvise a good deal of his or her piece while preserving its tune and following the main lines of its theme-and-variation structure and many individual "riffs." The main evidence for the oral origin of the epics lies in the "formulas" that pervade both of them: the epithets such as "swift-footed" (Achilles) and "shepherd of the people" (Agamemnon), whole lines such as the one about "rose-fingered Dawn" (twenty times verbatim in the *Odyssey*), and stock descriptions such as arming for battle or serving and eating food. Later epic poets, such as Apollonius in Greek and Virgil in Latin, seldom repeat phrases and almost never repeat lines, for they could write and rewrite their poems at leisure and then read them aloud or recite them from memory to an audience.

Even though writing has had effects on it, however, poetry seems essentially oral even today.[1] Meter and rhyme, if a poem has them, need to be heard, though perhaps to hear them in the mind's ear is enough for many readers, while others think it is important to go to an oral "reading" by a poet for the most authentic experience of his or her poems. It is true that there are genres of visible poetry, such as "concrete" poetry and the unpronounceable typographic playfulness of E. E. Cummings; there are "eye-rhymes" where groups of letters repeat but the sounds spelled by them do not; there are shaped poems like those of George Herbert that look like wings or an altar; and there have been poet-painters such as William Blake, who not only engraved illustrations on the same copper plate on which he engraved his poems but sometimes made the letters sprout tendrils and other decorative doodles. Calligraphy is a highly elaborated art form, especially in Muslim culture where images were banned from certain domains, and a poem written in calligraphic style might be considered a multi-media work of art; the same might be said for Chinese and Japanese calligraphy done with the brush. Readers of ordinary poetry, which can be presented accurately in any manner, usually find it more satisfying to read it in a finely bound edition on good paper, in attractive typeface, and carefully laid out. All this is true and worth thinking about, but it remains the case that poetry is by and large oral.

Later, I will touch on the question of what difference it might make whether poems are written in an alphabet or in a "logographic" system, but for now I want to argue that, to understand better the purely oral or auditory features of poetry, to "see" them better, it is a good idea to learn the International Phonetic Alphabet (or IPA), which was devised by linguists to provide one letter for each sound used by every language in the world. No poetry has been published in it, as far as I know, nor is it likely to establish itself as the standard alphabet in any country, and certainly not in Britain or America. Attempts at even modest reforms of the weird spelling system of English – if "system" is the word for it – have come to nothing, and the IPA would strike most native English-speakers as far too complicated and geeky to take up: for starters, it would require at least thirty-six symbols. If we all adopted it, moreover, there would be no point in holding spelling bees – a longstanding tradition, at least in America. But it is very helpful for a careful study of sounds in poetry, beginning with the concept of the syllable. It is also the convention adopted by the *OED* for its second edition (1989) and for its continually updated on-line version, so if you want to know how a word is or was pronounced, you will need to be familiar with it. It is not difficult, as about half of its characters will be familiar, but it requires a fresh look at how to spell words, and a little effort to extricate yourself from the grip of English conventions.

The IPA

The International Phonetic Alphabet is clearly Anglocentric, or at least Eurocentric, for many of the symbols in their simplest forms (without diacritical marks above or below them) are identical to the Roman alphabetic characters for the same sound. That makes it easier for us, but not so easy for speakers of, say, Russian or Mohawk. Its basic principle is simple: for each distinctive sound in any language – that is, each sound that is a "phoneme" in any language – there is one unique symbol; the exception is the set of diphthongs or double vowel sounds, which some phonologists consider phonemes and others do not. English, which has 44 phonemes, counting the diphthongs, needs 36 symbols;[2] Hawaiian, which has only 13 phonemes, needs only 13; Taa (or !Xóõ) in South Africa, which has at least 114 phonemes, many of them "clicks," has taxed the ingenuity of the IPA authorities, but they have come up with an impressive array of characters, one for each phoneme, such as ↓ŋΘʰ, which stands for a "bilabial voiceless ingressive nasal click with delayed aspiration," whatever that is.

Very few – if any at all – of the alphabets in common use around the world are isomorphic to the sounds they represent; very few, that is, map one letter to one sound and vice versa. The English alphabet, for example, among its many other oddities, could do perfectly well without the letter c, for it is already replaceable by k or s in most of its occurrences, and its peculiar partnership with h, as in "church," could be replaced by something better (in IPA it is tʃ or the combined forms ʧ or t͡ʃ). One alphabet that came close to perfection was the ancient Greek alphabet – not very surprising because the alphabet was invented for ancient Greek, and possibly even for ancient Greek poetry.[3] It is true that the Greeks drew heavily from the Phoenician system, but that system, some linguists have argued, was not really an alphabet but a syllabary with the vowels suppressed, or as Geoffrey Samson prefers, "a segmental script which ignores vowel segments."[4] All Phoenician words began with a consonant, and each Phoenician letter was named after a word that began with the sound it represents, so no letter could stand for a vowel. Vowels in Phoenician, as in its close cousin Hebrew and more distant cousin Arabic, mainly determine grammatical categories, rather like their function in "sing," "sang," "sung," and "song" in English, while consonants mainly determine "lexical" meaning, or basic dictionary-like sense. A speaker of Phoenician would seldom fail to know what word is meant by a succession of consonants. This feature is not true of Greek, or of any Indo-European language, where vowels are as crucial to the meaning as consonants, so the Greeks needed to add vowels. T wrt Nglsh w nd vls t, s y cn s.[5] The result was the first true alphabet, and it was fairly good. If you know how to pronounce the individual Greek letters, you can pronounce any word you meet in ancient Greek, and if you hear a word pronounced, you can (almost always) spell it right. The same was true of Latin and is still true, more or less, for Italian,

Spanish, Hungarian, and a few other languages, but it is far from the case, alas, in English.

The inventors of the IPA had the advantage over the Greeks, clever though they were, of knowing what a phoneme is. A phoneme, to put it somewhat loosely, is the smallest meaningful unit of sound in a language. (Linguists generally use "phone" for "sound" in the broad sense.) More precisely, a phoneme is the smallest contrastive unit of sound, or phone, that may bring about a change of meaning. Their existence can be brought to light by contrasting two words that differ by one phone, such as "kith" and "kin." In the IPA, they would be written /kɪθ/ and /kɪn/ (phonemes and phonemic spellings of words are conventionally put between slashes), and they make a "minimal pair" of words. Note that the th- sound is one sound, a voiceless interdental fricative, though we spell it with two letters for complicated historical reasons; the IPA uses one letter for it, the Greek letter theta (θ). Another minimal pair, with a minimal difference between them, is "kin" and "king." With "king," we have another example where two English letters correspond to one sound, a velar nasal "stop,"[6] and in IPA the word would be /kɪŋ/. The final letter here (ŋ) is the "eng," and the sound it represents, /ŋ/, differs from /n/ by only one "distinctive feature": they are both nasal stops, but they differ in their point of articulation, /n/ pronounced with the tip of the tongue at the alveolus (the hard ridge above the teeth) and /ŋ/ pronounced with the back of the tongue at the velum, the soft palate near the back of the mouth.

If this is too much information at once, we can slow down a little, and take a moment to salute the phonologists for their meticulous analysis of what the human vocal tract can produce. There is nothing you can do with your mouth, teeth, tongue, throat, uvula, or glottis that they haven't named, described, categorized, graphed, and measured in all directions down to the millimeter. For our purposes, we may pick and choose among their findings, and we need only be familiar with the symbols for the English phonemes and with a few other symbols that will come up when we discuss languages that have certain sounds which English-speakers sometimes make but which are not English phonemes or words.

Consonants and Almost-Consonants

We can begin with the box of nine stops (Figure 2.1).

These make a satisfying three-by-three column-and-row system, and show that at least some phonemes in English fall into patterns. On this grid, we can readily see how the stops differ from each other by one or two

	voiceless	voiced	nasal
bilabial	p	b	m
alveolar	t	d	n
velar	k	g	ŋ

Figure 2.1 The pattern of English stops

"distinctive features." Take /p/ and /b/, for example. Both are bilabial stops, involving both lips, and they differ in one distinctive feature, namely voice (the vibration of the vocal cords), or "vocal onset." With /p/ the vocal stream is interrupted; after an initial /p/ there is a tiny delay before the voice comes in. With /b/ there is virtually no interruption or delay. (There is more aspiration or "puff" with /p/, at least initial /p/, but this difference is slight and is not what distinguishes /p/ and /b/ as phonemes to our ear.) The same is true of /t/ and /d/, both alveolar stops, one voiceless, the other voiced, and of /k/ and /g/, both velar stops. There is one asymmetry in this box: the velar nasal /ŋ/ cannot begin a word in English, though it can do so in other languages.

We should add that these nine phonemes are *oral* stops. The air stream in the mouth is stopped for a second as they are articulated, but with the three nasals the air stream is not stopped but diverted through the nose. The nasals are classed among the "sonorants" because the voice keeps sounding during their production, while the other six stops are "obstruents": they obstruct the air flow.

Another interesting set of obstruent phonemes is the "fricative" consonants (Figure 2.2), so called because of the friction or turbulence the airstream makes when they are pronounced, a friction due to the constriction of the oral part of the vocal tract. They partially obstruct the airstream continually rather than stop it for a moment. English is a rather friction-rich language, for it has nine of these sounds; they are produced at five positions, because eight of them come in pairs, voiceless and voiced. We have just met the voiceless dental /θ/, found not only at the ends of words such as "kith" and "path" but at the beginnings of such words as "thin" and "theatre." Its voiced counterpart, found in "then," "weather," and "blithe," is written /ð/ and is called the "eth" (or maybe "edh" to indicate that the consonant should be voiced), a letter taken from Old English texts. These two are called "dentals," or, more precisely, "interdentals," because the tongue is inserted a little between the teeth. Though phonologists do not

	voiceless	voiced
dental or interdental	θ	ð
labio-dental	f	v
alveolar sibilant	s	z
post-alveolar sibilant	ʃ	ʒ
glottal	h	

Figure 2.2 The nine English fricatives

hesitate to call them distinct phonemes, they are hard pressed to find a minimal pair of words that contrast them; for word-initial examples, the best they can offer is "thigh" and "thy," but there are a few word-final examples, such as "teeth" and "teethe." That suggests that we might not need both of them, but they make a pair parallel to three other pairs, and native English-speakers would find something very odd in a speaker who mixed them up.

The two "labio-dentals" are made with the upper teeth against the lower lip: the voiceless /f/ and the voiced /v/. Minimal pairs would be "fat" and "vat," or "leaf" and "leave."

Notice, by the way, that when the final consonant is voiced, the syllable takes a little longer to say than when the consonant is voiceless. "Teethe" takes a little longer to say than "teeth," and "leave" takes a little longer than "leaf." Poets sometimes exploit this fact. Even though the length of time a vowel lasts is not the basis of English meter, as it was in ancient Greek and Latin, poets with sensitive ears will give thought to the rhythmic side-effects of these varying lengths.

Four of the fricatives are also called "sibilants," from Latin word *sibilus*, which meant "hiss." Two are made with the tongue very close to the alveolus, /s/ and /z/, and they contrast in such pairs as "sip" and "zip," or "faced" and "phased," the latter pair being a good example of the vagaries of English spelling. The other two are post-alveolar, the tongue curling up and back a little further, the voiceless /ʃ/ and the voiced /ʒ/. The first, sometimes called the "esh," is often written sh in English (as in "short" or "ash"), but it can show up as -ti- (as in "nation") or as -ssi- (as in "mission"), among other spellings. The second, sometimes called the "ezh," can be spelled with an -s- (as in "measure") or a -z- (as in "azure") or a -ge (as in "garage" or "rouge"). Contrasting pairs are fairly scarce (as /ʒ/ itself is fairly scarce), but we could contrast "leash" with "liege," or "dilution" with "delusion." Like the eng, the ezh cannot begin a word in English, unless it has been recently borrowed from French (as in "genre"). Under some systems, the feature "stridency" is posited to distinguish the sibilants from the other fricatives because the former are noisier, but there are other ways to distinguish them, as we have seen.

Farthest back in the mouth is the glottal fricative /h/, spelled almost always with an h. It is considered voiceless, as there is a little gap between the onset of the breath (from deep in the throat) and the following vowel, but it does not contrast with a voiced version, if such a thing is conceivable. It does contrast with words that begin with a vowel, as in "hitch" and "itch," or "heave" and "eave." Some phonologists argue that /h/ is a "pseudo-fricative" in English because it does not constrict the flow of air much, but we will keep it among the fricatives so it isn't orphaned.

There are two more related consonants, called "affricates," though some would say they are double consonants: the unvoiced ch- sound in "church" and the voiced j- sound and dge- sound in "judge." The first of these, as we noted earlier, could be written /tʃ/ if you think they make two sounds, or /ʧ/ if you think they make one sound. The voiced version is /dʒ/ or /ʤ/. You sometimes see /č/ for the unvoiced affricate and /ǰ/ for the voiced, though these characters are no longer standard.

There is a fricative phoneme in German, Dutch, Greek, and many other languages that English speakers are familiar with, but which does not qualify as a phoneme in English: the voiceless velar /x/ or, if pronounced a little farther back, the voiceless uvular /χ/. It's the gurgle we often make at the end of "uck" or "yech" when expressing disgust, or when carefully pronouncing the names of the many composers of the Bach family. Another not-quite-phoneme is the glottal stop (ʔ), the sound made in the middle of "uh-oh," a stoppage of the airflow in the back of the throat. There is one somewhat suspect minimal pair in English, where /ʔ/ contrasts with /h/: the difference between "uh-uh" ("no") and "uh-huh" ("yes"). Many speakers use the glottal stop in the middle of "mitten" or "bottle" or "couldn't," but they do not contrast in meaning with the other pronunciations.

Then there is a set of four strange sounds that foreigners have a lot of trouble with, classed together as "approximants": the semi-vowels /w/ and /r/, and the liquids /l/ and /j/. And not only foreigners, for they are often the last sounds babies master as they grow up speaking English. (My 3-year-old daughter liked to be taken to the stables to feed "cawwots" to the horses.) The last of these four is not the j in "just" but the consonantal y in "yellow." They are "almost-consonants": the tongue comes close to touching something and then holds back, but there is no turbulence as in the sibilants; or the tongue touches the alveolus (making an /l/) and curls, but there is nothing "plosive" like /t/ or /d/. The /r/ is the strangest of all, and bears little relation to what is indicated by the letter r in every other language: it is not trilled or flapped as in Spanish or Italian, for example, or uvulated as in French. During my year teaching English in Japan, I tormented my students by drawing cross-sections of the mouth on the blackboard and making them say "Larry went to the rally" until they insisted it was time for tea. Because the English r is so odd, IPA usually reserves the basic /r/ symbol for the trilled sound and relegates an upside-down version to English: /ɹ/. We deserve it, but in this book we can revert to the normal form, as long as we remember how unusual it is in the world.[7]

Those are the English consonants. Before we look at the vowels, we should note that the kinds of distinctions that make two phonemes contrast with each other in English may not exist in other languages, and vice versa. Modern Greek, for instance, does not have a /ʃ/ phoneme or its voiced counterpart /ʒ/, but you do hear these sounds when you listen to at least some dialects of Greek. What happens is that the /s/ is sometimes "realized" or pronounced like [ʃ] (I am putting it in brackets to indicate that it is a phone but not a phoneme in Greek); in those cases we say that [ʃ] is an "allophone" of /s/. They never contrast, and there are no minimal pairs of words differing only between [s] and [ʃ]. Conversely, Hindi distinguishes between two kinds of t- sounds, d- sounds, and n- sounds, neither of which is made at the alveolus, where we make ours (see Figure 2.3). One is dental, made with the tongue behind the teeth (but just touching the alveolus), much like the comparable sounds in French and the other Romance languages; the other is made with the tongue farther up and back in the so-called "retroflex" position, post-alveolar or a tad farther back. They have different symbols in IPA. When Hindi speakers transcribe English words into their alphabet, they are often unsure which letter to use for our /t/.

Ancient Greek had six stops corresponding to our three voiceless stops /p t k/, with an aspirated and non-aspirated form of each. When we pronounce the phoneme /p/ at the beginning of a word, for example, we give it a little puff – you can feel it with your hand held close to your mouth. If we put an /s/ before it, the puff vanishes. So "pit" is puffy, or aspirated, and "spit" is not. These two are allophones of /p/ in English, and we do not notice them. But the Greeks did. Their puffy version (written φ) was a distinct phoneme and contrasted with their unpuffy version (π). By New Testament times, the φ had become an [f], as it is today, and that is

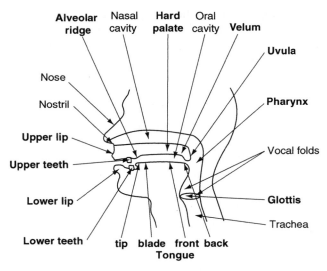

Figure 2.3 The vocal tract

how we pronounce Greek words that began with it (such as "phoneme" or "Phoenician") in English. We know it was originally an aspirated p (written p^h in IPA) in part because the Romans transliterated it "ph"; the Romans had the letter f in their alphabet and would have used it if they had heard an [f]. Similarly, θ (theta) was a breathy t^h (not like the IPA θ) and χ (chi) was a breathy k^h.

Vowels

Vowels are made with an open vocal tract, that is, a tract with no constrictions that stop, disturb, or deviate the airflow, which is the task of consonants. For that reason, they are a little harder to define. The position of the tongue is the determining factor, and that is described in two dimensions: (1) height (high, mid, and low, though the IPA prefers to say close, mid, and open), and (2) frontness or backness (front, central, back). In what follows, I will describe the vowel phonemes according to a standard American pronunciation. One of the troubles with vowels is that they vary more from dialect to dialect than consonants usually do; the standard or "received" British pronunciations are often different from American, and both have changed quite a bit over the centuries – another reason to keep the *OED* at hand.

High (close) front: /i/ as in "sheep" and /ɪ/ as in "ship," that is /ʃip/ and /ʃɪp/. The difference between these is sometimes said to be length (/i/ is longer) but there is also a slight difference in height (/i/ is higher). The higher sound is often labeled "tense," the lower one "lax." To indicate greater length, IPA often inserts a triangular colon (:), so "sheep" might be transcribed /ʃiːp/.

High (close) back: /u/ as in "goose" and /ʊ/ as in "foot." Again, the first of these might be a little longer, but it is also a little higher. Both are also "rounded," because the lips form an O-shape, more or less.

Mid front: /ɛ/ as in "bed." The symbol is a kind of Greek epsilon. We might expect /e/ for it, but that symbol is usually reserved for a closer (higher) vowel. We might also expect that closer vowel to show up in, say, "face," but when it does it is part of a diphthong, a pair of vowels compressed together, in this case /eɪ/.

Mid back: /ɔ/ as in "cloth" or "thought."
Low (open) front: /æ/ as in "bath" or "sad."
Mid (open) central: /ʌ/ as in "but" or "dumb."
Low (open) back: /ɑ/ as in "lot" and "palm." The symbol is a "script a," not to be confused with "printed a" (a), which represents a slightly different sound, found in diphthongs such as /aɪ/ in "price."

One phoneme remains, a mid central vowel, always short, and always unstressed. It is called the "schwa," a German spelling of a Hebrew word meaning "emptiness," and used by Hebrew scholars to refer to a symbol placed under a consonant to indicate the absence of a following vowel sound. The IPA character is /ə/, an upside-down e, and it stands for the vowel of virtually every unaccented syllable in ordinary rapid speech, no matter how it is spelled: "comma" /kɑmə/, for example, or "mention" /mɛnʃən/.

I have left out the diphthongs, the double-vowels such as the /aʊ/ sound in "pound" or the /aɪ/ sound in "light." Many phonologists consider these sounds phonemes because they also consider them to be single syllables, and they often contrast with "monophthongs" in minimal pairs. Thus "pound" and "pond" contrast with each other (/paʊnd/ versus /pand/), and so do "light" and "lot" (/laɪt/ versus /lat/). There are about eight of these in English, depending on the dialect.

Figure 2.4 provides a list of the IPA letters for American English, in more or less alphabetical order. There are thirty-six of them.

I am not urging poets to adopt the IPA for their next poem, for their Muses may shrink from it in dismay, but it is an interesting exercise to

Consonants				Vowels	
b	big, rib	r	read, dear	a	father
d	dim, mud	s	seat, miss	æ	hat
ð	this, lithe	ʃ	shave, rush	e	care
f	fill, tough	t	take, wait	ɛ	pet
g	go, wag	θ	thin, myth	ə	about, sofa
h	hill	v	vat, wave	i	beet
j	yard	w	wish	ɪ	bit
k	kill, coal, lock	z	zero, raise	o	bore
l	lady, mail	ʒ	measure, garage	ɔ	bought, ball
m	many, room	ʧ	church	u	boot
n	nut, win	ʤ	judge	ʊ	book
ŋ	sing			ʌ	but
p	put, tap				

Figure 2.4 The International Phonetic Alphabet for American English

transcribe an existing poem into IPA. Here are the first eight lines of Robert Frost's great sonnet "Design":

> aɪ faʊnd ə dɪmpld spaɪdəʳ, fæt ənd waɪt,
> ɑn ə waɪt hi:l- ɔ:l, hoʊldɪŋ ʌp ə mɔ:θ,
> laɪk ə waɪt pi:s əv rɪdʒəd sætən klɔ:θ –
> əsɔrtəd kærəktəʳz əv dɛθ ənd blaɪt
> mɪkst rɛdɪ tu bəgɪn ðə mɔrnɪŋ raɪt,
> laɪk ði əngri:dɪənts əv ə wɪtʃəz brɔ:θ –
> ə snoʊ-drɑp spaɪdəʳ, ə flaʊəʳ laɪk ə frɔ:θ,
> ənd dɛd wɪŋz kærɪd laɪk ə peɪpər kaɪt.

> I found a dimpled spider, fat and white,
> On a white heal-all, holding up a moth
> Like a white piece of rigid satin cloth –
> Assorted characters of death and blight
> Mixed ready to begin the morning right,
> Like the ingredients of a witches' broth –
> A snow-drop spider, a flower like a froth,
> And dead wings carried like a paper kite.

I have left out the accent marks, which are unnecessary here; they are little vertical strokes that precede the stressed syllables, as in "ənˈgri:dɪənts." I have included the colon-like symbols for length, though they are not really necessary here. I may have been too quick to use the schwa for unstressed syllables – "əngri:dɪənts" might have been "ɪngri:dɪɛnts" – since a poem will normally be recited more slowly and carefully than ordinary rapid speech and the pale schwas will gain color. And I may not have used the best method for indicating the vocalic r (as in "spider"); superscripts might not be necessary.

What does this transcript reveal? Is it worth the trouble of making it? A good reader, reciting the poem aloud from its traditional spelling (or "hearing" it mentally while reading it), will not miss anything important, but, once you get used to it, the IPA text may bring out visibly some resemblances that the English alphabet blurs. The four rhymes in "white," "blight," "right," and "kite," for example, are spelled two different ways, and the letter i in them is also the spelling of the very different recurrent vowel in "dimpled," "rigid," "mixed," "begin," "witches," and "wings." The /aɪ/ diphthong makes it harder to fool the eye. Similarly the /k/ phoneme replaces four different spellings of the sound it stands for: "characters," "mixed," "carried," and "kite." Whether these four instances amount to a salient pattern is debatable, but the IPA letters at least help you see it. If you only had the IPA text, too, you might take "raɪt" to spell "rite": doing so is both a boon, since "rite" would be very appropriate to the meaning of the line it is in, and a distraction, since the homophone "right" is the right word. Again, the IPA helps raise the possibility for you to evaluate.

So I think it is worth taking the time to transcribe a few lines into IPA now and then. Its main use in the rest of this book, however, is to clarify certain important features of meter and rhyme, and for that we need to look first at the syllable.

The Syllable

Our word processors have a syllabication function which will break up words of more than one syllable at the end of the line and indicate the break with a hyphen. With that function in place, we can forget about syllables, but in the old days when we used typewriters or pens, we had to stop and think whenever we needed to break a word, or we had to resort to a dictionary, which would tell us the right places to hyphenate: *dic-tion-ar-y, type-writ-er, syl-la-ble, hy-phen-ate.* We might have noticed that different dictionaries often did it differently, but as long as we had one authority or another we could continue typing with a clear conscience. If we got into a debate with someone about where to break a word, however, and we had differing dictionaries, it was often impossible to find a consistent principle by which to settle the matter.

Linguists, needless to say, are not content with this state of affairs, which is due in part to the absurdity of English spelling and in part to the complexity of English sounds. They also want a theory that applies to all languages. According to recent theories of the syllable, all four of these hyphenated words would be hyphenated differently, but then all four of them would have to be respelled in the IPA before their syllabic structures revealed themselves clearly. Dictionaries usually respect etymology, so where a phonologist, as we will see, would prefer *type-wri-ter*, dictionary-writers remember that *writ-* is the root, not *wri-*, and make it *type-writ-er*.

One reason we might be unable to settle a debate about where to put in a hyphen is that we might be hard pressed even to say what a syllable is. Certainly there are ambiguous cases. How many syllables does "flower" have? Two, we might say: it might be *flo-wer* or *flow-er* but in either case, it is two. But then what about "flour"? One, no? Dictionaries don't hyphenate it. But it is pronounced just like "flower," and is in fact the same word historically. "Bowel" and "fowl" rhyme in most people's pronunciation, as do "sower" and "sore" in that of some, but the first of each pair is thought to have two syllables, and the second, one. These doubtful cases, which the well-tuned ears of poets often notice, are due to the presence of approximants or semi-vowels. Other ambiguous cases are caused by "vocalic" nasals. Does "mechanism" have three syllables or four? Dictionaries never break up *–ism* into *-is-m*, though that is partly because it would look silly to relegate just one letter to the next line. Many phonologists, however, would say it has four syllables, because the nasal stop /m/ can be syllabic, because it is a sonorant: it can be sounded for a while, unlike non-nasal stops; as such, it is usually written phonetically as an m with a little vertical stroke under it: [m̩].

Aristotle, in the earliest discussion of it we have, defines "syllable" (συλλαβή, *syllabē*) as "a meaningless sound put together out of a soundless [element] and one having sound" (*Poetics* 1456b35-36), which we can translate closely enough as a sound comprising a consonant and a vowel.[8] In his view, consonants are soundless or mute, presumably because they cannot be sustained, though in modern parlance there are several kinds of "consonants" that may indeed be sustained, either with the voice (nasals) or with a turbulent air-stream (fricatives). It is possible that the very term "consonant" reflects Aristotle's account, for it comes from the Latin for "sounding with" – that is, with a sounding vowel. A consonant, supposedly, cannot "sound" without one. Aristotle fails to note, however, that a vowel alone, without a mute element, can also be a syllable. ("Vowel" comes via French from Latin *vocalem* ["vocal"], from *vox* ["voice"] – it is the element that speaks or voices.)

According to the current consensus of phonologists, central to a syllable (in English) is the "vocalic peak," normally a vowel or, if not a vowel, then a consonant that can be sustained with the voice, a "sonorant," such as the /m/ in "-ism" and the other nasals /n/ and /ŋ/, as well as the liquids /l/ and /r/. In some languages, a whispered vowel will do, such as the /u/ between voiceless consonants in Japanese; in *sukiyaki*, the first syllable is not voiced, but the lips form the /u/ and whisper it for one beat: it is not *skiyaki*. In other languages, fricatives such as /s/ and /f/ can create syllables, like our "paraverbal" sounds "shh" or "psst." This central vowel or equivalent is called the "nucleus." The other sounds of a syllable, if there are any (the nucleus alone is enough), have been called "margins," or "troughs" between the "peaks," and they consist of consonants, but we distinguish between the consonant or consonant cluster that begins a syllable – the "onset" – and the consonant or cluster that ends it – the "coda" (Italian for "tail"). The nucleus and coda together constitute the "rhyme," since this is what we refer to when we talk about rhyme in poetry – though the concept of "rich rhyme," as we will see in the next chapter, involves the onset as well; linguists sometimes spell it "rime" to indicate that it is a linguistic category and not the poetic term. They often use the lower-case Greek letter sigma (σ) for "syllable" (for συλλαβή), which meant "something taken together," such as a set of sounds or "letters."

In the little tree diagram in Figure 2.5, C stands for "consonant" or "consonant cluster," and V for "vowel." Both onset and coda could be empty or null and we would still have a syllable if we had a vowel or some other sustainable sound – a possibility, we noted, that Aristotle did not consider. The vowel V could be a diphthong or double vowel, usually written with two letters, such as "ou" or "ai."

The remaining question, of course, is where to dump the consonants between the nuclei: should they go into onsets or codas or be divided up equitably between them, or what? Should it be *que-stion* or *ques-tion* or *quest-ion*? The rule phonologists have agreed on, for reasons not initially obvious, is to put as many as possible of the non-nuclear sounds into an onset, including the onset of the next syllable, and as few as possible into a coda. That would seem to require *que-stio-n+*, with -*st*- given to the onset of the second syllable and the final -*n* donated to the onset of the next word. In scanning the meters of ancient Greek and Latin, we do take the next word into account, but phonologists want syllables to stay within their words, so they make an exception to the rule: whatever consonants come at the end of the word go into the coda of the final syllable. So the final -*n* stays with the second syllable.

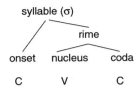

Figure 2.5 The structure of the syllable

There is another exception, much more interesting: the onset must obey the "phonotactic" rules of the language – that is, the rules of permissible sequences of phonemes. No word in English may begin with /tl/, for example, though it is perfectly all right in Greek. It is permissible in English to begin a word with /sl/ but not /sr/, while /ʃr/ is permissible but /ʃl/ is not, except in words recently borrowed from German or Yiddish, such as "schlep." If a combination is not allowed at the beginning of a word – that is, as the onset of the word's first syllable – then it is not allowed as the onset of any syllable within the word. So we would hyphenate "atlas" as *at-las*, though the Greeks (and it was their word originally) would hyphenate it *a-tlas*. As for "question," if we judged by the spelling, it would seem all right to send /-st-/ to the onset of the second syllable (*question*), since words in English may begin /st/. But in fact we don't pronounce the word that way: it is kwɛstʃ(ə)n. (The schwa [ə] is in parenthesis because it might be dropped, leaving only the syllabic -n (or n̩) to serve as the second nucleus.) No word in English may begin stʃ (it would have to be spelled stch or stsh), so it cannot be an onset anywhere. A word may begin tʃ, however, as in "chest" and "chin," so, by the rule that we assign as much as possible to an onset, we would break the word this way: kwɛs-tʃ(ə)n (*ques-tion*). It might seem better to make it kwɛst-ʃ(ə)n (*quest-ion*), and certainly more etymological, but the rule is the rule. So we would syllabify "dictionary" (dɪkʃənɛri) as *dic-tio-na-ry* and not *di-ctio-na-ry* because kʃ- is not a possible onset, though again, in a dictionary it may be best to leave the *-tion-* intact (as *dic-tion-a-ry*) since the word is constructed out of *diction* plus an ending.

Not all syllables are equal in "weight": some are "light" and some are "heavy." These terms are close in meaning to the more traditional terms "short" and "long," but phonologists prefer to assign "length" to vowels and "weight" to syllables. Roughly speaking, a syllable is heavy if it has either: (1) a long vowel or a diphthong in its nucleus, or (2) at least one consonant in its coda – or both; otherwise it is light. In English, length is not as distinctive a characteristic of vowels as it was in Greek and Latin, for instance. When we non-linguists speak of "long a" and "short "long e" and "short e," and so on, we are mainly distinguishing the shape of the vowel, that is, whether it is high or low, or front or back, or tense or lax, and only secondarily its actual length, that is, how long it takes to say it. Weight is measured in units called "morae" (singular "mora," Latin for "delay" or "unit of time," whence our word "moratorium"): a light syllable has one mora, a heavy syllable two. For some purposes, such as formulating laws of change in historical linguistics, it was found that a third category is needed, "super-heavy" syllables, which have three morae, such as a diphthong followed by a coda with one or two consonants,[9] but two categories are enough for understanding poetic meters that are based on syllable weight, since all meters, no matter what feature they are based on, are binary; they have only two values. In a binary system, the rule for calculating weight with morae is this: (1) count the first segment, or phoneme, in the nucleus as one mora, and (2) if there is anything after it in the syllable, whether in the nucleus (such as the second part of a diphthong) or in the coda (a consonant or two), add another mora.[10]

In "dictionary" (dɪk-ʃə-nɛ-ri) the first syllable is heavy, because it has two morae (ɪ+k), the other three light, while in "atlas" (æt-ləs), both syllables are heavy. The two syllables in "heavy" (hɛvi) are both light, whereas "light" (laɪt) is heavy, even super-heavy, as it has a diphthong in the nucleus and a consonant in the coda. This technical account of the syllable will be useful to have at hand in analyzing certain kinds of meter, and even more in analyzing rhyme.

Prosody, Meter, and Feet

Prosody is the study of versification or meter, the regular patterns of sounds in poetry. Linguists often use "prosody" in a broader sense to refer to the sound patterns or rhythms in prose or in everyday speech as well as verse, but, even though the word looks as if it is akin to "prose," it originally had to do with verse and we will be using it in that respect. It comes from Latin *prosodia*, which meant "accent of a syllable," from Greek *prosōidia* (προσῳδία), which meant "tune to which speech is intoned" or "melodic accent," from *pros-* ("to, in addition to") and *ōidē* ("song"). *Prosōidia* was translated by the Romans as *accentus*, which gives English "accent," from *ad* ("to") and *cantus* ("song"). The Greeks had to consider the length of a syllable, the tone or pitch of a syllable, and "breathing" ("rough" or "smooth"), none of which was indicated in writing until Hellenistic times or later. To analyze or "scan" the meter of ancient verse is a complicated task, as there are many rules and a huge variety of meters, most of which are impossible in English and the modern European languages, which are based on different features.

For students of English poetry in high school and university, "meter" means the set of four kinds of "feet" that divide up a line, and the number of them in each line. "Free verse" is an exception because it doesn't have feet, or at least not regularly repeating feet, though it may have a looser sort of rhythm. Of these four kinds (occasionally a few more are added), two of them are two-syllable feet and two are three-syllable feet, and they are distinguished from each other by where the accent or stress falls: iambic, trochaic, anapestic, and dactylic. "Accent" and "stress" are the usual terms for the phonological feature in English that determines the meter, but a clearer name for it is "loudness": the voice gets louder on an accented syllable. This is the case not only in poetry, of course, but in everyday speech. The word "accent" is accented on the first syllable, as are "students," "English," "meter," "looser," "feature," "loudness," "louder," and "syllable." All but the last of these are trochaic words or trochees (stressed-unstressed, or loud-soft), like the great majority of two-syllable words in English, while the last one, "syllable," is a dactyl (loud-soft-soft). We have used only one iambic word, or iamb, in this paragraph so far: "divide." In the previous paragraph, we had "refer," "respect," and "intoned," all soft-loud. Anapests (soft-soft-loud) are fairly rare, and are usually compound or prefixed verbs such as "understand," "comprehend," "correspond," "interrupt." Dactyls in the last few sentences include "poetry" as well as "syllable."

Sometimes, a fifth kind of foot is also taught, the spondee (loud-loud). If there are any such words, they would be compounds, usually nouns, such as "baseball," "racetrack," "shortcake," or "zigzag," but these are actually stressed a little louder on the first syllable. Some versification experts would deny that the spondee is really a foot of the same sort as the other four, since we do not find lines of all spondees – at least not in the modern European languages – as we find lines of iambs, trochees, dactyls, and anapests; a spondee might show up in a foot here and there, as a substitute for another kind of foot, but if there were two or more of them they would be reinterpreted as part of another meter.

In verse, of course, a metrical foot may include two or three words, or a word may span two or more feet. The phrase "in the house" is an anapestic foot, though in an iambic or trochaic setting the word "in" could be given a stress. The word "university" has five syllables, with the stress in the middle, and in a poem it could be assimilated in various ways. In an iambic pentameter line (five iambs), for example, it could be this:

    /   /   /   /   /

The u|niver|sity | is on | the hill

In dactylic tetrameter (four dactyls), it could be this:

  /   /   /   /

Taking a | walk through the | great uni|versity

And it could be this in anapestic tetrameter (four anapests):

   /   /   /   /

Univer|sity class|es are hard|er than that

If you find the meter of a poem hard to figure out, or scan, a good trick is to look for a polysyllabic word and say it as you would say it in normal speech. The stress will fall on a stressed position in the line – if it doesn't, then it isn't meter – and you can work backward and forward from there. There may still be ambiguities. "The university is on the hill" might give you pause because there are only two fully stressed syllables in the line, *-ver-* and *hill*, but when you note that the initial "The" is unlikely to receive the stress, and English does not use four-syllable feet such as soft-soft-soft-loud, you will readily scan the line as iambic.

Here are the names of the four feet again, plus spondee, and their etymologies, all from Greek. Here "x" means unaccented or soft and "/" means accented or loud.

Iambic foot, or **iamb**: x / or di-dum. The words, like all the others here, are originally Greek. We get the word from French *iambe* < Latin *iambus* < Greek *iambos*, of uncertain origin. It may share an ending with *dithyrambos*, a kind of song (and dance) associated with the god Dionysus, but the origin of that word is also obscure. The *OED* connects it to the verb *iaptō* ("assail, attack"), because the oldest iambic poetry in Greece (by Archilochus and Hipponax) was sharply satirical, but this theory is questionable.

Trochaic foot, or **trochee**: / x or dum-di French *trochée* < Latin *trochaeus* < Greek *trokhaios [pous]* ("running [foot]") < *trokhos* ("running, course") related to the verb *trekhō* ("run").

Spondaic foot, or **spondee**: / / or dum-dum. French *spondée* < Latin *spondeus* < Greek *spondeios [pous]* ("[foot] used at a libation") < *spondē* ("libation") < *spendō* ("make an offering, perform a rite"). Greek sacrifices were solemn affairs, and presumably a slow and even pace was thought fitting.

Dactylic foot, or **dactyl**: / x x or dum-diddy. Latin *dactylus* < Greek *daktulos* ("finger"), of uncertain origin, but perhaps from PIE *deik-* ("show, point to") > Latin *dicere* ("say, tell") > "dictate," "contradict," etc.; also Latin *digitus* ("finger" = the pointer) > "digit"; and Latin *-dex* as in *index* ("forefinger") > "index," "indicate," etc. The Greek idea was that the long bone and the two small bones of a finger represent the long and two shorts of the dactylic foot; the trouble is that, depending on which finger is pointed in which direction, a finger could equally well represent an anapest. If you hold your left hand in front of you and point to the right, you get a dactyl, reading left to right. It is a happy accident, presumably, that the word *daktulos* itself (δάκτυλος) scans as a dactyl.

Anapestic foot, or **anapest**: x x / or diddy-dum. Latin *anapaestus* < Greek *anapaistos* ("struck back, rebounding," i.e., a dactyl reversed) < *anapaiō* ("strike back") < *paiō* ("to strike"). The Greeks occasionally called it *antidaktulos*.

Why do we call these units "feet"? "Foot" is obviously the same word as that for the human appendage. It is cognate with Greek *pous*, Latin *pes*, and Sanskrit *padá* ("step" < *pád* ["foot"]), all of which could mean a metrical unit or part of a verse. Some scholars have assumed that the term arose because people kept time to verse by tapping their feet, but surely it is more likely that the Greeks and others danced to verse. One of the feet, the trochee, refers to a running pace, and many of the Greek odes – perhaps all of them originally – were choral odes, danced to by a *khoros* (χορός), which meant a round dance and a place for dancing, as well as a choir. The Muses were dancers as well as singers. It has been argued recently by A. P. David in *Dance of the Muses* that even Homer's epics were originally danced to!

There was a charming set of diagrams on a website called RhymeWeaver .com which used ballet slippers for unaccented syllables and work boots for accented ones. It almost suggested that the Greeks wore different footwear on different feet, but it also reminds us vividly of the origin of meter in dancing, and perhaps marching.

We said that accent in English meter, no less than in spoken English, is a matter of loudness. Normally, though not invariably, when we make a syllable louder, we also raise it a little in pitch (up a few notes on the musical scale) and increase its length a little (sustain it a bit longer in time). There is good evidence that the accent of ancient Greek and Sanskrit was a matter of pitch more than stress, and that these languages inherited it from Proto-Indo-European; it lingers in some modern Indo-European languages such as Lithuanian and Serbian. But Greek and Sanskrit, like Latin, based their meters not on pitch and not on loudness but on length – on how long it takes to say a syllable. For this reason, many descriptions of English meter (as well as German and other "accentual" meters) speak of "long" and "short" units and use the symbols‒ and ᴜ for them when scanning, but such accounts are misleading. Though louder syllables tend to be a little longer, length is not the basis of English meter.

Meter as Template

There are several theories of meter competing among each other today, but most of them include the idea that meter is a template, an abstract pattern that actual lines of verse approximate. Some theories leave it at that; others try to explain the templates themselves, whether historically or through a set of abstract principles or procedures that "generate" them.

Here is a plausible definition: Meter is an abstract structure by which one phonological feature (or sound-feature) of a language – usually stress, pitch, or length – is reduced from several levels to two, to a *binary* pattern of marked and unmarked syllables in regular alternation. English words in everyday speech, for example, have at least three levels of stress or accent (loudness), as we shall see in a moment, but English meter is concerned with only two: accented or unaccented syllables. English meter is also concerned with the number of syllables, so it is usually labeled accentual-syllabic. It may be possible to have a meter that is only accentual (as in Old English and other old Germanic languages) or only syllabic (as in French and Japanese); it is certainly possible to have a meter based on neither accent nor syllable-count but units of length (as in Greek and Latin). We shall look at these possibilities later on.

When spoken, a polysyllabic word such as "indispensability" has at least three different levels distributed across its seven syllables, and some analysts would say four; I lean toward four myself:

3   4   2   4 1 4 3
in|di|spen|sa|bi|li|ty

The greatest stress (1) falls on the third-last syllable (-bi-), while the third syllable (-spen-) is a bit louder than the first or final (as becomes clear in the word "indispensable"):

3   4   1   4 3
in|di|spen|sa|ble

If you think there are only three levels, the ones I have numbered 2 and 3 will be 2, and the 4s will be 3s. In verse, in either case, the pattern of "indispensability" is reduced to two levels: where / is the stress marker and x indicates unstressed, "indispensability" is scanned as / x / x / x / or dumdy-dumdy-dumdy-dum. The word is itself a line of trochaic tetrameter "catalectic," that is, it can be divided up into four *metra* or feet of trochees (loud-soft) with the last one cut off or truncated:

```
/ x      / x     / x   /
indi    spensa   bili  ty
```

Two examples of trochaic tetrameter catalectic are William Blake's "Tyger, Tyger, burning bright" and Jane Taylor's "Twinkle, twinkle, little star."

Some theorists of meter try to preserve the greater differentiation of stress in the spoken language, and in actual recitation or performance of verse, by scanning with as many as four stress options. Carper and Attridge, for example, in an attractive introductory book, *Meter and Meaning*, posit two kinds of "beats" (emphasized and unemphasized) and two kinds of "offbeats" (emphasized and unemphasized), and they annotate many lines of verse with symbols for each of these. Their observations are usually very responsive to the distinctive characteristics of the lines, but their system is a kind of compromise between scansion, which is the application of a binary pattern or template, and performance, which might well resort to three levels, or even four. They acknowledge the binary template with their basic division of "beat" and "off-beat," but then try to simplify and systematize the possible realizations of a line by rather arbitrarily bifurcating these two positions. They conflate, in other words, meter and rhythm, or template and performance, but it makes things clearer to keep them distinct.

In a vivid simile, the poet Robert Lowell likened meter to "the bone structure of the body," while rhythm is "not just the flesh and blood, it's the whole character, the whole flux of things that aren't visible at all."[11]

Iambic Pentameter

The best-known and most prestigious meter in English is iambic pentameter, the basis of blank verse, which is the unrhymed line of Shakespeare's plays and Milton's *Paradise Lost*, as well as the basis of the rhymed couplet of "heroic" and other varieties from Chaucer onward.

Hamlet speaks to Polonius, whom he has just killed: "Thou wretched, rash, intruding fool, farewell" (3.4.31). This line scans easily and is perfectly regular:

```
            1   2    3    4    5   6  7    8    9  10
```
Thou wret|ched, rash, | intru|ding fool, | farewell.

It has ten syllables, and all the even-numbered ones are stressed. If you had any trouble scanning it, you would only have to look at one of the three polysyllabic words, especially "intruding," to get things right, but even if you had no idea what meter this might be, you would still say it right if you said it, as you would certainly say it, with the normal accents on the words. Difficulties seldom arise in lines like this one, with polysyllabic words, or with little words such as "the" that are seldom stressed.

On his way to England, Hamlet comes upon two armies fighting over a tiny piece of land and begins a soliloquy with this line: "How all occasions do inform against me" (4.4.32). This line too is easily scanned and recited, but it has eleven syllables:

```
        1   2    3    4  5    6    7  8    9  10     11
```
How all | occa|sions do | inform | against | me

It is still iambic pentameter, and quite regular, but it has an unstressed syllable at the end; it is labeled "extrametrical" because it is not counted as part of the pentameter structure. A line that ends with such an unaccented syllable is said to have a "feminine" ending, while lines that end on an accented syllable, like "Thou wretched, rash, intruding fool, farewell," have a "masculine" ending. These terms come up in discussions of rhyme, as we shall see, and ought to be abolished in English as they arose in French, which had and still has grammatical genders. These extrametrical syllables, in any case, are very common in iambic pentameter and various other meters.

Here is another line, the most famous in *Hamlet*, that has an extrametrical syllable at the end but also has something else: "To be, or not to be, that is the question" (3.1.56). The first three feet are obviously iambic, but what about the fourth foot? Is it iambic too? Do we say "that IS the question"? It seems unnatural to do so, and no actor I have heard or read about ever said it that way. It is surely a "trochaic inversion," a trochee substituted for an iamb, and it is surely effective dramatically in this line. Such substitutes are common in iambic pentameter, especially in the first foot. The very next line of Hamlet's speech, in fact, begins with one: "Whether 'tis nobler in the mind to suffer."

```
       /   x    x  /   x  /    x   /    x  /  x
```
Whether | 'tis no|bler in | the mind | to suf|fer

The fact that such inversions and other irregularities are much more common in the beginning of the line than in the ending may express a general principle about the structure of all lines of verse: that meter is looser at the outset and stricter at the close.[12] The Homeric line of dactylic hexameter, for example, almost always concludes the same way, a "cadence" in the final two feet with the pattern long-short-short long-long.

Once in a while you can be misled by what appears to be a trochaic inversion but is not. Polonius, warning Ophelia to stay at a distance from Hamlet, says he has heard that Hamlet has "Given private time to you, and you yourself" have freely listened to him (1.3.92). If you took "Given" as a trochaic foot, then the whole line appears trochaic, but with six stressed syllables:

/ x   / x   /   x   /   x   /   x   /
Given | private | time to | you, and | you your|self

That would make it a trochaic hexameter catalectic, uncomfortable here in an iambic pentameter setting. Something must be adjusted somewhere, and the fewest distortions of normal English are either (1) to make the first foot an anapestic substitution (or consider one of the two unstressed syllables "extrametrical") –

x x   / x   /   x   /   x   /   x   /
Given pri|vate time | to you, | and you | yourself

– or (2) to compress the first word into a single unstressed syllable. It makes little difference in the performance which way you think of it as long as you get "given" in quickly. It seems likelier that "given" is compressed, in the same way "heaven" is often taken as one syllable in poems and Christmas carols, to /gɪvn/ (in IPA) or even /gɪn/, which was the way it was pronounced in some dialects, and spelled "gin," "geen," "gein," or the like.

The opening line of Macbeth's great speech, "Tomorrow and tomorrow and tomorrow" (*Macbeth* 5.5.19), has a final unstressed syllable, but what is interesting about it metrically is that it forces us to put stresses on "and" twice. "Tomorrow" has three syllables with the central syllable stressed (soft-loud-soft) – there is a name for it, amphibrach, but it is not needed in English scansion of meter – so one way – the only good way – to get it into an iambic line three times is to confer a stress on "and" twice.

x / x   /   x / x   /   x / x
Tomor|row and | tomor|row and | tomor|row

This metrical elevation of normally unaccented syllables is called "promotion." Most actors would not promote the two instances of "and" to the same level as the three instances of "-mor-," but they would have to do something to acknowledge the stress pattern, perhaps simply by dwelling a little on each "and." Then again, an actor might do something surprising and overpromote each "and," and pause after each "tomorrow," as one way to bring out the tedious and meaningless concatenation of Macbeth's days. These various performances illustrate the distinction usually drawn between meter and rhythm: meter is the fixed binary pattern, though there are occasional ambiguities, while rhythm is what results when a speaker pays attention both to the meter and to the meaning of the line.

Here is a more challenging line from Milton's *Paradise Lost* (*PL* 2.621): "Rocks, caves, lakes, fens, bogs, dens, and shades of death." It ends iambic, but what about the six monosyllabic words in the first three feet? They have equal weight as items on a list, so it seems almost inescapable that we have three spondees:

$$/ \quad / \quad / \quad / \quad / \quad / \quad x \quad / \quad x \quad /$$
Rocks, caves, | lakes, fens, | bogs, dens, | and shades | of death

It would be very artificial to force the first three feet into iambs, though I think it would be natural to pause slightly after each foot, and perhaps stress a little more heavily, or rise in pitch on, "dens," the last word before the unstressed "and," and which rhymes with "fens." Some sort of registration of the prevailing iambic wind may be all we can allow in this remarkable slow line.

There is no way, however, to assimilate the third of the next three lines to iambicity:

> Why should a dog, a horse, a rat have life
> And thou no breath at all? Thou'lt come no more,
> Never, never, never, never, never.

They are, of course, a part of King Lear's heartbreaking lament over the dead Cordelia (5.3.305–07).[13] The breaking of the iambic pattern with the five "nevers" emphasizes – if emphasis is needed – Lear's recognition of the absolute finality of her death.

Iambic pentameter is an abstract pattern, a set of expectations, that the actual lines approximate. If they seldom deviate from the template, they run the risk of sounding mechanical and jingly, like a nursery rhyme, so a good poet will deviate when the meaning is enhanced by doing so or the lines made more interesting, dramatic, or memorable. Sometimes poets push the line to the breaking point. Whether they succeed in making great poetry out of such fracturing depends on many things besides meter, needless to say, but without at least the hovering presence of the metrical pattern the departures from it would have no effect.[14]

This may be the place to mention that some scholars have thought that the Old English four-stress line, which we will look at shortly, still haunts iambic pentameter: English verse, they say, hearkens to its ancient birthright of four stresses. So we might scan Hamlet's soliloquy like this:

/   /   /   /

To be, or not to be, that is the question:

/   /   /   /

Whether 'tis nobler in the mind to suffer

/   /   /   /

The slings and arrows of outrageous fortune,

/ /   /   /

Or to take arms against a sea of troubles

/   /   /   /

And by opposing end them. To die, to sleep . . .

Some of these lines are more plausibly scanned than others in this system. The little words "in" in line 2, "of" in line 3, and "by" in line 5, for instance, no longer need to be "promoted," but then sometimes a syllable between two unstressed ones will have to be "demoted," or the three syllables will have to be elided and huddled into one position. The scansion of line 1 seems arbitrary, for it might just as well go like this:

/   /   /   /

To be, or not to be, that is the question:

And "against" in line 4 would seem to deserve a stress. In actual performance an actor might well produce four strong stresses in these lines, but I don't see how he could do it to the lines from *King Lear* without weird distortions. The four-stress theory, whatever else may be said for it, seems to conflate scansion with performance.

Other English Meters

We have already mentioned trochaic tetrameter, and in particular the truncated or catalectic kind, frequent in nursery rhymes, such as "Jack and Jill went up the hill" or "Eeny meeny miney mo." Here is the first stanza of Blake's "The Tyger":

   /   /   /   /
Tyger, Tyger, burning bright,
  /   /   /   /
In the forests of the night;
    /   /   /   /
What immortal hand or eye,
    /   /   /   /
Could frame thy fearful symmetry?

This is very easily scanned, but note that in line 2 "In" and "of" get promoted to receive the accent. All that matters is that they occupy odd-numbered positions (1 and 5) and are surrounded by weak syllables ("In," of course, begins a line, but both promoted syllables precede "the"); in these circumstances they resemble the "and" (twice) in Macbeth's line. Note, too, that the fourth line begins with an "upbeat" or unstressed syllable, which might tempt us to declare the line iambic; we should resist that temptation because the trochaic environment is well established in the first three lines. It may not be a coincidence that line 3 "enjambs" or carries over syntactically into line 4, so we might not pause as long between them as we do between the earlier lines, despite the comma after "eye." (Blake's punctuation is notoriously quirky.) So we might discount "Could" as extrametrical, but it does serve as a kind of metrical glue between lines 3 and 4.

Poe gives us a much longer trochaic line in "The Raven":

/   /   /   /   /   /   /   /
Once upon a midnight dreary, while I pondered, weak and weary,
/   /   /   /   /   /   /   /
Over many a quaint and curious volume of forgotten lore –

On the basis of the first line, with its internal rhyme at the halfway point, and many later lines, we might be tempted to relineate this octometer poem into tetrameters, but that project would run into snags as early as line 2, as we would have to break it between "curious" and "volume," resulting in a tight enjambment of adjective and noun. It is hard to miss the sound-effects Poe deploys, such as the pairings of alliterating adjectives in both lines. ("Quaint" and "curious" alliterate, of course, as their IPA spellings make obvious: /kwent/ and /kjʊriəs/.) Even the two little irregularities in the meter of the second line are similar:

    / x x   / x x
    many a . . . curious

The two quasi-dactylic feet here almost rhyme in their two upbeats with their /iə/ vowels, and these vowels can be readily "resolved" or compressed into a single syllable /jə/.

The triple meters in English (anapestic and dactylic) are far less common, but some are memorable, such as Clement Moore's "Visit from St. Nicholas" in very regular anapestic tetrameter:

<pre>
     x   x /   x x   /   x   x /   x   x /
   'Twas the night before Christmas, when all through the house
     x x   / x   x / x   x / x x   /
   Not a creature was stirring, not even a mouse[.]
</pre>

By ending on a stressed syllable, anapests invite rhyme; it is difficult to find an anapestic poem that does not make use of it.

Here is Tennyson's "Charge of the Light Brigade" in dactylic dimeter:

> Cannon to right of them,
> Cannon to left of them,
> Cannon in front of them
>   Volleyed and thundered[.]

There is no need to mark the syllables, but we should take note that the fourth line is "catalectic" – one syllable is dropped – and Tennyson seems to have dropped it so the final word could rhyme (on "hundred") a few lines later. In fact, he tinkered with several lines after these for rhyming purposes, because dactylic meter is challenging to find rhymes for. (One might argue that the first three lines "rhyme" on the same two words, but they are unstressed, and self-respecting rhymes must rhyme on a stressed syllable.)

Accentual Meter

A quite different kind of meter governed Old English poetry, such as *Beowulf*, before the arrival of French, with its syllable-counting meters, in 1066; it also governed poetry in other Germanic languages, such as Old Norse, Old High German, and Old Saxon. What counted in this kind of meter, according to a longstanding theory repeated in introductory books, was a strong stress or accent: four to a line. Unaccented or weak syllables did not count, and were not counted; a line could have anywhere from none to ten or so, though almost always there were at least four. Old Germanic verse, to be more precise, consisted of pairs of half-lines or hemistichs, each called a "verse," each more or less independent of the other metrically but linked by alliteration; two verses, then, made up a line. The first stressed syllable of the second half-line, called the "stave," set the alliteration for the first half – that is, it almost always alliterated with one or both of its stressed syllables; usually both of them alliterated, but the second syllable in the second verse seldom did so: **leo**mum ond **lea**fum; / **lif** eac ge**sceop** (*Beowulf* 97, strong syllables in boldface).

These "rules" are inferred from studying the surviving texts; there is no explicit account of them from the Old English period. But we can also infer from the texts some complications of this simple theory, such as the fact that there appears to be a secondary stress besides the strong and weak ones, normally on the second syllable of a compound word, such as *land-fruma* ("land-leader") (*Beowulf* 31), *leod-cyning* ("people-king") (54), and *Healfdene* (a name) (57), which would each be weighted 1-2-3, or perhaps 1-2-4, but in any case strong-secondary-weak, sometimes notated as "Ssw." The existence of the secondary stress might seem to have no bearing on the principle that each verse has two strong syllables and a varying number of weak (or weaker) ones, but it seems that a verse cannot end with a certain sort of weak syllable unless there is a secondary stress between the strong stresses. Stresses, too – both strong and secondary – predominantly fell on heavy syllables, and that pattern suggests there was a "quantitative" basis as well as accentual. (In Old English, as in other Germanic languages, heavy syllables tend to draw stresses in ordinary speech.) On the assumption that the verses were "isochronic" – that is, they took the same length of time to recite or chant – some scholars, notably J. C. Pope (*The Rhythm of Bewoulf*), have made elaborate attempts to put the lines into musical notation, with half-notes for the heavy stresses, quarter notes for secondary stresses, and eighth notes for weak stresses, but with lots of variations, quickening of tempos, and so on, to accommodate the stubbornly excessive numbers of weak syllables. Other scholars think it is impossible to score Old English poetry that way, and that we should drop the assumption of isochrony.

Experts also disagree as to the relevance of the category "foot." About a quarter of all verses in *Beowulf* are trochaic, two feet to the verse, a proportion that rises to about half if certain "resolutions" of weak syllables are allowed so they can count as one heavy syllable; those frequencies establish the trochaic foot as a norm, according to syllable-counting advocates of the foot. But that still leaves a lot of irregular feet, if they *are* feet, including feet that don't look like any feet we know unless some syllables are discounted as "extrametrical." The term "anacrusis" is often invoked here, a word used in classical metrics, though not by the ancients themselves, to refer to extra syllables at the beginning of a line that do not figure in the main meter; it comes from Greek *anakrousis*, which meant "a pushing back," especially of a ship backing water, and then "a striking up" before music or verse (as we might say "strike up the band") or "upbeat." In my far-from-expert view, if a theory requires so many syllables to be compressed or hustled offstage as extrametrical or hypermetrical or cases of anacrusis, in order to preserve a simple norm or core, then surely the theory is suspect. The experts continue to debate.[15] I suspect there is an irreducible messiness to *Beowulf,* and perhaps to all the other Germanic poems based on heavy stresses, that no formula will clean up. In any case, here is a three-line sample from *Beowulf* (2688–90), in which the hero faces the dragon in his final battle. The little acute accents over some of the vowels are the conventional way of marking them as long. The letters þ (thorn) and ð (eth) were both used for both voiced and unvoiced th-sounds, though here the þ is used only initially and the ð more often medially. (In the IPA, we saw, the ð was adopted for the voiced variant.) I use the right-leaning slash (/) for the strong stress, the left-leaning slash (\) for the secondary stress, and x for unstressed syllables.

> /   x   /   \ x   /   x   / x
> Þá wæs þéodsceaða   þriddan síðe
>
> Then was (the) people-scourge, for the third time,
>
> /   x   / \ x   /   x x   /   x
> frécne fýrdraca   faéhða gemyndig·
>
> the fierce firedragon, violence-minded;
>
> /   x x   x x /   x   x x   /   /   x
> raésde on ðone rófan   þá him rúm ágeald

it rushed at the brave one, when it was yielded room

If we were to analyze the meter with familiar feet, we might want to call the first two lines trochaic tetrameter with some extrametrical syllables or perhaps dactylic substitutions, but our attempt to foot it would fall flat in the third line. Some of these syllables may be "extrametrical"; some may be generated by some rule or other, still not agreed on by the specialists. We might imagine a singer of *Beowulf* plucking a harp loudly twice per verse alongside his stressed syllables, at a fairly regular pace (but perhaps not at a strictly isochronic pace), and shoveling in as many unstressed syllables as he

needed in between them (but with a few constraints or pressure
them out in certain ways).[16] The old Germanic bards were origin
poets and illiterate, and they probably did not altogether memori
songs but partly improvised them, as we think Homer and his pred
did with Greek epic. If they recomposed their poems each time they
chanted them, they would need flexibility in the rules. Homer, it is true,
recited his poems in an elaborate isochronic meter with strict rules governing syllable substitutions, but he too had a large repertory of devices,
notably formulas like "swift-footed Achilles," to give him elbow room for
improvising. *Beowulf* seems less formulaic than the *Iliad* (though, of
course, it is much shorter), and perhaps the lax rules – or lack of rules –
for unstressed syllables is the reason it seems so.

It is striking that rap and/or hip-hop songs (or chants), which emerged
in the 1970s, repeat several features of Old English verse. Most of them
have four strong stresses per line, with any number of unstressed syllables
between them, though the lines, for the most part, are not divided into
hemistichs. Instead of alliteration, of course, they use rhymes or semi-
rhymes on the downbeats. It is crucial in rapping to stay on beat, which is
often underlined by percussion: that creates isochrony of the lines. Beowulf
would feel right at home.

Syllabic Meter

Greek, Sanskrit, and Latin based their meters on "quantity," the length of
time it takes to pronounce a syllable. The vernacular languages that
evolved from Latin (Italian, French, Spanish, Portuguese, Catalan,
Provençal, and several others) developed a metrical system based on the
number of syllables regardless of length *or* stress. They were, in that
regard, the opposite of the Germanic meters, which by and large counted
only stresses. It is sometimes said that French verse, for example, is almost
entirely a matter of getting the right number of syllables into the line,
without regard to the accents of the words, which are lightly spoken
anyway (in comparison with English or German). To give the line some
structure, a caesura or break may be required, notably in the middle of the
twelve-syllable line called the alexandrine, and the lines usually rhymed at
the end. It is conceded by French metricians that the rhyming syllable
receives a stress (or *accent tonique*), and so does the sixth syllable, just
before the caesura, though perhaps a somewhat lighter one. Otherwise it
was a matter of counting syllables, though there were intricate rules for
determining whether a potential syllable was sounded or not, based on

the pronunciation of words centuries ago or their etymological history in Latin.

Some metricians have doubted that a simple count of syllables with prominent ones at the end of half-lines can possibly be the basis of metrical verse, even with rhymes, and it is true that in the verse of Romance languages there are discernible patterns of stress in phrases. Here, for instance, is a famous couplet from Racine's *Phèdre* (1.3.305–06), with the syllable count:

> 1   2   3   4   5   6   7   8   9   10 11 12
> Ce n'est plus une ardeur ‖ dans mes veines cachée:
> It is no longer a fever   hidden in my veins:

> 1   2 3   4   5   6   7 8   9   10 11 12
> C'est Vénus toute entière ‖ à sa proie attachée.
> It is Venus altogether   crouched upon her prey.

The break is indicated by the double bar (‖), which in classical alexandrines falls at midpoint; poets of the Romantic era began to move it around. Even a reader with a little French might wonder about syllable 10 in the first line, since in spoken French the e would be silent, but in verse as in song such an e, called variously *e muet* ("mute"), *e atone* ("unaccented"), or *e caduc* ("defunct"), is brought to life when it precedes a consonant, even the plural s; all the other examples of silent e in this couplet remain silent because they precede vowels.

So we have the right number of syllables, divided properly into hemistichs, and a fine two-syllable rhyme. Is that it? No: surely there is an anapestic meter here, though delicately expressed:

> x x   / x   x /   x   x   / x   x /
> Ce n'est plus une ardeur ‖ dans mes veines cachée:

> x   x / x   x   /   x x   / x x /
> C'est Vénus toute entière ‖ à sa proie attachée.

Here is the opening line of a famous poem by Victor Hugo ("Extase"), also in alexandrines:

> J'étais seul près des flots, ‖ par une nuit d'étoiles.
> I was alone by the waves,   on a night of stars.

The word *une* has two syllables here, as its *e caduc* is followed by a consonant in the next word. It seems there is also a pattern of light stresses, anapestic in the first hemistich like those by Racine, but with a graceful variation in the second hemistich. We might, in other words, understand a *coupe* (or "cut") in the middle of the first hemistich, though it is less clear if we can posit one in the second.

<pre>
    x x /   x x /   x x x /   x /
J'étais seul│ près des flots, ‖ par une nuit d'étoiles.
</pre>

Syllable-counting alone, then, even with regularly placed caesuras and final rhymes, would seem to be too minimal a sort of metricality to exist in reality. Without going so far as to deploy regular feet, French poets were attentive to phrases in order to subtly shape their lines.[17]

We might note, before leaving French verse, that, even though the alexandrine was the usual line in epic poems, the Homeric and Virgilian line of dactylic hexameter forbade a caesura in the exact middle. It most often comes in the third of the six *metra*, but it may fall elsewhere. This difference may say something about French classicism and its love of symmetry and balance, but it is in that respect not very classical.

By the conventions of Italian prosody, the hendecasyllable or eleven-syllable line, the line of Dante and many poets after him, must have a relatively strong stress on the tenth syllable and a secondary stress most often on the sixth but sometimes on the fourth and eighth. To take the opening line of the *Inferno*:

<pre>
 x   x x x x   / x x x / x
Nel mezzo del cammin di nostra vita
In the middle of the path of our life
</pre>

Even though stresses in Italian tend to be lighter than in English, when the natural stresses of *mezzo* and *nostra* are figured in, we have a line of iambic pentameter if we "promote" *del* in the second foot:

<pre>
 x / x / x   /   x / x / x
Nel mezzo del cammin di nostra vita
</pre>

Spanish prosody is also based on syllable count, but with stress patterns like those of Italian. The hendecasyllable line has a strong stress on the tenth syllable, like the Italian line, and two or three lighter stresses, almost always on even-numbered syllables. In this line of Garcilaso de la Vega's, the secondary stresses would seem to fall on the second and sixth syllables, but perhaps also on the eighth; the result is another iambic pentameter:

<pre>
 x   / x / x /   x /   x / x
El dulce lamentar de dos pastores
The sweet lamenting of two shepherds
</pre>

Japanese Syllabic Verse

One reason purely syllabic versification systems are rare[18] is that in most languages syllables come in several varieties, or at least two: light and heavy. Where all you do is count syllables, moreover, it is difficult to retain a sense of regular repetition among lines longer than seven or eight syllables, perhaps because of "Miller's Law," which states that the number of objects a human being can hold in working memory is seven, plus or minus two ("Magical Number Seven").

Japanese verse may evade both difficulties, as the Japanese syllable is defined as a mora (symbolized by μ), and even by the definition of syllable we have set out earlier in this chapter most Japanese syllables would have one mora. The language lacks consonant clusters. Its native speakers have notable difficulty learning to pronounce English clusters, and English speakers find it amusing to see how their words get transliterated into the *katakana* syllabary (with one symbol for each mora-syllable, all in the form CV): our two-syllable word "cluster," for example, comes out ク ラ ス タ ― or *ku-ra-su-ta-a*, which, counting the long sign at the end (which accommodates the vocalic -r), has five morae.

The Japanese verse line has for centuries been either five or seven morae long, usually alternating. The short tanka form, which goes back to the eighth century, is in the pattern 5-7-5-7-7, while the haiku, much more recent in origin, is 5-7-5. If Miller is right, we can readily manage lines of seven morae and seven-minus-two morae, even if they don't group themselves into larger units. The spoken accent of Japanese is pitched, rather gently, and a large portion of words have no accent at all. So, possibly, Japanese verse comes much closer to being truly syllabic than the putatively syllabic verse of French and the other Romance languages.

Here is a haiku by the greatest of its masters, Bashō (1644–94):

> Haru tatsu ya
> Spring starts:
> shinnen furuki
> new-year old
> kome go shō.
> rice five *shō*.

The second line, however it looks to us, has seven morae, for *shinnen* has four, as the -*n* in what we would call the codas of both syllables counts as a mora: *shi-n-ne-n*. The third line has five, as the long -*ō* in *shō* makes that count as two (a *shō* is a container or unit of measure a little larger than a quart). A persuasive case has been made[19] that these lines, and the three lines of all haiku, have the same length, eight morae each: lines one and three have five uttered morae and three silent morae (that is, a pause taking three beats), and line 2 has seven uttered morae and one silent mora:

Haru tatsu ya * * *

μ μ μ μ μ μ μ μ
shinnen furuki *

μ μ μ μ μ μ μ μ
kome go shō. * * *

μ μ μ μ μ μ μ μ

The pause at the end of line 3 might not be noticeable in performance, since one would pause at the end of the haiku in any case, but experiments with tanka showed that speakers paused for three beats at the end of both short lines.

The *ya* in line 1 of this haiku is nearly untranslatable. It is classed as a *kireji*, a "cutting-word," one of several particles found in haiku; this one might be called the emphatic particle, calling attention to what precedes it, as if to say "look!" or "lo!" retrospectively. A three-mora pause would let the two preceding words sink in. What follows this cut, which might be indicated by a colon[20] or exclamation point, is often descriptive or explanatory. The only verb is *tatsu* in line 1, which can mean "start," "stand," or "rise up," among other things; the rest of the poem is a little list of two-noun phrases which pivots on the second line with a seeming oxymoron, "new-year old." If line 1 ends with a *kireji* and a little pause, line 2 would seem to enjamb or carry over syntactically to the third, since *furuki* ("old") modifies *kome* ("rice"), and this kind of adjective precedes the noun. Whether we are to imagine Bashō as pleased that he still has five *shō* of last year's rice on hand as the new growing season begins or worried that five *shō* is all he has to sustain him until the harvest is not for us to settle here, as we are concerned only with the meter. My knowledge of Japanese is slender, but I see nothing in the last two lines that would make us group them one way or another metrically, as there is not much syntactic structure, and a fairly even stress or pitch across the morae seems almost required.[21]

With two features that might or might not be counted, stress (or accent) and syllable (or mora), we can draw a little schematic box (see Figure 2.6).

We have seen how pure forms of accentual and syllabic verse are rare, if they exist at all, and even in a system that counts both accents and syllables, some have argued, syllables and even feet yield in importance to accents, so this box is overly simple. And it leaves out quantitative meter altogether.

	+ count syllable	− count syllable
+ count stress	accentual-syllabic **(Modern English)**	accentual or strong-stress **(𝔒𝔩𝔡 𝔈𝔫𝔤𝔩𝔦𝔰𝔥)**
− count stress	syllabic *(𝒮𝓇𝑒𝓃𝒸𝒽)* (Japanese)	no meter *(free verse)*

Figure 2.6 Four basic types of meter

The reader, too, might want to leave out quantitative meter, and turn to the next chapter, as the subject involves quite a few concepts and technical terms that take time to assimilate. (It is smoother sailing after this.) I believe, however, that an acquaintance with the dazzling variety of Greek and Latin meters, on very different principles from those of English or French, will expand one's sense of what is possible in poetry. These meters display much closer ties to music and dance than modern verse does, and, of course, Greek and Latin poetry is the main fountain of European poetry. It's good to know about them. Many English poets, too, have been inspired by their intricate quantitative forms to create beautiful effects in their own language.

Quantitative Meter

Ancient Greek and Latin meter is based on the "quantity" of a syllable – that is, on how much *time* a syllable takes to be uttered, and that depends both on the natural vowel length and on the number of consonants that follow the vowel, whether in the coda of the same syllable or in the onset of the next, for within a line of verse the breaks between words do not affect the weight of a syllable. A word might end with a light syllable, but if there is a consonant in the onset of the next word, that light syllable becomes heavy for metrical purposes. Meter is binary: there are two options as to length, though in actual performance no doubt the two lengths were somewhat variable. A heavy syllable takes twice as long to say as a light syllable.

The name "Agamemnōn" (Ἀγαμέμνων) is metrically ∪ ∪ — — (light-light-heavy-heavy); the third syllable (*mem*) has a short *e* (epsilon), but it is followed by a consonant (*m*) (the *n* belongs to the fourth syllable), and the *o* in the final syllable is long (omega). If the name had been "Agamenōn" (Ἀγαμένων), the third syllable would be construed as *me* because the *n* belongs with the fourth syllable, the result being a light third syllable and a name that scans ∪ ∪ ∪ —. That would ban the name from Homer's *Iliad* and *Odyssey*, the dactylic meter of which could not accommodate it. So one way to scan is to see if there are *two* consonants after a vowel, whether in the same word or not; if so, make that syllable heavy. (Some letters, such as ξ (= ks) and ψ (= ps), represent two consonants.) There are a couple of exceptions to this rule, but we may ignore them here.

Throughout this book, I have usually transliterated Greek into a variant of the Roman alphabet rather than the IPA, as it makes clearer the correspondences between Greek letters and our own, which are derived from Greek, while to use the IPA would require some needless decisions about exact pronunciation, especially of vowels.

Greek had an accent as well as a distinction in length, an accent more pitched than stressed, indicated here by the acute over the epsilon, but it is not a factor in meter, though it may have played a secondary expressive or decorative part. (I take up this possibility in the appendix.) The Latin accent was probably more stressed than pitched, as is English, but again it was not a factor in scansion until Latin poets more or less gave up quantitative meter (based on Greek practice) and took up accentual or "qualitative" meter in the fourth or fifth century.

Greek and Latin verse was divided into *metra* (plural of *metron*), or what we would call "feet," of various types, though some *metra* contain what we would consider two feet. The iamb (∪ —) and its opposite, the trochee (— ∪), have two syllables but three beats; musically, we would score them in three-four time. You could waltz to iambic or trochaic verse, if it were recited slowly enough. The spondee (— —) has two syllables but four beats, and we would score them in four-four time. The dactyl (— ∪ ∪) and its opposite, the anapest (∪ ∪ —), have three syllables and four beats. These five kinds of feet are familiar in English verse scansion, as we saw, and we usually make do with them alone (if we even need the spondee), but classical poets exploited several other kinds, such as the cretic (— ∪ —) and its opposite the amphibrach (∪ — ∪), the bacchiac (∪ — —), the ionic (∪ ∪ — —), and the choriamb (— ∪ ∪ —). The name "Agamemnōn" (∪ ∪ — —), an ionic foot, has six beats (see Figure 2.7).

Ag a mem nōn

Figure 2.7 Timing an ionic foot

Some of the most common verse types can be described as sets of similar *tra*, such as dactylic hexameter, the verse form of epic from Homer in Greek to Virgil in Latin. As its name implies, it consists of six dactylic *metra*:

$$— \cup \cup \mid — \cup \cup \mid — \cup \cup \mid — \cup \cup \mid — \cup \cup \mid — X$$

The X at the end stands for the "anceps," a metrical space for one syllable either long or short; it is considered "long" in final position because the singer ("Homer") probably paused slightly on it. "Anceps" is Latin for "doubtful" (Virgil uses it as an epithet of *fortuna*); etymologically it means "two-headed," from *ambi-* ("both") and *caput* ("head").

But things are a bit more complicated than this in epic. In any foot (or *metron*), a heavy syllable can be substituted for the two lights (but not the other way round), though in the fifth foot this substitution is rare. Since a heavy equals two lights (more or less), the epic line is constant in time (twenty-four beats), though of course a performer would doubtless vary the time as the meaning and structure of the lines invited him to (probably him, maybe her). The final two feet of the line almost invariably took this form, without substitutions: $— \cup \cup \mid — X$. To our ears that pattern, knocked on a wall or door, sounds incomplete and invites a spondaic response, but to the Greeks and Romans it sounded like a concluding cadence.

Here is a lovely line from Homer, a formula recurring verbatim twice in the *Iliad* and twenty times in the *Odyssey*:

ἦμος δ' ἠριγένεια φάνη ῥοδοδάκτυλος Ἠώς

ēmos d'ērigeneia pʰanē rhododaktulos Ēōs

When the early-born rose-fingered Dawn appeared

Here it is scanned:

$— —$ $— \cup \cup — \cup$ $\cup —$ $\cup \cup$ $— \cup \cup$ $— X$

ἦμος δ' ἠριγένεια   φάνη ῥοδοδάκτυλος Ἠώς

ēmos d'ērigeneia   pʰanē rhododaktulos Ēōs

What is particularly nice about this line is that the famous epithet "rose-fingered" has the word "dactyl" in it; *daktulos* means "finger," and metrically the word is a dactyl – indeed it occupies the fifth *metron*, which must be dactylic (see Figure 2.8).

Another common verse type was iambic trimeter, used in tragedies and comedies for speeches and dialogue, as opposed to choral odes. From the name you might think it is a short line, with six syllables, but in fact each of

ē- mos d'ē- rige-nei- a pʰa-nē rhodo-daktulos Ē- ōs

Figure 2.8 Timing the dactylic hexameter line

the three *metra* had two iambs, and the first iamb in each could turn into a spondee or even an anapest:

$$\text{X} - \cup - \mid \text{X} - \cup - \mid \text{X} - \cup -$$

where X is the anceps, the main space where substitutions could occur. That gave quite a lot of flexibility in the form that Aristotle said came the closest to spoken Greek.

Here are the opening two lines of Euripides' *Bacchae*:

ἥκω Διὸς παῖς τήνδε Θηβαίων χθόνα
Hēkō Dios pais tēnde Tʰēbaiōn kʰtʰona
I have come, Zeus's son, to this land of Thebes

Διόνυσος, ὃν τίκτει ποθ' ἡ Κάδμου κόρη
Dionysos, hon tiktei potʰ' hē Kadmou korē
Dionysus, whom once Cadmus' daughter bore

The first line makes the anceps long in each *metron*:

$$- - \cup - \mid - \; - \cup \; - \mid - \; - \qquad \cup -$$
ἥκω Διὸς παῖς τήνδε Θηβαίων χθόνα
Hēkō Dios pais tēnde Tʰēbaiōn kʰtʰona

The second line substitutes two shorts for the first anceps, and keeps the other two long:

$$\cup\cup - \cup \; - \mid - \; - \cup - \mid - \; - \cup -$$
Διόνυσος, ὃν τίκτει ποθ' ἡ Κάδμου κόρη
Dionysos, hon tiktei potʰ' hē Kadmou korē

There were other kinds of meters based on *metra*, but for many other meters "*metron*" is not an adequate term, as the whole lines, though composed of varying *metra*, feel like units themselves. The name for such a unit is the *colon* (plural *cola*). We have nothing like this in English, except in imitations of Greek or Latin verse. There were scores of different cola. A common example is the glyconic (named after the poet Glycon [Γλύκων]), which goes like this:

X X — ∪ ∪ — ∪ —

You could call this a line consisting of a double anceps, a dactyl, and a cretic, but that seems arbitrary. It is better to give the whole colon a name.

If you add a long syllable at the end you get what might be called a hypermetric glyconic –

X X — ∪ ∪ — ∪ — —

– but it deserves its own name, hipponactean (named after the poet Hipponax). The Sapphic stanza is based on a long line of eleven syllables:

— ∪ — X — ∪ ∪ — ∪ — —

It could be analyzed as a cretic (— ∪ —) followed by a hipponactean but with one of the anceps syllables omitted. Or it could just be called the Sapphic line, which, when you've heard a few of them, seems to have a distinct character. Here is the opening of Sappho's ode to Aphrodite:

— ∪ — ∪ — ∪ ∪ — ∪ — —

Ποικιλόθρον' 'αθάνατ' 'Αφρόδιτα

Poikilot^hron' at^hanat' Ap^hrodita

Beautiful-throned immortal Aphrodite[22]

The Sapphic stanza has three of these long lines followed by a short line like the last two *metra* of the epic meter (— ∪ ∪ — X), which gives a closing cadence.

Another form brilliantly exploited by Greek and Roman poets was the elegiac distich or couplet. The word *elegos*, found in Euripides, refers to a song of lamentation without reference to form, but *elegeia* (feminine) or *elegeion* (neuter) came to refer to a particular verse form without reference to content, a couplet in which the first line is a dactylic hexameter (the epic line), and the second is what we might loosely call a dactylic pentameter with a strong caesura or break in the middle (or, strictly, a diaeresis, as the break comes between feet); more exactly, the second line is a pentameter made up of two identical halves or hemistichs consisting of a pair of dactyls and a single long syllable – or, if you like, a line consisting of two dactylic trimeters catalectic ("cut off").

— ∪ ∪ | — ∪ ∪ | — ∪ ∪ | — ∪ ∪ | — ∪ ∪ | — **X**
— ∪ ∪ | — ∪ ∪ | — ‖ — ∪ ∪ | — ∪ ∪ | —

In the second line, the two parts are separated by a word break and are considered disjunct metrical units, though the repeated pattern here obviously appealed to many poets and their audiences for several centuries. In the hexameter line, a heavy syllable may be substituted for the two lights (i.e., a spondee for a dactyl), as in Homer and the other epic writers, though there is a strong tendency to avoid doing so in the fifth *metron*; in the pentameter line, a heavy may be substituted for two lights in the first half but not in the second. There should be a feeling of closure at the end of each pentameter line, and together the two lines have something of the effect of the rhymed couplet in English and other modern languages. Sometimes, this form is called "hexameters," but that seems a somewhat misleading term, as the second line could count as a hexameter only if the two single long syllables are considered *metra* in themselves – which, in a sense, they are, if you pause for a beat after each one.

This couplet form was used for almost any subject: the earliest Greek instances (Archilochus, Tyrtaeus) were about war or love more often than death. The Alexandrian poet Callimachus used it extensively, as a kind of anti-epic, and he inspired the Roman love elegists (notably Propertius, Tibullus, and Ovid), who employed the form for sophisticated and satirical explorations of the erotic. In the opening poem of his *Amores*, Ovid insists that he tried to write a heroic epic but Cupid interfered by cutting a foot out of his second line: "Arms, and the violent deeds of war, I was making ready to sound forth – in weighty numbers, with matter suited to the measure. The second verse was equal to the first – but Cupid, they say, with a laugh stole away one foot" (trans. Grant Showerman). In a later poem of the set, the goddess Elegea limps. The very form of the elegiac distich enacts the "cutting off" of epic, twice in the second line.

The form has been revived periodically, notably by the great German poets Goethe, Schiller, and Hölderlin, mainly for meditations on serious themes; it has been far less prominent among English poets.

Its brevity and self-enclosed character suited epitaphs or memorials, and one of the greatest of these is by Simonides of Ceos on the Spartans who died at Thermopylae:

$$— \;\; — \quad\;\; — \quad — — \cup\cup — \cup\cup — \quad\; \cup\cup — \mathrm{X}$$

ὦ ξεῖν’, | ἀγγέλλ|ειν Λακε|δαιμονί|οις ὅτι | τῇδε
Ō xein’, angellein   Lakedaimoniois hoti tēide
O stranger, report (to the) Lakedaimonians that here

$$— \cup\cup \;\; — \quad — \;\; — \quad\; — \cup\cup \;\; — \;\; \cup\cup \;\; —$$

κείμεθα, |τοῖς κεῖ|νων ‖ ῥήμασι | πειθόμε|νοι.
keimet^ha, tois keinōn   rhēmasi peit^homenoi.
we lie,   to their   words obedient.

Of its many translations into English, I have seen only one in the original meter, by George Campbell Macaulay:

> Stranger, report this word, we pray, to the Spartans, that lying
> Here in this spot we remain, faithfully keeping their laws.

Among the points to take away from this discussion of quantitative meter are: (1) that Greek (and Latin and Sanskrit) developed a great profusion of meters, both *metra* and cola, which English (and other modern European languages) cannot replicate; and that is because (2) the basis of quantitative meter is length and not stress or even syllable count. There is a line in *The Bacchae* that has fifteen light syllables in a row. Try reciting fifteen syllables in a row in English without imposing some sort of metrical pattern on them. Another point you can't help taking away is that everything has a name in ancient metrics. I apologize for all the technical terms, but they are hard to avoid, and if nothing else they testify to how seriously the ancients took their verse forms. Poetry, chanted, sung, and often danced to, deeply pervaded their lives in ways we can scarcely imagine.

Notes

1. There is, of course, poetry by and for the deaf, where meter and even visual rhyme correspond to oral effects.
2. The number most frequently given is 44, but dialects may vary by 1 or 2, especially in vowel-phonemes, and there has been disagreement over the status of the 2 "palato-alveolar affricates," found in "church" and "judge": are they 1 phoneme or 2? The consensus now is that they are 1. See Lass, *Phonology*, 26–27; Odden, *Introducing Phonology*, 56. English can get by with fewer than 44 IPA characters because it has 8 double-vowel phonemes or diphthongs, such as the /aʊ/ sound in "house," which can be represented with 2 IPA characters.
3. Barry Powell, in *Homer and the Origin of the Greek Alphabet*, has argued that the Greek alphabet was invented by a single man (Palamedes) in order to write down Homer. That theory seems too good to be true, but Powell makes a plausible and erudite case for it.
4. Sampson, *Writing Systems*, 82.
5. To write English we need vowels too, as you can see.
6. I have put "stop" in quotation marks to indicate that, in my opinion, there is something misleading about calling it a stop, which is the standard term among phonologists. The air flow in the mouth is indeed stopped by the nasal consonants (/m/, /n/, /ŋ/), but the air flow is not stopped altogether: it is deflected through the nose. If your nasal passage were really stopped, as when you have a cold, those three sounds would be the only ones you could *not* make.

7. For an introduction to the complexities of "rhotic" or r- sounds across many languages, see Roca and Johnson, *Course in Phonology*, 74–81; for a fuller discussion, see Wiese, "The Phonology of /r/."

8. The word in brackets, "element" (*stoikheion*) is usually translated as "letter," and indeed it was the regular word for "letter," but its earlier meaning was a "member of a row," and then "element" or "unit": Aristotle may not be as confused as translators make him seem. See Aristotle, *Poetics*, ed. Lucas, p. 200. "Letter," of course, is not apt here; we would prefer "phoneme," or at least "sound," but the concept of the phoneme was not available to Aristotle and "sound" (*phōnē*) would have led to troubling phrases such as "soundless sound." *Stoikheion* comes from a root meaning "walk" or "march" (in a row), which also shows up in *stikhos*, meaning "line" and then "line of verse," as we see in English "hemistich" ("half-line") and "distich" ("couplet").

9. See Lass, *Old English*, 36.

10. A brief and lucid account of the syllable and morae may be found in Fabb, *Linguistics and Literature*, 30–33.

11. In Brooks and Warren, *Conversations*, 33.

12. See Fabb, *What is Poetry?* 31.

13. This is the Folio text. The earlier Quarto version gives the second line an extra foot: "And thou no breath at all? O thou wilt come no more."

14. I recommend Robert Shaw's book *Blank Verse* for many astute insights into the history of that form in English.

15. A good summary of the debates as of 1991 is by Stockwell, "On Recent Theories of Metrics." A thorough (and demanding) study is by Russom, in Beowulf *and Old English Metre*, where he presents his "word-based" theory, too complicated to go into here.

16. Fabb and Halle, in *Meter in Poetry*, say "The *Beowulf* meter differs from all other meters reviewed in this book in that it systematically disregards all unstressed syllables" (267). This seems too simple, and disregards decades of work on the subject.

17. I have profited from the discussions of French verse in Berthon, *Nine French Poets*, xxi–xliii; Flescher, "French"; and especially Dane, *The Long and the Short of It*, 37–54.

18. Fabb and Halle, in "Pairs and Triplets," argue that some sections of Biblical Hebrew verse may be the only purely syllabic verse in the world!

19. By Cole and Miyashita, in "The Function of Pauses."

20. As Henderson suggests, in *Introduction to Haiku*, 189.

21. For a discussion of two more haiku, see Chapter 8 on "Translation."

22. "Beautiful" is not the best translation of the *poikilo-* part of the compound epithet here (better might be "intricate" or "spangled"), and –*tʰron* might not be the correct reading.

CHAPTER THREE

Rhyme

The most common meaning of "rhyme" is the sameness or identity of sound between two words at the end of lines of verse, an identity that includes a stressed vowel and whatever follows it, if anything: a consonant or two, another syllable or two (if unstressed), even another (unstressed) word. So, in a million poems and songs, "moon" and "June" are united by rhyme, or "love" and "dove." Bisyllabic rhymes are stressed on the second-last syllable, as in "marriage" and "carriage," or "spoken" and "awoken." Trisyllabic rhymes are stressed on the third-last syllable, such as "history" and "mystery"; they are often deployed for comic purposes, such as when Byron rhymes "gunnery" with "nunnery," or "goddesses" with "bodices" (*Don Juan* 1.38, 41). Tetrasyllabic rhymes show up in Ogden Nash's poems, for example, when he pairs "antidisestablishmentarianism" with "antiquarianism" ("No, You Be a Lone Eagle").

When we study sonnets in school or university, we learn "rhyme schemes" such as the Petrarchan (e.g., abba/abba//cdecde) and Shakespearean (abab/cdcd/efef/gg) which indicate the sets of line-final sounds. We learn that in his plays Shakespeare did not rhyme, for the most part – he usually wrote blank verse, and often prose – though even in blank-verse plays, he would often rhyme on the final two lines of a scene: "The play's the thing / Wherein I'll catch the conscience of the King." If we write rhymed poetry ourselves, or translate rhymed poetry from other languages into English, we soon learn certain stubborn facts about English, such as that there is only one good rhyme for "death."[1]

Rhyme is so frequent in English poetry, or used to be, that the word was loosely used to refer to any poetry, rhymed or not, and even today the sort of poems found on greeting cards or "occasional" verse read at parties or weddings will almost always be rhymed. Limericks and other humorous verse, such as Ogden Nash's, have rhymes, because much of their humor depends on them. Though we may know that such august authorities as Shakespeare and Milton wrote their major works in blank verse, we may still incline toward taking rhyme – "fine tinkling rhyme," as Ben Jonson has it (*Fortunate Isles* 180) – as a prime characteristic of poetry: second only, perhaps, to meter. Rhyme, however, is not found in the verse of the great majority of the world's languages. It was not a feature of Greek or Latin verse, and the oldest poetry we have in English, such as *Beowulf,* alliterates but does not rhyme. There is no ancient word for it. How rhyme arose in Europe we will discuss later, but it is well to keep in mind that rhyme, in the usual sense of the word, is not inevitable in poetry, and certainly not central to it, however much it has flourished in English and most other modern European languages. The main point of this chapter is to sharpen our sense of it, and to broaden our understanding of it, and I will try to step back from it a little so that it seems somewhat strange.

As we saw in the previous chapter, linguists who have written about the structure of the syllable recently, even when they are not discussing poetry, use the word "rime" to refer to a syllable's latter part. They sometimes spell it "rhyme," but many linguists want to keep their use of the word distinct from the way it is used in descriptions of poetry. However they spell it, they respect the usual English meaning of "rhyme": two syllables rhyme when the final stressed vowel and the final consonant or consonants (if there are any) are alike. What precedes the vowel – what linguists call the "onset" – is not taken into consideration. Figure 3.1 shows the diagram of the syllable again.

The **C** of the onset stands for a consonant or consonant cluster; it may be "zero" or absent. The **V** of the nucleus must be a vowel or diphthong (a double-vowel such as the **ou**- sound in "mouse"), or in some cases (rare in English) it might be a vocalic version of a consonant, such as the nasal m of "spasm." The **C** of the coda ("tail") may be a consonant or consonant cluster; it may also be absent. The nucleus alone is essential to a syllable.

This **CVC** template will serve as a handy way to describe the various kinds of correspondence or sound-similarity between two syllables, that is, "rhyme" in the broadest sense of the word, well beyond the common

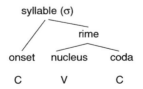

Figure 3.1 The structure of the syllable

English restriction to the nucleus and coda. In what follows, I am expanding a great deal on the excellent but terse discussion in *The Princeton Encyclopedia of Poetry and Poetics*.

There are eight possible sound-correspondences between any two syllables, depending on whether one, two, all three, or none of their components matches. Whether or not the matching syllables come at the ends of their lines of verse is of no relevance to this taxonomy, but of course, in most poetry, rhymes are end-rhymes, or perhaps it is better to say that we don't ordinarily consider two rhyming words to be genuine rhymes unless they appear at the end of their lines. Then again there are exceptions, where metrical or syntactical patterns invite us to take them as constructing lines within a line, such as these examples from Coleridge's "The Rime of the Ancyent Marinere" (1798): "The wedding-guest he beat his breast" (41), "For days and weeks it play'd us freaks" (47), and "It crack'd and growl'd, and roar'd and howl'd" (59); or this from Poe's "The Raven" (1845): "Once upon a midnight dreary, while I pondered, weak and weary." What we take as a line, we see in these examples, often depends on type-setting; set differently, Poe's long line would make two lines of trochaic tetrameter. In Welsh, Irish, and several other languages, there are verse forms that require internal rhymes that do not necessarily mark syntactic pauses. And even in forms that do not require them, internal rhymes can be striking, as in this line from Sonnet 126 by Shakespeare: "[thou] Dost hold time's fickle glass, his sickle hour."

If we consider rhymes over more than one syllable, the number of possible correspondences grows very large: for a pair of two-syllable words, assuming that the coda of the first such syllable is distinct from the onset of the second (CVCCVC), we would have sixty-four possibilities, and, figuring in approximate or close correspondences, the number is at least twice that. Most of these possibilities, happily, do not have names, but some do.

The underlined letters below represent the components that correspond between two syllables in different words.

1 **CVC**

This is "rhyme" in the strict sense, true rhyme, where the nucleus and the coda (VC) are the same but the onset differs. For example: **rhyme / time / chime**, or **death / breath**, or **sea / free.** Note that, in the last pair, the coda consonant is absent or null, but we write it into the formula as a place-holder. These are the two parts of the syllable that linguists call "rime" or "rhyme." In English poetry, this is simply "rhyme," but in French poetry it is called *rime suffisante* ("sufficient rhyme"), but if the coda consonant is absent it is called *rime pauvre* ("poor rhyme"). In some other Romance languages, such as Portuguese, "poor rhyme" means rhyme on two words of the same grammatical category (such as **death / breath**, both nouns), and "rich rhyme" means rhyme on two words of different categories (such as **sea / free**, noun and adjective). This idea seems absent from English versification theories, and we reserve "rich rhyme" for the next category.

2 **CVC**

This is "rich rhyme" (French *rime riche*), where the entire syllable is the same, at least back to the last consonant of the onset cluster, if there is one. For example: (a) homophones (with the same sound but different spelling) such as **right / wright / rite / write, do / due / dew, time / thyme** (the poet Shenstone called it "pun-provoking thyme"), or bou**quet** / de**cay**; and (b) homonyms (with the same sound *and* spelling) such as **port / port** (where the meaning is different); also (c) **port / sport**, or **lake / flake**. It is not very common in English verse, and some critics dismiss it as having a "poor" effect, but *rime riche* is prominent in French poetry, notably in the Romantic era, where it is almost normal. The French call the onset consonant the *consonne d'appui*, the "support" or "prop" consonant. Of the first eight couplets of Victor Hugo's "Nox," to pick a French poem at random, seven have rich rhyme: *pensée / glacée, noir / manoir, oblique / République*, and so on.

A variant would move the support consonant earlier, followed by a different consonant: **cloud / crowd** or **spoke / stoke**; we might call it "displaced rich rhyme." It could be displaced further still – moved a whole syllable earlier: **moon / maroon, wracked / react**, or **sort / support**. One could have "very rich rhyme" if the onset **C** is a cluster and two consonants in it correspond exactly (as with **trip / strip** or **scream / stream**) or correspond closely (**dream / stream**), the latter overlapping with the "displaced" variety, and these also could be displaced further in various types: **drive / derive, prong / prolong**, or, shuffled a bit, **trend / pretend**. If a single support consonant is similar but not exactly the same, we get something between "sufficient" and "rich" rhyme, maybe "weak rich rhyme" (if that's not a mixed metaphor): **bound / pound, goat / coat, cheat / sheet**, or, in Victor Hugo's poem, *filles / chevilles*. Another interesting pairing, again by Hugo, is *pierre* and *prière* (in "In the Ruins of an Abbey"): it is almost as if the double r has split apart and one of them moved forward (but *pierre* has one syllable and *prière* has two). There are obviously several degrees of richness, depending on how closely the support consonants or clusters echo each other. We might also attribute richness to the coda if it is also a cluster, as in **first** / **burst**, and greater richness if the onset cluster is similar, as in Blake's rhyme **grasp** / **clasp** (in "The Tyger").

We are concerned in this classification mainly with single syllables, but of course polysyllabic rhymes are common, so we might extend the term "very rich rhyme" to cover two or more syllables, such as **candle** / **scandal** or **machinery** / **scenery**. In these examples, the unstressed syllables follow the stressed one; rarer are cases where a rhyming unstressed syllable, usually the schwa (ə), precedes it: **evoke** / **revoke** or **relay** / **delay**.

A well-known example of a three-syllable but two-stress rhyme comes from Coleridge's "Kubla Khan": "So twice five miles of **fertile ground** / With walls and towers were **girdled round**" (note that the **g-** of **ground** gets recycled with **girdled**). The French call rhyming on two syllables *rime léonine* ("leonine rhyme") after a Pope Leo or a monk named Leoninus, but it seems fitting to think of two-syllable rhymes as lion-like; if so, then Coleridge's trisyllabic rhyme might be called "elephantine," though I am not recommending it.

A rhyme on a single stressed syllable is sometimes called a "masculine" rhyme, while a rhyme on two syllables, and particularly if the second syllable is a grammatical ending with no secondary stress, is called a "feminine" rhyme. Examples of the latter: **thinking** / **drinking, stated** / **fated, spoken** / **broken**, but also by extension **candle** / **scandal**, etc. Various fanciful notions have gotten loose as to why these gendered terms apply to rhymes – such as that finality or simplicity is masculine, while tentativeness or subtlety is feminine, but the terms come from French, where all nouns have genders, and many nouns that refer to things that really are gendered come in two forms, the feminine of which adds an e (and often doubles the preceding consonant). So a *chien* is a male dog, a *chienne* is female; a *chat* is a male cat, a *chatte* is female; and among names *Michel* is a male name, *Michelle* female. This final e today is silent or "mute" (*e muet*) or "defunct" (*e caduc*), but it was not always so, and in French poetry and song it is sounded if it precedes a consonant in the next word. French poetry had a strict rule until the twentieth century that masculine and feminine rhymes had to alternate, the *loi de l'alternance des rimes*; another rule forbade rhyming a masculine with a feminine noun even if the mute e stayed mute (for example, *mer* could not rhyme with *mère* – too bad, because the sea is our mother). No such rules hamper poets in English, and most English rhymes are monosyllabic; "masculine" and "feminine" are not very apt terms for English poetry and might better be reserved for French and other languages that mark gender in a similar way.

Traditional Chinese poetry shows another feature that might be the basis of rich rhyme, though the term is not used of it. The Chinese languages are tonal. Mandarin has four (some would say five) phonemic tones or pitches that distinguish otherwise identical homophones: *mā* (with a high level tone) means "mother," *má* (with a rising tone) means "hemp," *mǎ* (with a falling and rising tone) means "horse," and so on. (Cantonese has more tones.) End-rhyme is prominent in Chinese poetry, and in some forms there are rules about the kinds of tone that can appear in the rhymes. If the tones are identical, we might call it rich rhyme.

In most European poetic traditions, these first two types, "rhyme" and "rich rhyme," are usually found at the end of lines, and together they constitute what we usually mean by "rhyme." The following types are not usually called "rhyme" and are as likely to be found scattered throughout lines as placed prominently at the end of them.

3   CV*C*

Where only the coda corresponds, we have "consonance" in the strict sense. For example: **back / neck / sick / rock / luck / speak / dark**, etc. The term "consonance" is also used more loosely to refer to repetitions of consonants anywhere in the words. A dense example based on **s, t,** and **l** is found in Keats's "Ode on a Grecian Urn": "Thou foster-child of silence and slow time." Where two CV*C* syllables fall at the end of the line, the relationship has been called "near rhyme," "slant rhyme," "half rhyme," "off-rhyme," and various other kinds of rhyme. Robert Pinsky's translation of Dante's *Inferno* uses this to approximate the *terza rima* of the original: **tell / feel / well, sleep / stop / up,** and **night / thought / it**. If the nucleus vowel is similar but not identical, we might call it "rich half rhyme," "rich coda-rhyme," or the like, as in **stop / up** or **foot / about**. Even richer would be cases where the codas are identical clusters: **birth / forth**.

Some apparent cases of this kind of rhyme could be called "historical rhyme" or "conventional rhyme." Two words that once truly rhymed may have deviated over the centuries so that only the coda rhymes, if there is one, but they are still considered proper rhymes. Examples would be **wind** (as in "west wind") / **behind, love / prove**, and **eye / symmetry**. It may also be the case that two words rhyme fully in one dialect but only in their coda in another dialect. In the conventional "dialect" of poetry, they are nonetheless full rhymes.

Old Norse and Icelandic poetry permitted coda-only rhyme, and sometimes required it, usually internal to the line, and often on syllables internal to the words; for English examples: a ra**ft** of dri**ft**wood, the wo**rd** hoa**rd** of the ba**rd**. It was called *skothending*, a term whose first part might be related to English "shoot," so it meant something like "shot-in rhyme" or "inserted rhyme"; other sources say it meant "skewed rhyme," "glancing hit," or "half-hitch." (It contrasted with *aðalhending* or "noble" rhyme, rhyme in the usual sense. *Hending* by itself first meant "catching.") Traditional Arabic poetry typically rhymed only on the coda, a final consonant kept constant throughout the poem.

4   <u>CVC</u>

Sometimes called "frame rhyme," this pattern might also be called "rich consonance." For example: **back / buck**, or the disyllabic **linger / longer**. Here only the nucleus vowel differs. Where onset clusters correspond exactly, we might call such pairs "very rich consonance," as in **truth / troth** and **plight / plot**; the same is true, and richer still, when coda clusters also correspond, as in **brisk / brusque** or in Hopkins's phrase **ghost guessed**. Wilfred Owen called this relationship "pararhyme" and used it often in his own poems: / **loads / lids / lads, ferns / fawns, simmer / summer**; some of them are slightly off, the consonants differing by one distinctive feature: **crisp / grasp, number / remember**; or a consonant in an onset cluster might match a single consonant: **brambles / rumbles**. A recent example of very rich consonance, though with only one of the words at a line-end, is this by Tracy K. Smith: "nothing / to shrink from, nothing to shirk."

Perhaps the most richly elaborate examples of consonance are found in Welsh poetry. Some traditional forms of *cynghanedd* or "harmony" required patterns wherein from two to seven consonants in the first half of a line must be repeated in the same order in the second half, on top of which some stressed syllables alliterated and there were internal and external full rhymes. G. M. Hopkins, who wrote traditional Welsh poetry, sought effects in his English poems reminiscent of *cynghanedd*, such as the final line of "God's Grandeur": "**W**orld **br**oods with **w**arm **br**east and with ah! **br**ight **w**ings."

5 CV̱C

This is "assonance," the opposite of "frame rhyme"; here only the nucleus is the same. For example: **pack / rat, skim / milk**. If the same consonants are used but in opposite order, we might call it "rich assonance": **top / pot, feel / leaf, step / pets** (or **pest**). More loosely, assonance is repetition of vowels anywhere in the line: Yeats's "widening gyre," or Pope's wonderful "With gun, drum, trumpet, blunderbuss, and thunder." And Keats's line, "Thou foster-child of silence and slow time," illustrates assonance as neatly as consonance. Where the vowel is the same but the final consonant is similar, we have a kind of near rhyme; it is called "generic rhyme" in studies of Scots Gaelic and Welsh poetry, where there were rules that dictated what consonants belonged to what permissible groups – for example, voiceless stops (spelled p, t, c) or voiced fricatives, liquids, and the nasal n (bh, mh, gh, dh, l, r, n). For rhymes in Tagalog, a Philippine language, there are two sets of equivalent final consonants (in IPA: p, b, s, t, d, k, and g, versus l, m, n, ŋ, r, w, and j). Contemporary rap lyrics often rhyme in this way. The end-rhymes in a recent hip-hop song stanza are: **bub, drugs, love**, and **rubbed**, with an internal rhyme on **hug**; all the final consonants or consonant clusters are voiced.

Spanish poetry had something called "assonantal rhyme" over two syllables, like this: CV̱CV; so these words, accented on the penultimate (second-last) syllable, would rhyme assonantally on i-a: *tranquila, ida, hija, caballeria*. When Shakespeare's Benedick says "I can find out no rhyme to 'lady' but 'baby'" (*Much Ado About Nothing* 5.2.31–32), he admits it is an "innocent" or childish rhyme; it is not a rhyme in English terms at all, but it is an assonantal rhyme. Early Shakespeare editors missed his humor and "corrected" "baby" to "badie," "bady," or "baudy." A slightly extended version of assonantal rhyme over two words is found in Shakespeare's Sonnet III, which ends by rhyming "I assure ye" with "to cure me."

The loose sense of assonance, as the repetition of vowels anywhere in the line, reaches the sublime, or maybe the ridiculous, in the prose poems of Christian Bök. For example: "Westerners revere the Greek legends. Versemen retell the represented events, the resplendent scenes, where, hellbent, the Greek freemen seek revenge whenever Helen, the new-wed empress, weeps" (from *Eunoia*). Brilliant though this may be as an escape from a self-imposed straitjacket, it is really an eye-assonance, based on a single letter rather than a single vowel sound or phoneme.

6 $\underline{C}VC$

This pattern is called "alliteration" if it falls on the first syllable (or only syllable) of a word: **big** / **bad** / **boy**, or Coleridge's "Five **m**iles **m**eandering with a **m**azy **m**otion." If the onset consonant is a cluster, we might call the result "rich consonant alliteration": **sti**fle / **sti**ng, or "And **str**etch my feet forth **str**aight as **st**one can point" (Coleridge), or (doubled and interlaced) "**dr**agonflies **dr**aw **fl**ame" (Hopkins); or it might be a similar cluster, as in Tennyson's "**bl**oom-**br**ight." If the pattern falls on a syllable later than the first of a word, it is a form of consonance. Old English poetry relies on alliteration, as we saw in the last chapter – typically three alliterative words per four-beat line: "**m**urnende **m**ōd. / **M**en ne cunnon" (*Beowulf* 50). By convention, all initial vowels alliterate with each other, or we could say the null or zero onset alliterates with itself. A modern example from Tennyson's "Locksley Hall," with four vowel-alliterations: "I am the heir of all the ages." We might have "rich vowel alliteration" on words whose initial syllables correspond VC (null onset but identical nucleus): **ache** / **ate**, **eager** / **evening**, or "the **old oa**ken bucket."

Blake does something interesting over two syllables in "The Clod and the Pebble," where he creates a super-reverse-rhyme spanning from line 4 to line 12: "despair" and "despite" (both nouns) ($C\underline{V}CVC$, where the central C is a cluster). Or, since the rhyming syllable is unstressed, it might be better to assimilate it to the onset cluster of one syllable ($\underline{C_vC}VC$); we might call it "very rich alliteration."

Classical verse did not often alliterate, but striking examples can be found, as in the Sappho couplet quoted later in this chapter, or the line from the *Agamemnon* discussed in Chapter 2, "*di^thronou Dio^then kai diskēptrou*," with initial $\underline{CV}$ corresponding in polysyllabic words, a sort of "reverse rhyme," as we see next.

7 $\underline{CV}C$

Here we have "reverse rhyme" (or perhaps "front rhyme"). For example: **ba**ck / **ba**t, **fee**t / **fea**r, **sli**p / **sli**m, Poe's "**wea**k and **wea**ry," or Swinburne's compound "**hea**vy-**hea**ded." Both the onset and nucleus are the same. The **sli**p / **sli**m example approaches "rich reverse rhyme" since the onset is a cluster. We might call this resemblance "rich alliteration" (again) or "extended alliteration"; it is fairly systematically deployed in the poetry of some languages, such as Finnish. We could extend "reverse rhyme"

forward as well, making the coda similar but not the same, as in **dame /
deign** or **force / forth**.

8   CVC

Finally, there is the null case, where none of the sounds is the same. I
suppose we could have "rich null rhyme" if one or more of the components
are similar (**rude / boat**), but we would soon approach one or more of the
seven preceding types.

These eight categories and their polysyllabic extensions look distinct and
logical enough, and they make a useful template for considering the variety
of sound similarities in verse (or prose, for that matter), but in practice
there are gray areas where categories overlap or fade into one another. In
most of them we were able to push components into "rich" or "extended"
similarities, and they could be pushed further.

In a brief essay of 1940, "On Musicality in Verse," Kenneth Burke looks
at a range of similarities and differences among English sounds, and how
they are enlisted by poets beyond the usual categories. He notes, for
example, "If you place the lips in the position to make the sound m,
from this same position you can make the sounds b and p. Hence, when
looking for a basis of musicality in verse, we may treat b and p as close
phonetic relatives of m. The three are all in the same family: they are
'cognates.'"The phrase "bathed by the mist," which Burke takes from
Coleridge, is an example of what he calls "concealed alliteration" on the
"cognate" sounds b and m, and in fact it is two alliterations, as the th-d of
"bathed" and the st of "mist" are also "cognates." He explores several other
phrases and lines of verse, and invokes such musical parallels as diminution
and augmentation. The modern theory of the syllable was unavailable to
him, and he does not use technically precise terms from phonology, but he
had a good ear and good ideas. Prompted by this essay, we might try to
rank similarities between phonemes, even roughly to quantify them.

Take /p/ and /b/, for example. As we noted in the previous chapter, both
are bilabial stops, and they differ in one "distinctive feature," namely voice,
or "vocal onset" (see Figure 3.2). With /p/, the vocal stream is interrupted;
after an initial parting of the lips, there is a tiny delay before the voice
comes in. With /b/, there is virtually no interruption or delay. So we could
say that /p/ and /b/ differ by one degree; they are what Burke might call
"close cognates." The same is true of /t/ and /d/, both alveolar stops, one
voiceless, the other voiced; and of /k/ and /g/, both velar stops. Each of
these pairs has a variance or differential of 1.

	voiceless	voiced	nasal
bilabial	p	b	m
alveolar	t	d	n
velar	k	g	ŋ

Figure 3.2 The English stops

Then there is the bilabial nasal stop /m/. It is voiced, of course, so it would seem closer to /b/ than to /p/, so we might say /b/ and /m/ differ by 1, but /p/ and /m/ differ by 2. (The arbitrariness of these numbers should be apparent by now, but they'll do as a first approximation.) Similarly, /n/ is the nasal alveolar stop, and is closer to /d/ than to /t/, and "ng" (written /ŋ/ in the IPA), the nasal velar stop, is closer to /g/ than to /k/. These nasal sounds are called stops, as we noted in the last chapter, because they stop or block the air from passing through, or even entering, the mouth, but nothing really stops: the voice can keep vibrating and air keep passing for quite a while, because the air is diverted through the nose. This feature makes them sonorants, and poets can exploit their continuous sonority, sometimes to brilliant effect, as Tennyson does in "The moan of doves in immemorial elms, / And murmuring of innumerable bees" ("Come Down, O Maid"), a pair of lines in which every consonant is voiced and most are continuants in the sense I have been using.

We have set a value of 1 for a single horizontal move on this diagram. What about the difference between, say, /p/ and /t/? They are both voiceless stops, and their points of articulation are fairly close together. If /p/ and /b/ differ by 1, and /p/ and /m/ differ by 2, then perhaps we should say /p/ and /t/ differ by 2, and /p/ and /d/ differ by 3 (since they differ by voice as well as point of articulation), and /p/ and /n/ differ by 4. In other words, horizontal moves cost 1 point, vertical moves 2 points, and diagonal moves 3 points. So /p/ and /k/ differ by 4 (since lips and velum are farther apart than lips and alveolus), and /p/ and /g/ differ by 5, while /p/ and /ŋ/ differ by 6. Those values may be too high, because, for example, the physical distance in the mouth may not matter as much as how the phonemes sound to the ear, and the difference between voiced and voiceless consonants may seem greater than other factors (or may not). But this exercise in score-keeping is still worth pursuing a little further, even if we don't take the results too seriously.

So a word such as "pup" (setting aside the vowel for now) would have a score of 0, while "pub" would have a score of 1. "Pun" is worth 4, and "pung," if there is such a word, is worth 6. ("Bung" does exist, and is worth 5.)

The /s/ phoneme is alveolar, even though the tongue does not quite come into contact with the alveolus (the hard ridge just above the teeth), so it belongs with /t/, /d/, and /n/; it is voiceless, so it is closer to /t/ than to /d/ or /n/; it is a fricative, not a stop – that is, it is a continuant – so it resembles [n] a little, but it is not nasal. Let's say it differs from /t/ by 2 and from /d/ by 3 and from /n/ by, well, 3, or maybe 4. The sh-phoneme (ʃ in IPA) is post-alveolar, almost "retroflex" – that is, the tongue comes close to touching the palate at the upper and rear edge of the alveolar ridge; that would put it one step farther from, say, /t/. (Hence perhaps the phonotactic taboo in English against beginning words with sht-, except for a few borrowed from Yiddish or German, sometimes spelled scht-.) The nine fricatives in English, we might argue, are alike in their frictional quality, so they would not differ from each other by more than 2. The proximants might also be considered similar, and some of them correlate somewhat with stops. I think /w/ would go with the bilabials, though phonologists would describe it as labial-velar because of the position of the tongue, and /l/ would go with the alveolars, but /j/ and /r/ are vaguer: /j/ is classified as palatal, but it could be associated with the alveolars (since the top middle of the tongue comes close to the alveolus, though closer to the hard palate), and /r/ with the /ʃ/ (since the tongue, in some versions of /r/, curls up toward the hard palate).

Then there are a dozen or more vowels, some in the front, some in the rear, some high, some low, and some at various points in between. Though phonologists consider all vowels to be "dorsal" (made with the upper body of the tongue), the high front ee (IPA i) seems closer to the labials, or maybe alveolars, than to the velars; hence "peep" would have less internal variance than "pop"; "gawk" would have a lower numerical score than "geek." (The fact that many people pronounce "just" as if it were "gist" is a clue to our numerical system, because all three consonants [four, arguably, since j is /dʒ/] are alveolar, whereas the u vowel [IPA ʌ] is back and low; the "principle of least effort" – or laziness – leads us to move the vowel upward and frontward so it is nearer the consonants before and after it.)

Assuming we can assign numerical values like these across the board, we can gain a measure of similarity across whole lines of verse. We are not claiming that similarity is necessarily better, of course, or more beautiful, effective, or expressive, but similarity underlies harmony, and harmony is often a factor in our aesthetic judgments.

Let's look again at Pope's amusing line:

> With gun, drum, trumpet, blunderbuss, and thunder.

It is in iambic pentameter (with a final unaccented syllable), or possibly trochaic pentameter (with unaccented extra-metrical initial syllable), but in either case it has six stresses, for "drum" must receive a fairly full stress even though it falls on the weak half of the foot; perhaps "–buss" can be lightly stressed to make up for "drum" even though it falls in strong position. Every stressed vowel is the same, the lower mid central /ʌ/, a rather dull sound (as in "dull" itself, perhaps not accidentally). All the consonants but the initial g- are bilabials, alveolars, or, in the case of th (IPA /θ/) interdentals (or linguo-dentals), and all but six are voiced. Each noun has a nasal /m/ or /n/ after the vowel, except in the syllable "-buss"; the /dr/ of "drum" leads to the /tr/ of "trumpet" (the two consonant clusters differing by 1 point); the /p/ of "trumpet" leads to the two /b/ sounds of "blunderbuss"; the two-syllable "-under-" in "blunder-" is repeated in "thunder"; and the voiceless /s/ in "-buss" prepares the way for the /θ/ of the last word of the line, "thunder," which echoes the unstressed /θ/ of the first word of the line. It is striking that the only noun with any voiceless stops, three of them, is "trumpet," surely the sharpest and clearest of these noise-making things. This line, then, has a very low number on the scale we have been postulating, though I hesitate to suggest just what it is. The move from /g/ to /n/ in "gun" costs 3 points, but from /n/ to /d/ and from /d/ to /r/ each costs only 1 point; from /dr/ to /m/ costs 3 and /m/ to /tr/ costs 4, but we might reduce that cost by stepping back and noting that the whole syllables /drʌm/ and /trʌm/ differ from each other by only 1. In sum, many of the consonants are akin, and the accented vowels are all alike.[2]

We might say, then, that Pope's line has high harmony or smoothness, with almost no jumps between points of articulation. And yet it is all about the violent sounds of warfare! It gives the impression of onomatopoeia, but only the dull thudding of cannon at a distance might sound like this line; I think it does not resemble the sounds the noun referents would make in a real battle except perhaps "thunder," and that is not strictly a weapon or military instrument.[3]

Its brilliance is only enhanced in its context. Pope's target here is Sir Richard Blackmore, who wrote a lot of bombastic epics which

> Rend with tremendous sound your ears asunder,
> With gun, drum, trumpet, blunderbuss, and thunder.
>
> ("First Satire of Second Book of Horace," 25–26)

The couplet is an extraordinary tour de force, and I won't ruin any more of it by stapling numbers to its phonemes, but I would point out that the end-rhymes are what we called "weak rich bisyllabic rhyme," since /s/ and /θ/ are "cognate" in Burke's sense, both voiceless fricatives made a few millimeters apart. And how nice that "trumpet" richly alliterates with "tremendous."

The second line of Pope's couplet, we noted, is highly assonant: every stressed vowel is the same. A very interesting example of assonance on the final stressed syllable of the line may be found in the poem "Die Gebüsche" ("The Thicket") by Friedrich Schlegel. Here it is in German:

> Es wehet kühl und leise
> Die Luft durch dunkle Auen,
> Und nur der Himmel lächelt
> Aus tausend hellen Augen.
> Es regt nur *eine* Seele 5
> Sich in der Meere Brausen,
> Und in den leisen Worten,
> Die durch die Blätter rauschen.
> So tönt in Welle Welle,
> Wo Geister heimlich trauen; 10
> So folgen Worte Worten,
> Wo Geister Leben hauchen.
> Durch all Töne tönet
> Im bunten Erdentraume
> *Ein* leiser Ton gezogen, 15
> Für den, der heimlich lauschet.

Note the end-words of the even-numbered lines. They are all "feminine" endings: the stress falls on the second-last syllable, though that is true of the odd-numbered lines as well. The vowel sound is identical: the diphthong **au**, pronounced like the **ou** (IPA aʊ) in English "sound." Following that stressed sound is an unstressed syllable spelled with the letter **e**, pronounced like the minimal unstressed vowel schwa (ə), followed the first six times with the coda **n**. The onsets of that final syllable vary from zero to **g, s, sch** (pronounced ʃ), **ch** (the velar fricative x), and **m**. I don't remember encountering anything else quite like this pattern of assonance. Since the poem is about the one soft sound (*Ein leiser Ton*) that permeates all of nature, it is a lovely enactment or performance of the theme to make the alternate lines end with the same diphthong set among different consonants but with the same feminine cadence.

Having never seen a translation of this poem into English, I was determined to make one. I tried to deploy the same sound, the vowel sound of "sound" (as well as German *Laut*, meaning "sound," which is conspicuously absent from the poem), but soon concluded it would be extremely difficult to approach the meaning if I confined myself to that sound. So I settled for the long **ee** sound (i), which had more possibilities.

The Thicket

Cool and soft the air blows
Through darkening fields,
And only heaven smiles
Through thousands of bright eyes.
One soul alone is active
In the roaring of the seas,
And in the gentle words
That rustle through the leaves.
So waves resound in waves
Where in secret spirits grieve;
So words respond to words
Where by spirits life is breathed.
One soft sound through every sound
Of earth's bright-colored dream
Sustains its sound for him alone
Who secretly gives heed.

I also sacrificed the feminine endings, more frequent in German than in English because German verbs, nouns, and adjectives are often inflected with unstressed endings. The mysterious vowel sound that only a few heedful souls can hear, I admit, is not the same sound in my poem as it is in the original; far from it. I can't decide whether that matters or not.

We have been assuming throughout this discussion that rhyme, in both the narrow and broad sense, must fall on a stressed syllable if it is to be felt as rhyme at all. Unstressed syllables may be consonant or assonant as a kind of sonic background in harmony with the stressed ones in the foreground, but if they are not it hardly matters, as they usually pass below the threshold of attention in ordinary reading or hearing, and most if not all unstressed vowels have the schwa- sound (ə). But some recent poets, notably Seamus Heaney, have placed end-words that "rhyme," if we can call it that, on unstressed syllables only. "Mint," for example (1996), written in abab quatrains, begins this way:

> It looked like a clump of small dusty nettles
> Growing wild at the gable of the house
> Beyond where we dumped our refuse and old bottles:
> Unverdant ever, almost beneath notice.

"Nettles" and "bottles" seem to "rhyme" well enough. We might call it "extended consonance" in the narrow sense (see [3] above), even though, to be precise about it, it is only the unstressed final syllable that repeats exactly, including -tt- as its onset. It is not hard, however, to hear the nearly vowelless -les [lz] as an extension of -tt- as the coda of the preceding syllable and thus take the final words as having one syllable. Between "house" and "notice" we have a bigger gap. It is true that the vowel of "house" is a diphthong, and thus moves a little along the line toward becoming disyllabic, like "notice" (remember the discussion of "flower" versus "flour" and similar pairs), but there is no getting around the -t- stop in "notice." This pair makes a kind of consonance, but only with the help of the unstressed second syllable of "notice." I suppose you could pronounce "notice" with a softly flapped and voiced -d- sound to move the whole word toward one syllable, and perhaps in Irish English that pronunciation is common, but it sounds forced to my ears and out of keeping with the double -tt- sounds of the other pair.

The first section of Heaney's "Mycenae Lookout" (1996), written in "rhymed" couplets, includes these lines:

> Of bodies raining down like tattered meat
> On top of me asleep—and me the lookout
> The queen's command had posted and forgotten,
> The blind spot her farsightedness relied on.   (7–10)

We are invited to accept "meat" and "lookout" as rhymes, but if "lookout" is a trochee then the only sound-similarity rests on the coda (-t) of an unstressed syllable (-out); there is no way to stretch "meat," which is not a diphthong, into two syllables or to compress "lookout," which is a compound, into one. (This rhyming of a stressed syllable with an unstressed one somewhat resembles the Welsh form called *cywydd*.) The next lines end with "forgotten" and "relied on": I'll leave it to the reader to decide how closely they rhyme. Heaney's poems are full of tongue-delighting lines such as "I saw damp panniers disgorge / The frond-lipped brine-stung / Glut of privilege" ("Oysters," 1979), and his celebrated translation

Beowulf (2000), with its heavy alliterative stresses, culminated a lifetime of fascination with sounds and sound-echoes, so it would seem that his strained quasi-rhymes are not lazy or desperate resorts but are meant to teach us something about sounds by pushing the notion of "rhyme" to the limit, if not beyond it.

In a recent poem, "Memphis," a poignant, puzzling, but witty poem that seems to be spoken by an Egyptian lion, Paul Muldoon creates a series of ingenious rhymes, all of which, I think, could be a given a name from our set of categories, unlike some of Heaney's, but they stretch the categories in interesting ways.[4] The poem consists of two quasi-Petrarchan sonnets of irregular line-lengths, each with the rhyme-scheme abcb/abcb//def/def, and with the b-rhyme shared by the two stanzas. So "Amenhotep" rhymes with "upturned tub," "Ramses" rhymes with "ramps," "Sekhmet" rhymes with "schemata," and "pyramids" rhymes with "beermats." The eight b-rhymes are: manage, mange, menage, munch, haunch, hunch, hinge, inch. It is almost as if Muldoon set himself a goal: to have almost no perfect rhymes, but to make up for their imperfections with rich sound-links of many other kinds. The b-rhymes, for example, alliterate within their stanzas, the first four on m-, the second four on h-, except for the glottal stop beginning "inch" (it follows a vowel). Whatever else may be said about this glitzy display, these twenty-eight rhyme words compose a lesson in sound-similarities, and are very funny as well.

The History of Rhyme

Ancient Greek and Latin verse seldom, if ever, rhymed. We can find some impressive sound-effects in several poems, such as this remarkable pair of lines from Sappho (140a), probably part of a longer poem but very effective by itself. It is an exchange between a chorus of maidens lamenting the dying Adonis and the goddess Aphrodite (Cytherea), who loved him:

> — — — ∪∪— —∪ ∪ — —∪∪ — —
> κατθνάσκει, Κυθέρη᾽, ἄβρος Ἄδωνις· τί κε θεῖμεν;
> katt^hnaskei, Kut^herē᾽, abros Adōnis; ti ke t^heimen?
> [He] is dying, Cytherea, sweet Adonis; what are we to do?

> — — — ∪ ∪— —∪∪— —∪ ∪ — —
> καττύπτεσθε, κόραι, καὶ καταρείκεσθε κίθωνας.
> kattuptest^he, korai, kai katareikest^he kit^honas.
> Beat [your breasts], daughters, and tear [your] tunics.

That is all they can do for him: there is no bringing him back to life. But they can also chant, they can cantillate in harsh and eerie sounds. This couplet has ten k- sounds, eight of them at the beginning of words (alliteration), three of which begin with the *kata-* prefix, hard to translate but perhaps acting something like an intensifier: "he is dying away," "beat against," and "tear apart." It has six θ- sounds, which I have transliterated t^h, which represents an aspirated or more plosive t, not so different from initial t in English; these are similar, of course, to the non-aspirated t-sounds, written with a tau (τ), of which there are five here (counting two that are doubled). There are four r- sounds, which were not like the English r but closer to the r of Spanish or Italian, a flap or trill, much like a d-sound, which is found in *Adonis*. The numerical "harmony" score would be low – that is, very harmonious – yet the k- and t^h- sounds make it sound, as it should, harsh, almost a stammer or cry.

I have written in the metrical scansion as well. Try chanting it aloud a few times, dwelling twice as long on the heavy (long) syllables as on the light (short). Don't worry about distinguishing the t- sounds from the t^h-sounds; it is not a phonemic distinction in English, and English-speakers find it difficult. But try to raise your voice a few notes on the accented syllables, which are sometimes the light ones.

Or consider these lines from Euripides' *Bacchae*, which conclude a tumultuous exchange between the god Dionysus and his bacchantes after he has destroyed the king's palace (601–03):

U U U —
ὁ γὰρ ἄναξ
ho gar anax
For the lord

U — U — U — U — U
ἄνω κάτω τιθεὶς ἔπεισι
anō katō tit^{h}eis epeisi
turning [things] upside down comes against

U U U U U U— U —
μέλαθρα τάδε Διὸς γόνος.
melat^{h}ra tade Dios gonos.
this house, the son of Zeus.

A loose translation that preserves something of the original meter and assonance might go like this: "It is the lord, / the son of Zeus, attacking the palace and / leveling everything down to the ground." The many sound-repetitions of the Greek are certainly effective, and certainly intentional, though none of them is a rhyme in the strict sense.

For a subtle display of sound-repetitions in Latin verse, here is an elegiac couplet from Ovid's *Amores* 3.9.7–8. They are about Cupid coming to mourn the dead poet Tibullus:

—U U— UU— — ——— U U——

ecce, puer Veneris fert ēversamque pharetram
See, the son of Venus bears an overturned quiver

— —— ———UU —U U—

et fractos arcus et sine luce facem.
and broken bows and torch without light.

Some scholars argue that Greek verse did include end-rhyme, and as evidence they cite pairs of lines like these from the *Iliad* (2.87–88):

ἠΰτε ἔθνεα εἶσι μελισσάων ἀδινάων
ēute et^{h}nea eisi melissāōn hadināōn

πέτρης ἐκ γλαφυρῆς αἰεὶ νέον ἐρχομενάων
petrēs ek glap^{h}urēs aiei neon erk^{h}omenāōn.

In Lattimore's translation,

Like the swarms of clustering bees that issue forever
in fresh bursts from the hollow in the stone[.]

Since this is the first "Homeric" – or extended – simile in the whole epic, we might expect some sonic razzle-dazzle. What we get is a rhyme of sorts on two long syllables with an identical opening consonant (-*nāōn*), making it a seemingly "rich" rhyme. But does this apparent couplet really count as a rhyme? It certainly does not seem deliberate. The –*āōn* ending is very common in Homeric Greek, as both syllables together compose a normal genitive plural ending; in fact it occurs again at the end of the third line following this pair (κλισιάων / *klisiāōn* 91). Two lines earlier, too, the final word is λαῶν / *lāōn* 85), part of a formula for a king, "shepherd of the people," which occurs over fifty times in the *Iliad* and the *Odyssey*. In fact, the next line ends with the same word, "people," in a different case (λαοί / *lāoi* 86). This array of supposed rhymes or near-rhymes looks entirely random, as do the very few other instances scholars have put forward. In fact, there may be fewer of them than we would predict if they really were random, given the length of the two epics and the inflection-rich character of Greek; I am tempted to say that these few instances of rhyme attest to deliberate avoidance of it, if Homer or his later editors even noticed them. In any case, they don't amount to much.[5]

The ancient word for this sort of pseudo-rhyme based on grammatical endings is homoeoteleuton (ὁμοιοτέλευτον) or "similar ending"; Aristotle discusses it in his *Rhetoric*, and gives examples, though it grew more frequent in Latin. It is also called "case-rhyme," though it ought to be called "inflectional rhyme," because case is a feature only of nouns and adjectives, while these homoeoteleutic effects sometimes depend on verb-inflections, which indicate person, number, tense, aspect, and mood, but not case. I think Greek and Latin poets took no interest in end-rhyme, and even spurned it if it accidentally turned up, because the sound-echoes of homoeoteleuton seemed trivial: nothing surprising or interesting results from it.

Modern English, by contrast, has very few endings, so rhymes almost always fall on a root, something lexical or meaningful rather than grammatical, and since roots have no particular connection with each other, the fact that they rhyme with other roots is an arbitrary fact about the language that poets can exploit for interesting, even startling, effects. Alexander Pope, for example, begins *An Essay on Man*, addressed to his friend the Viscount Bolingbroke, with this couplet:

> Awake, my St. John! leave all meaner things
> To low ambition, and the pride of Kings.

It comes with a little shiver of surprise, and is even a sign of political daring, to find "Kings" the rhyme-mate of "things," and "meaner things" at that. Hamlet, as we saw, was planning dangerous mischief when he decided a play is just the thing for it. Shelley will rhyme them again, in the plural, to good effect in "Ozymandias." The two words did not always rhyme, as the "–ing" in "king" was originally an unstressed ending (seen in Old English *cyning*) but is now taken to be part of a one-syllable root, identical to the whole word.

Though they are each other's only serious match, and have been paired countless times, it is still interesting, if no longer very surprising, that "death" and "breath" rhyme. They didn't rhyme in Old English, but they have converged as if they were meant for each other – which they are. Another seemingly destined pair, so often mated that they are now the type or exemplar of clichés to be avoided, is "love" and "dove," though they have each hooked up with many other words. Their similarity too is the result of independent linguistic evolution. They may have rhymed in Old English, but their cognates in our fellow Germanic languages do not (German *Liebe*

and *Taube*, Dutch *liefde* and *duif*). Compared to meaningful rhymes like
these – and their very overuse testifies to their meaningfulness – the fact
that two Greek nouns have the same bisyllabic ending in the genitive plural
is trivial.

The importance of rhyme in modern European languages, and its
seeming inevitability, has led legions of modern translators in several
languages, such as Pope in English, to think rhymed couplets, or what
they liked to call "heroic couplets," were just the thing for Homer's Greek
(or for Virgil's Latin), but Homer manifestly does not compose in couplets,
rhymed or not (nor does Virgil). Greek and Latin had a beautiful metrical
form for unrhymed couplets, the elegiac distich, and many classical poets
were masters of it, such as Ovid, as we can see in the one from the *Amores*
we have just quoted, but it is a violent straitjacketing of Homer and Virgil
to force couplets of any kind onto them, and especially rhymed ones.

For reasons scholars have not entirely agreed on, at some point in the late
classical period rhyme began to appear in Latin verse and in the verse of the
Romance vernacular languages that were steadily deviating from the literary language, though it was not for several centuries that rhyme flowered,
notably in the Occitan (or *Langue d'oc*) poems of the troubadours in the
eleventh century. Perhaps the most charming moment of Goethe's *Faust,
Part II* (1832), appears in the medieval courtyard scene where Faust has
brought Helen to safety after rescuing her from death at the hands of her
unforgiving husband, Menelaus. She and Faust have been speaking in
blank verse during this scene, like good Greeks, but Lynceus the watchman
makes his announcements in rhymed couplets. Helen is struck by them,
and asks Faust,

> Tell me why the speech of that good man
> Had something strange about it, strange and friendly:
> Each sound seems to accommodate the next,
> And when one word has settled in the ear
> Another follows to caress the first.   (9367–71)[6]

Faust suggests they practice, and after a few tries Helen, that expert in
caresses, is mistress of rhymes. Goethe himself had mastered classical verse-
forms (the scene before this, an imitation of a Greek tragedy, begins in
excellent iambic trimeters) and knew very well that rhyme is a medieval or
late-classical innovation: Helen would never have heard it in Sparta or
Troy.

The origin of rhyme in "Vulgar" Latin and the early vernaculars almost
certainly had to do with the weakening of the Latin inflection system,

which made homoeoteleuton more frequent (because the endings began to resemble each other) and soon almost inescapable. The weakening of endings probably had to do with the growing importance of stress, and that in turn may have been the result of another change, the weakening of quantitative differences in Latin vowels and the strengthening of qualitative ones. In classical Latin (as in classical Greek), the five vowel sounds each had two forms, long and short, and this fact had much to do, we saw, with whether a syllable in poetry was heavy or light; a language with a clear distinction in quantity or length invites the kind of meter (quantitative) that Latin and Greek deployed. As Latin evolved, differences in vowel length shifted to differences in vowel quality, which are due to the placement of the tongue in the mouth when the vowel is sounded and not (or not as much) to how long the sound takes. So Latin *amīca* ("friend," female), with a long vowel where the stress fell, evolved into Italian *amica*, Spanish *amiga*, and French *amie*, all of which have preserved the original long ī- sound, but Latin *pĭlu* ("hair"), with a short stressed vowel, evolved into Italian *pelo*, Spanish *pelo*, and (most oddly) French *poil* (IPA pwal).[7] The number of vowel contrasts shrank to nine, then seven. Latin always had a stress pattern, but as the length duality evaporated stress grew in importance. For many centuries, even well past the Renaissance, quantitative meter was still employed by learned poets writing in classical Latin, but in the vernaculars it no longer worked well, and other devices were sought to give shape to the verse lines, and particularly to mark line endings. Occitan poets may have learned about rhyme from Arabic poetry in Spain, but rhyme of one sort or another seems to have been hit upon independently in several parts of Europe.

French, though it lost the vowel-length duality along with the other Romance languages, is a lightly stressed language, so its verse does not usually fall into the stress patterns so familiar in English: iambic, trochaic, and so on. The number of syllables is definitive, and the placement of pauses, but there is nothing else to define the line in the way, say, five iambic feet define the blank verse line in English. (That said, as we noted in the last chapter, it is hard for French verse to avoid metrical patterns altogether.) Until recently, at least, there was nothing like blank verse in French; poetry had to rhyme, if only to give shape to the line, and quite a few fussy rules, as we saw, were imposed to make the rhymes more exact, and "rich."

Arabic poetry rhymed for as long as we have record, and it is probably not a coincidence that Arabic has few inflectional suffixes, though it does have a rich set of vowel changes among its root consonants that function like inflections, and these changes may generate rhymes. The oldest recorded rhyming verse, dated around 1000 BCE, is Chinese, which is also a language with no endings; nearly all words are monosyllabic, and it follows that there are lots of homophones, although some verse forms required rhyming words to have the same tone or "tonal contour," one of four or more kinds. There seems to be a correlation between a language's lack of grammatical endings and its propensity to rhyme, but I don't know if anyone has done a thorough survey.

The word "rhyme" has a murky and disputed history. Most of the technical terms used in descriptions of poetry come from Greek, such as "poetry" itself, and "rhyme" certainly looks Greek enough, with its initial rh-, as if it were related to "rhythm," which is certainly Greek. But the spelling is recent. From the earliest appearances of the word in English in about 1200 until about 1600, it is invariably spelled without the -h-: we find "rym," "rim," "ryme," and "rime," but never "rhyme" or "rhime"; some people still spell it "rime" today. English got it from Old French, where it was also spelled "rime" or "ryme." This evidence would be odd, though perhaps not impossible, if the word passed from Greek through Latin into Old French and then into English, however else it was altered. One of the two contending theories about its origin argues that it was not born with that -h- but acquired it only after scholars mistakenly decided it must be related to "rhythm" and respelled it accordingly. On this theory, it really derives from a Germanic word like Old High German and Old English *rīm*, which meant "number, counting, reckoning"; it was taken into Old French, probably from Frankish (very similar to Old High German), and then passed into the other Romance languages (as *rima*) and into Middle English (as "rime" or "ryme"). This Germanic word goes back to PIE *re- or *rei-, which meant "reason" or "count," a root with many offspring, such as Latin *ratio*, itself the mother of many words. According to the *OED*, the oldest meaning of "rym" or "rim" was not "rhyme" in the modern sense but "meter" or "measure" in verse. How it got to mean rhyme is speculative, but perhaps it was through this sequence of senses: "count" > "series" > "series of rhymed syllables" > "rhymed verse." That seems a bit of a stretch, but the "number" theory seems to be the dominant view of the etymologists today.[8]

The other theory, and the one that seems to have convinced seventeenth-century scholars to respell it, is that "rhyme," earlier "rime," goes back to Old French *rime*, with a variant spelling *ritme* (the -t- being silent), which comes from Medieval Latin *rithmus* < Latin *rhythmus* < Greek *rhythmos*. Medieval Latin *rithmus* meant *versus rithmici* (*versus* is plural here), "rhythmical verses" – that is, verses in meter based on "rhythm" or stress (accent) – as opposed to *versus metrici*, which were "metrical verses" based on measures of length (either long or short), as in classical Latin. Such "rhythmical" or stress-based verses happened to have end-rhyme, unlike metrical verses, and so the term came to mean "rhymed verse(s)" and then "rhyme" itself. The Russian word for rhyme, рифма (*rifma*), originally spelled риѳма (*rithma*), seems to be based on the same theory.

Both theories have difficulties, such as the fact that French *rime* is feminine whereas both *rhythmus* and *rīm* are masculine, and that the posited form *ritme* in Old French is not attested anywhere. If nothing else, these incompatible theories show that rhyme, a new thing under the sun, was very slow to acquire a name. Even today, in modern Greek, there is no good word for "rhyme," though some recent Greek poets have used rhymes; it has to make do with the octosyllabic word ὁμοιοκαταληξία (*omiokatalixia*), meaning "similar-endingness."

Though rhyme has been a staple of English poetry since the time of Chaucer (*c.* 1343–1400), and largely because of Chaucer, it has periodically drawn the scorn of poets. The most famous instance is Milton's prefatory note to *Paradise Lost*, where he calls rhyme "the invention of a barbarous age, to set off wretched matter and lame metre." To "judicious ears," he goes on, rhyme is "trivial and of no true musical delight"; and the heroic poem that follows is an example of "ancient liberty," free of "the troublesome and modern bondage of rhyming." Though we may not wish *Paradise Lost* any different from what it is, in magnificent blank verse, it is strange to see Milton implicitly reject his own twenty-three sonnets, "L'Allegro," "Il Penseroso," "On the Morning of Christ's Nativity," and "Lycidas." He was a master of rhyme. So was Ben Jonson, who nonetheless complained against it in "A Fit of Rhyme against Rhyme." As "the rack of finest wits," he writes, rhyme twists words and cheats verse and fetters vowels together. "Greek was free from rhyme's infection," but it has been downhill since the Greeks, and he wishes the fool who invented it to suffer cramps in his joints forever. The poem, of course, is in rhyme, as is every other non-dramatic poem of Jonson's. In 1950, the American poet Charles Olson, in an influential essay called "Projective Verse," writes about the necessity of breaking away from rhyme (as well as meter) in favor of the "breath," the syllable, and the line, but even he cannot resist a striking rhyme in the opening of his magnum opus, *The Maximus Poems*: "I, Maximus / a metal hot from boiling water, tell you / what is a lance, who obeys the figures of / the present dance."[9] Certainly by Olson's day, and well before it, there was a widespread feeling among poets, not only in

English, that rhyme had been played out, along with regular meter and
stanza forms, if only because it seemed that every word in the language that
is capable of being a rhyme had already been rhymed with every other word
that could be rhymed with it, and many times over. But there may be
occasional surprises. "The old horse dies slow," William Carlos Williams
says, in the opening line of his enigmatic little poem titled "When
Structure Fails Rhyme Attempts to Come to the Rescue" (1948). If the
horse is an allegory for rhyme as the vehicle of poetry, as it seems, Pegasus is
now a wingless broken-down nag; there is no fresh fodder left, and there are
no rhymes in sight. Or maybe just one: the horse "does what he can, with /
unabated phlegm, / ahem!" The horse keeps producing these rhyming
sounds, but they don't sound good anymore. Williams may have been the
first and last poet to rhyme "phlegm" with "ahem," a synecdoche, perhaps,
for how little is left in the treasury of rhymes worth listening to.

But rhyme dies slow. We saw the acrobatic examples in Paul Muldoon's
poem. When free verse was still new, of course, there were rhymed protests
against it, but the ones I have found would seem to have given ammunition
to the innovators. Ella Wheeler Wilcox, for example, in "Old Rhythm and
Rhyme" (1912), overflows with both:

> They tell me new methods now govern the Muses,
> The modes of expression have changed with the times;
> That low is the rank of the poet who uses
>   The old-fashioned verse with intentional rhymes.
> And quite out of date, too, is rhythmical metre;
>   The critics declare it an insult to art.
> But oh! the sweet swing of it, oh! the clear ring of it,
>   Oh! the great pulse of it, right from the heart,
>   Art or no art.

"Rhymes" rhymes with "times" here for the millionth time, and later in the
poem "rhyming" rhymes with "chiming," of course. But it is too easy to
mock this sincere outpouring of love for the old beauties of poetry, and it is
worth remembering, a hundred years on, that the loose modes we take for
granted now were felt as a loss by more people then than read the newer
modes now, so much has the audience for poetry shrunk. Rhyme-lovers
still buy Hallmark cards and enjoy popular songs. And Wilcox goes on to
make a pertinent point – that there are rhymes and rhythms in nature: in
the regular waves and tides of the ocean ("that old poet," as she calls it), in
the winds in the trees, and so on. She might have pointed out to William
Carlos Williams that at least rhyme is a horse, and not a new-fangled
automobile with no meter but a speedometer and no sound but a honk.

Rhyme and meter can be dismissed as artificial, as opposed to the "breath," and form can be pronounced to be the ever-unique partner of ever-unique content, but then again we all breathe regularly, our heart beats regularly, we walk on two feet, and if we want to dance with our tribe we had better have someone keeping time. And in a language with the average number of phonemes lots of words rhyme, and children love them.

Though *vers libre* was not to arrive in France for another generation, Sainte-Beuve wrote a paean to rhyme in 1828 ("À la Rime") in fifteen six-line stanzas, which rivals Wilcox's poem in its gush, but with a remarkable collection of metaphors for rhyme and its powers. Here is the first stanza:

Rime, qui donnes leurs sons	Rime, you who give their sounds
Aux chansons,	To songs,
Rime, l'unique harmonie	Rime, unique harmony
Du vers, qui, sans tes accents	Of verse, which, without your tones
Frémissants,	Vibrating,
Serait muet au génie	Would be mute to the spirit

The three rhymes are all *rimes riches*, as we would expect, and so they remain, with a few exceptions, throughout the poem. Without rhymes, Sainte-Beuve says, verse would not speak to the *génie* (the "genius" or spirit), and if that sounds vague he gives a lovely example in the next stanza: it is the "last farewell of a friend / The other friend / Half repeats from afar." Rhyme is also a prow, a plow, a bridle, a spur (perhaps Williams was reading this), a clasp in the sash around the breasts of Venus or in the belt around the chest of a warrior, the narrow neck of a fountain, a yoke to which the once-rebellious Sainte-Beuve now willingly submits – and much more. The poem is a florid compendium of analogues, some of which, I think, deserve more attention than a reader would naturally give them as they fly by. He is addressing Mademoiselle Rime, flattering her with every conceivable metaphor, and showing off his own rimes as if they were a flock of their joint children.

The Russian poet Alexander Pushkin read this poem and was prompted to write two of his own on the subject. The first, in a similar stanza to Sainte-Beuve's, is known by its first line, "Rhyme, sonorous friend" ("Rifma, zvuchnaia podruga") (1828), and in it Pushkin speculates how the Greeks would have felt about Rhyme if she had appeared in their midst. Homer or Hesiod would have told a story about Apollo, god of poetry, abandoned by the other gods because he had offended Zeus, and how he suffered in his loneliness, but

> Remembering their first meetings,
> Mnemosyne came
> To sweeten his suffering.
> And Apollo's girlfriend
> In the dark grove of Helicon,
> Gave birth to the fruit of [his] raptures.   (trans. Wachtel)

And their daughter is named Rhyme. Two years later, in a poem called simply "Rhyme" ("Rifma"), he revised Rhyme's genealogy to make her the daughter of Apollo by Echo, with Mnemosyne (Memory) playing the midwife. Though the girl grows up obeying "memory's strictness," the "sensitive" Echo seems a more likely choice as the mother. Rhyme can aid the memory, no doubt, but there is a suggestion that memory must prevail over rhyme if a poet is not to be distracted by random similarities and wander off his path. As if to embody that point, Echo does nothing in this second poem – it does not rhyme. It is written in that very classical form, the elegiac distich, which we discussed in Chapter 2. Pushkin seems to have had second thoughts not only about who would be the more appropriate mother of Rhyme, but about how valuable rhyme would have been to the Greeks as well. Mnemosyne must have reminded Pushkin that the elegiac couplet hardly needed more structure or ornament than the Greeks and Romans gave it without the help of rhyme.

Poets, then, have had much to say about rhyme, for it or against it, and an interesting book might be written that follows that thread, but we will leave this account of rhyme by noting that, even though free verse and various kinds of unrhymed stanzaic forms, not to mention occasional uses of blank verse, are now dominant in English poetry and the poetries of many modern languages, rhyme still has its advocates and has even enjoyed a little revival. The "New Formalism" of younger poets of the 1980s is now some thirty years old and may have passed its peak, but there seems greater openness in many journals to publishing various kinds of traditional as well as experimental forms, including rhyme. Rhyme has thriven, too, in translations of verse, perhaps most gloriously in Richard Wilbur's great translations of ten of Molière's comedies between 1955 and 2009. As a poet-translator once told me, "When I translate into rhymes, my heart is happy."

Notes

1. It is, of course, "breath." They make a perfect pair: Shakespeare rhymes them three times in the same scene of *Richard II*. But there is nothing else but names (Seth, Macbeth) and "saith," the archaic form of "says." Poets have long

recognized this fact, but Keats seems to defy common sense in the first stanza of "Eve of St. Agnes," written in Spenserians (ababbcbcc), where he puts "breath" at the end of line 6 (the first c rhyme), "death" (inevitable) in line 8, and then, alas, "saith," the weakest rhyme word in the strongest position, at the end of the alexandrine.

2. See M. H. Abrams' essay "The Fourth Dimension of a Poem," where he speaks of the importance of feeling poetry in the mouth.

3. We should also note that the first four nouns grow increasingly long, as if in a battlefield crescendo, until "thunder" ends the line. I owe this observation to Midge Goldberg.

4. "Memphis" first appeared in *The Nation* 301:16 (October 19, 2015): 35.

5. There are a few instances in Aristophanes, such as *Clouds* 711–15, of humorous passages that supposedly rhyme, but even here the rhymes are on the unstressed (or rather unpitched) grammatical endings. They are surely intentional, but they are not much like rhymes on semantic or root syllables in rhyming poetry in other languages. The dozen or so proposed examples of "rhyme" in pairs of lines in Virgil's *Aeneid* are no more impressive, if a little more frequent, than those in Homer: they are all grammatical endings.

6. Translation by David Luke, in *Goethe: Faust: Part Two* (Oxford World Classics, 1994).

7. I have taken these examples from the thorough discussion in Alkire and Rosen, *Romance Languages*, 5–12.

8. See the etymological dictionaries by Calvert Watkins (English – *American Heritage Dictionary*), Jacqueline Picoche (French – *Le Robert*), and Günther Drosdowski (German – *Duden*).

9. "Projective Verse" in Olson, *Selected Writings*. Quotation from *The Maximus Poems*, p. 1. This passage is also in iambic pentameter, more or less.

CHAPTER FOUR

Onomatopoeia and Sound Symbolism

"Onomatopoeia" is one of the technical terms we most easily remember, perhaps because it is such an odd word, oddly spelled, and which could be a trochaic trimeter line by itself, but more probably because its meaning, as it is usually defined and illustrated, is easy to grasp and fun to think about. "Splash, squeak, chirp, buzz, boom, zap, crinkle, hiss, whisper, pop, hum, murmur" – these words, and many more, which imitate real sounds, are said to be "onomatopoeic" (or sometimes "onomatopoetic"). The definitions found in the handbooks start with words like these as instances of onomatopoeia in the strict sense, as "a word, or a combination of words, whose sound seems to resemble closely the sound it denotes,"[1] and then usually go on to describe an extended or more subtle sense, as a characteristic of words that suggest by their sound-shape any feature of what they mean, not just sound: it could be size, form, speed, solidity, duration, or almost anything else. The broader sense overlaps with "sound symbolism," the most general term for the natural, or apparently natural, connection between sounds and their meanings or referents; it is sometimes called "sound iconicity."

"Onomatopoeia" is indeed an odd word, for its original meaning in Greek does not imply anything about sound similarity or mimicry. *Onoma* (ὄνομα) means "name," later both widened to "expression" and narrowed to "noun," while *poiia* (ποιία) means "making," from the same root that gives us "poem" and "poet." The compound could be translated simply as "word-making," and when we make new words (such as the verb "google" or the nouns "biffles" and "bling") we do not necessarily base them on any associated sound or any trait of the meaning. Aristotle uses *pepoiēmenon* (πεποιημένον), the neuter perfect participle of "make," to refer to a new word: a "made thing" or "made-up thing" (*Poetics* 1457b2, 33). Some translators render it "coinage," but that is to introduce a distracting metaphor.[2] The two examples he gives, *ernugas* for "horns" and *arētēra* for "priest" (the latter used three times by Homer), are not onomatopoeic

86

in the modern sense; they came about by metaphor or metonymy without regard to their sounds: *arētēra*, for example, means "one who prays, a pray-er" (hyphenated), from *arē* ("prayer").

The first instance of the word "onomatopoeia" itself that has come down to us is found in the *Geographia* of Strabo (14.2.28). While talking about barbarians, he pauses on the word *barbaron*. He thinks it "was first sounded out thus according to onomatopoeia (κατ' ὀνοματοποιίαν)" because barbarians had trouble speaking Greek, implying that they sounded like "bar-bar": they were babblers. He then names three Greek verbs for poor speaking and calls them ono-matopoeic as well: *battarizein* ("stutter"), *traulizein* ("lisp"), and *pselli-zein* ("falter in speech"); and then gives five more nouns for sounds, such as *klangē* ("clang"). Strabo thus established the word "onomato-poeia" as about sound mimicry, the sense it has retained ever since. Quintilian introduced it into Latin, as far as we know, in his *Institutes of Oratory*, the most influential treatise on rhetoric that has survived from the ancient world. He defines it in broader terms than the imitation of sounds, but it still has to do with a natural fitness of some sort between sound and meaning, and his examples are all imitations – two examples from Greek: *linxe bios* ("the bow twanged") and *siz' ophthalmos* ("the eye hissed") (1.5.72), both unique instances from Homer; and three from Latin: *mugitus* ("lowing, mooing"), *sibilus* ("hissing"), and *murmur* ("murmur") (8.6.31). It was a virtue of the Greeks, he says, that they invented many such words, but Latin writers scarcely dare to try it, and rely only on onomatopoeic words already long established. Quintilian seems to think that onomatopoeia is appropriate only in the earliest phases of a language, when there aren't many words yet, and that the Greek language more or less began with Homer.[3]

So not only do we inherit the sense of "onomatopoeia" established by Strabo and Quintilian, but the word trails with it a notion about the origin of language itself: that the first speakers made up words that echo or imitate natural sounds, and then made up more words by expanding these words and/or applying them metaphorically or metonymically – that is, by analogy or extension. This is somewhat like the theory Socrates advocates in Plato's *Cratylus*. There he tells his friend Hermogenes that "Cratylus is right in saying that things have names by nature, and that not every man is an artificer of names, but only he who looks to the name which each thing by nature has, and is able to express the true forms of things in letters and syllables" (390d–e). Socrates goes on at tedious length to give one etymology after another, most of them absurd by modern standards (he seems not to take them very seriously himself); they are not onomatopoeic in the narrow sense, but rather expressive of something appropriate to their meaning. Toward the end, he enters the field of what has since been called "sound symbolism," where he says that "the letter rho (ρ) appears to me to be the general instrument expressing all motion" ("sound" would be better than "letter" here), and the original namer of things noted "that the tongue was most agitated and least at rest in the pronunciation of this letter" (426c,e) (the rho was trilled, unlike the standard pronunciations of English r); by contrast delta (δ) and tau (τ) expressed binding and staying in place, lambda (λ) expressed liquidness and smoothness, nu (ν) expressed inwardness, and so on (427b–c).[4]

These speculations ought to have given onomatopoeic and other naturalistic etymologies a bad name, but it is difficult to let go of the belief that the word you have used all your life for a thing is the most appropriate word for it, especially if you know only your native language, and in every language there is a set of words that are incontestably onomatopoeic. Throughout the Middle Ages and well into the Enlightenment era, most scholars argued for a naturalistic basis of vocabulary, or even a divine basis, since it was widely assumed that God had given language to Adam. It was also widely assumed that God taught Adam Hebrew, though the Book of Genesis does not say so, and that Hebrew was the language everyone on earth spoke before they pridefully undertook to build the tower of Babel and God confounded their speech (Genesis 11.1–9). In fact, Genesis implies that God did not teach Adam Hebrew or any other language, but simply endowed him with the capacity for it, for God brought all the beasts and birds to Adam "to see what he would name them" (2.19). God no doubt had his own names for all of them, but either he did not know Adam's language (though they somehow speak together later, after the Fall), or he did not know what Adam would come up with as he was shown beast after beast and bird after bird. Did Adam contemplate the inner nature of each creature and somehow intuit its most fitting name? Or did he agree with modern linguists that words have an arbitrary relation to their meanings? John Hollander's charming poem "Adam's Task" seems to make Adam a member of the arbitrary school. As the creatures appeared before him he came up with names like these:

> Thou, verdle; thou, McFleery's pomma;
>   Thou; thou; thou—three types of grawl;
> Thou, flisket; thou, kabasch; thou, comma-
>   Eared mashawk[.]

It was a long day for Adam, with little time to contemplate anything, so he must have tossed off at random the first sounds that came to his tongue. (But who could McFleery have been?)

At any rate, some sort of naturalistic theory, usually about onomatopoeia, governed most theories of language origins until the early twentieth century. Charles Darwin was repeating a commonplace when he wrote in *The Descent of Man* (1871), "I cannot doubt that language owes its origin to the imitation and modification of various natural sounds, the voices of other animals, and man's own instinctive cries, aided by signs and gestures" (p. 673). It is hard to credit any other theory, in my opinion, but if language is as old as some linguists now think, perhaps as old as our species (300,000 years or more), or even only as old as, say, a few thousand years before the exodus from Africa (perhaps 50,000 years ago), it is hopeless to attempt to reconstruct its original form, though some linguists have tried to do so. We can certainly track the continual infusion of imitative sounds into ancient and existing languages, but this is secondary to the mainly arbitrary or conventional vocabulary of all languages, which are products of tens of thousands of years of evolution during which all traces of the original words – if there even were "original" words – have long since melted away. Just how much effect the continual influx of onomatopoeic words has, however, and how large that influx has been, is not easy to determine. I think both are greater than most linguists believe.

The cornerstone of modern linguistics is what the Swiss linguist Ferdinand de Saussure called "the arbitrary nature of the linguistic sign." The sign is composed of two parts, the "signifier" (the sound or image) and the "signified" (the concept), and with a few exceptions, he says, there is no "inner relationship" between them.[5] So the concept TREE is called "tree" on one side of the Channel and "arbre" on the other, and across another border "Baum." There is nothing in the shape or color or size or anything else in a tree to commend one of these sounds over another: they are equally good, and equally arbitrary. It is important to note that the "signified" is not the "referent," the tree itself, in Saussure's view, but rather the concept of the tree, and while the concept may owe its outline to the existence of real trees, its full semantic character also depends on other concepts, such as BUSH and FOREST, in the same domain, and their relationships may vary from language to language. The key word is "system." Signifiers in a language are composed of phonemes whose sole virtue is that they are distinguishable from the others: /p/ and /b/ are different in one feature (voice), and that is enough to make them distinguish various pairs of words from each other, such as "pin" and "bin," or "flap" and "flab." (A dozen phonemes are all a language needs to generate a rich vocabulary, though most languages have quite a few more.) Signifieds also enter into a system, less easily specifiable than the system of phonemes, but based like them on differences: animate/inanimate, male/female, young/old, large/small, raw/cooked, and so on. As for phonemes, Saussure claims, their actual sonic character is of no importance – what counts is how they assemble into an indefinitely large number of different signifiers.

What about onomatopoeia? Saussure considers onomatopoeic words along with interjections (such as "ouch") as the two kinds of expression that might be held up as evidence against the rule of arbitrariness. But, he says, "onomatopoeic formations are never organic elements of a linguistic system. Besides, their number is much smaller than is generally supposed."[6] Many supposed formations are fanciful, or they are the result of evolution from earlier forms that don't seem onomatopoeic at all, while even the authentic examples (such as "tick-tock") are "only approximate," based as they are on a limited number of phonemes, and they too evolve under the laws of sound change and morphological change that admit of no exceptions. He says much the same thing about interjections. Either they are not really part of the linguistic system, or the system soon digests them.

Saussure has had critics among distinguished linguists, but his assumptions have been taken as definitive among the great majority of phonologists and semanticists.[7] One of his assumptions, widely repeated, is that there are only a few onomatopoeic words in any language. Is that true? Even if we take the term in the narrow sense, as imitations of sounds, there must be hundreds of them in English, at least, and more of them are invented every year. Here is a sample of fifty of them: babble, bark, bleep, boom, burp, buzz, chirp, click, crack, crackle, crinkle, croak, croak, crunch, cuckoo, fart, gargle, glug, grumble, gulp, gurgle, hiss, hum, mumble, murmur, piss, plop, pop, purr, scratch, scream, shriek, sizzle, slurp, smash, snap, spit, splash, squeak, stammer, stutter, swish, thud, thump, tinkle, twitter, whisper, whistle, zap, zip, zoom. All of these, I think, are used as both verbs and nouns, and many can readily generate adjectives and adverbs, so they are not quarantined from the syntactic system of English and can infect other words.

"Boom," for instance, now pairs with an alliterative partner, "bust," to describe stock-market cycles; it has entered other languages: *le boom, el boom, der Boom*; we also have "boomlet." Using it as a verb or verbal adjective, we say "the thunder boomed" and "he spoke in a booming voice." Among metaphorical extensions, to be "buzzed" is to be high or stoned, to be "pissed" or "smashed" is to be drunk, and you can make quite a "splash" at a public event very far from a swimming pool. "Click" as noun or verb may have first (in the seventeenth century) referred to the sound of a door or lock closing, or a gun cocking; later, it was the sound of a camera shutter opening; then, as a verb (in the twentieth century), it could mean "to fall in with someone or agree completely," as in "I clicked with her on our first date"; then, in the 1980s, we learned to "click on" an icon on our computer with a mouse, even to "click through" a series of icons or screens, to "left-click," or "right-click," or "double-click," and the word has also spread to other languages: French *cliquer*, German *anklicken*. Twitter now permeates cyberspace with its tweets, making it a "twittersphere" in which the President can unleash his "twitterstorms." And so on. There must be hundreds more such words, including many with influences that work their way far into their home language, and then into others.

Similar lists could readily be drawn up by native speakers of any other language. In French, for instance: *plouf* ("splash"), *prout* ("fart"), *chut* ("shh"), *gloups* ("glug"), and so on.

We might add that a few words with nothing remotely onomatopoeic in their origin may have acquired onomatopoeia by association with certain sounds. J. D. Sadler has provided a delightful example: "The German word *Gesundheit* means 'good health' and is the equivalent of our 'God bless you,' but one reason that we use it so enthusiastically after a sneeze may be that it *sounds* so much like a sneeze."[8]

A narrower set would be quasi-words like "bow-wow" or "moo" or "cock-a-doodle-doo," and perhaps a few of the fifty just listed would fall into this category. But then this category is also leaky, as most if not all of them could readily be promoted to words: "the cow mooed" and "the dog bow-wowed." "Ka-ching," the sound of a cash register, is now in wide use; it was the title of a popular song by Shania Twain in 2003; after such cash registers disappear, the word might still be current, leaving most people puzzled as to how it came about. Still further beneath normal word-status would be expressive "paraverbal" interjections, some of which might be onomatopoeic to a degree. There are a surprising number of these. One is conventionally spelled "tsk-tsk" or "tut-tut," but it is really an alveolar "click" (a kind of sucked alveolar t), made fairly loud, and not an English phoneme; used orally it is not strictly a word, though it has a meaning (disapproval or regret), but spelled out it can be promoted like "bow-wow." You could say "She tsk-tsked her pupils." "Uh-huh" (yes) and "uh-uh" (no) differ by one phoneme, /h/, but the two parts of "uh-uh" must be separated by a glottal stop, which is not an English phoneme. So must the two parts of "uh-oh" or "oh-oh" (expressing alarm or worry). "Hmmm" (for musing or considering) seems not to have a vowel, though it has often been spelled "hum"; the same is true of "hmph" or "hmmph" (indignation or disappointment), conventionally spelled "humph." (I once said "hmmph" when none of the students in my class came up with something I thought they should have known, whereupon one of them said, "Class, we've just been hmmphed at!") There are quite a few others, such as "phew," "whew," "ahem" (throat clearing), "shhhh" (leading to the verb "shush"), "psst" (to get someone's attention), "ugh," "yuch" (with the non-phonemic voiceless uvular fricative χ) or "yuck," its less intense cousin "ick," "ha-ha" and other laughter sounds, "brrr" (shivering, with a staccato series of glottal stops), "mmm" (pleasure or satisfaction), "ouch" and "ow," "wow," "oops" and "woops," "phooey," "hooray" and "yay," "boo," "yipes," and "yum," which is often now joined with "yuck" as a seemingly natural pair of opposites. Our spelling system does not do justice to some of these sounds, and when they are spelled out they sometimes engender new words, such as "tsk," via readers who don't know what sounds they awkwardly represent. (A friend of mine once joked that he was "taken to tsk" by his girlfriend.)

The most amusing of these sounds is the "raspberry" or (in America) the "Bronx cheer," used for derision or jeering. It has been described as an unvoiced linguo-labial trill, and an IPA symbol has been found for it (r̼), though it seems not to be a phoneme in any language. There is no good way to spell it in the Roman alphabet (prrprrprrp? pfrfrfrfrp?). It is called a "raspberry" because of British rhyming slang, whereby the term is a modifier of an unspoken word (here "tart") that rhymes with another ("fart"), which is what it means, though in this case it seems likely that "raspberry" also suggests "rasp," a good enough description of the sound. From "raspberry," we get the noun and verb "razz" (for "jeer").

Saussure would reply that all of these words, insofar as they are words at all and not just paraverbal sounds, are "only approximate." Even an imitation of a natural sound, such as "cock-a-doodle-doo," he would say, is conventionalized, as we can prove by listening to what French and German roosters say: *cocorico* and *kikeriki*. To Saussure we could reply that, of course, these imitations are only approximate: what else could they be if they must be concocted out of a limited number of phonemes and produced out of the human mouth?[9] All onomatopoeia is partial, ranging from fairly exact to subtle and dubious.[10] And the evidence of varying rooster cries cuts both ways: they vary indeed from language to language, but they do not vary by all that much. For example, in Hungarian it is *kukuriku*, in Japanese *kokekokkō*, in Persian *ghughuli-ghughu*, in Hindi *kukruukuu*, in Sudanese *kongkorongok*, in Thai *ake-e-ake-ake*, and in Tagalog *kukaok* or *tik-ti-laok* or *ta-tala-ok* or *ko-ko-ro-kok*.[11] These may sound quite different to some ears, but to mine they sound much alike; at any rate, no language, I believe, represents rooster cries as "moo" or "bow-wow" or "peep" or "neigh." It is partly a matter of taste or intuition whether and to what degree to call a word onomatopoeic (or natural) versus arbitrary (or conventional). Linguists in the dominant Saussurean tradition often rightly accuse "naturalists" of imaginary claims, but, if these naturalists are often guilty of "hearing things," their Saussurean opponents often seem deaf. In his otherwise excellent *Linguistic Guide to English Poetry*, for example, Geoffrey Leech writes, "although English *whisper* and French *chuchoter* are both felt to be onomatopoeic, there is scarcely any phonetic likeness between them."[12]

Partly in response to Saussure and the arbitrarians, and partly to rethink the sometimes questionable researches of nineteenth-century Cratyleans, several distinguished linguists, such as Otto Jespersen and Roman Jakobson, have made a case for the phenomenon of sound symbolism, beyond the narrow domain of onomatopoeia. Among many examples they and others have canvassed, we can discuss only two or three here. One is the widespread use of the high front vowel /i/, or other vowels close to it, to indicate smallness, affection, or intimacy. The Romance languages attach endings such as *-ino, -ito,* and *-illo* (masculine), or *-ina, -ita,* and *-illa* (feminine), to nouns to make "diminutives": a *señorita* is a young (or maiden) *señora; zucchini* is the plural diminutive of *zucca* ("pumpkin"); a *guerrilla* is a little *guerra* ("war"). In English, we use words like "teensy-weensy" or "itty-bitty" to mean something very small; the Scots use "wee." There is also a pattern in deictic words – that is, words that point to various positions with respect to the speaker – whereby the terms for nearer things tend to have a higher and more frontal vowel than those for things farther away: "this" and "that," "these" and "those," "here" and "there"; French *ceci* and *celà*; and so on.[13] There are some counter-examples, of course, one of which is striking: "big" versus "tiny." "Tiny" has a diphthong (/ai/) that begins with a low or open vowel made farther back, so it ought to mean "big," whereas "big" ought to mean "small" (and "small" itself ought to mean "big"). In fact, however, when "tiny" (and variant "tine") entered English, it was pronounced with a high front vowel, but the Great Vowel Shift changed long /i/- sounds to /ai/- sounds in most dialects, and, since about 1800, "teeny" has been in circulation to mean "smaller than tiny."

"Big" is an exception among words in its semantic field, such as "great, vast, grand, huge, enormous, giant, gigantic, humongous," but there it is – a big exception. Any big exception may embarrass the sound-symbolism school, but it need not refute it. It is a question of statistics: we would need to know how many words in common use (and "common" too is a quantitative term in this context) fall or do not fall under plausible symbolic categories in order to see whether there is a salient trend or not. It would be a long and tedious research project.

A possible phenomenon that belongs somewhere in the realm of sound symbolism is what we might call "rhyme-attraction." The older forms of "breath" and "death" did not rhyme, but they do now; they are each, in fact, the other's only good rhyme. Did they fall into sonic orbit around each other? "Womb" is Germanic in origin, and did not at first rhyme with "tomb," which comes to English from Greek via Latin and French. Did their natural pairing of meanings help bring about pairings of sound? And was "doom" a factor in the pronunciation of "tomb"? "Doom" seems the perfect sound for its meaning, and if it did not affect "tomb" it might well have attracted "gloom," which did not at first rhyme with it. A rhyming phrase like "ill will" might have kept "ill" in the sense of "bad" circulating longer than it otherwise might have. And there are quite a few alliterative pairs, such as "kith and kin," "wrack and ruin," "odds and ends," "from pillar to post," and "head over heels," where the two partners may subtly affect each other's sense. Such semantic effects of sound-shape causes might seem arbitrary, but if so they are arbitrary in a different sense from Saussure's usage.

Those who advocate the importance of sound symbolism often cite certain patterns such as the st- cluster at the beginning of words having to do with stiffness, staunchness, steadiness, or stamina ("stand, stout, sturdy, staff, stick, stock," German *stehen, Stamm*, etc.). Though some of these words go back to the same Proto-Indo-European root, others seem drawn into this semantic field out of a sense that the initial sound is appropriate to the meaning. Four other such sets, in English at least, are: (1) dr- words having to do with water or the conspicuous absence of it: "drip, drop, drizzle, dribble, drink, drench, dregs, drool, drown, drain, dry, drought"; (2) gl- words referring to light: "glare, glitter, glisten, gleam, glimmer, glance, glimpse, glass, glacier, glaze, glow, glossy, glad" (which used to mean "shining"), "glade" (as an open sunny space); (3) sl- words about slippery or slimy things: "sled, sleek, slick, slide, slime, slough, sludge, slug, slink, slip, slope" (derived from "slip"), "slither, slush, slobber"; and (4) sn- words concerning the nose and the expressions it makes:

"snout, snort, snore, snooze, snarl, sneer, snoop, sneeze, sniff, sniffle, snuff, snot, snivel, snooty, snob, snub." Again, many of these words are not related to one another etymologically but seem to belong together anyway, drawn by what Anderson calls "conspiracy rules."[14] Skeptics point out that these patterns are confined to a single language or family of languages, though, again, I don't know whether anyone has had the patience to trawl through, say, a hundred languages to see if there are any trans-linguistic tendencies toward such patterns.[15]

And what about certain humorous coinages, such as "ramshackle" from seventeenth-century British English; "bamboozle," "flabbergast," and "hullabaloo" from eighteenth-century British English; and a large set of nineteenth-century American inventions: "bloviate," "absquatulate," "discombobulate," "rambunctious," "hornswoggle," "skedaddle," and "shenanigan"? These could hardly be called onomatopoeic, but they seem highly expressive of their meaning, and not entirely "arbitrary." "Discombobulate" we might call an "autonym," as it is itself a discombobulated word.[16] A more recent Americanism, "gobbledygook," also sounds like what it means, in a way, because what it means is "incomprehensible jargon."

For a last example, take the set of doublets of the "zigzag" type. Unless the two parts rhyme (as they do in "helter-skelter" or "razzle-dazzle"), the first invariably is a high front vowel and the second a low back vowel: "chit-chat, clip-clop, dilly-dally, ding-dong, fiddle-faddle, flim-flam, flip-flop, hip-hop, kitty-cat, knick-knack, mish-mash, ping-pong, pitter-patter, rick-rack, see-saw, shilly-shally, sing-song, splish-splash, teeter-totter, tick-tock, ticky-tacky, tittle-tattle, wig-wag, wishy-washy." If there are three or more parts, the final vowel is farther back: "tic-tac-toe" or "eeny meeny miney moe." We could add "bric-à-brac," which we took from French, and such nursery-rhyme bits as "A tisket, a tasket." I don't know why we feel this is the right order of sounds, but we do; they are so well ingrained in our habits that reversing them sounds weird. We may reverse them, of course, to make a humorous point, such as: "He is so reactionary that his watch goes tock-tick."

The debate about a natural or symbolic source of sounds continues. My own view is that the Saussurean or arbitrary school has the better of the argument, but not by much, for it is too quick to fence off onomatopoeia and sound symbolism as anomalous and unimportant, underestimating as it does both the number of words that are not arbitrary or random and the way they have of proliferating and attracting other words. No doubt all words, however they come about, get absorbed into a phonological system and then undergo sound-changes over the centuries according to general laws, attenuating whatever natural basis they may have had, yet, even as this system digests and transforms its onomatopoeic nutrients, they in turn continuously modify the system they enter. To what extent they do so, even after centuries of discussion, still seems unsettled. Perhaps we could say that the same signifier can be both arbitrary and natural. Noam Chomsky has famously argued that all humans have an innate syntactic machine in their brains, a "universal grammar" that underlies the syntactic structures of all possible "natural" languages. More recently, he and Jerry Fodor and others have argued that we are also endowed with universal semantic categories or concepts, perhaps quite a few of them. Since the human mouth, tongue, throat, nose, and diaphragm are also innate and universal, isn't it possible that there are universal phonological categories, tied to meanings? It may be questionable, and Chomsky does not make this claim, but I believe that not all the returns are in yet on this question.

Onomatopoeia and Poetry

It may be, too, that the arbitrariness and systematicity of a language's sounds – where any signifier might mean any signified, and all that matters is that the sounds contrast clearly with one another so a sufficient set of phonemes is available to make words out of – are pretty much all that is needed for the "normal" or more practical uses of language, such as communicating information, giving orders, asking questions, and the like, so when we think of those uses we hardly even think of onomatopoeia or sound symbolism. In more playful, artistic, ritualistic, and self-con-scious uses, on the other hand, this other dimension looms larger. When we give directions or gossip with our friends, we seldom pun or rhyme or imitate bird calls, but when we pass into the other mode, where the language itself becomes a focus of attention, it is no longer a transparent line of transmission but an interesting thing in its own right, with various links to the real world.

However this may be, poets seem to belong to the naturalistic school, or at least they try to make their own poetic language express the true nature of things. Nearly all discussions of onomatopoeia quote these famous lines from Pope's "Essay on Criticism" (364–73):

> 'Tis not enough no Harshness gives Offence,
> The Sound must seem an Eccho to the Sense.
> Soft is the Strain when Zephyr gently blows,
> And the smooth Stream in smoother Numbers flows;

But when loud Surges lash the sounding Shore,
The hoarse, rough Verse shou'd like the Torrent roar.
When Ajax strives, some Rock's vast Weight to throw,
The Line too labours, and the Words move slow;
Not so, when swift Camilla scours the Plain,
Flies o'er th'unbending Corn, and skims along the Main.

Generations of readers have found these lines brilliant instances or enactments of what they describe. But we should examine ourselves as we examine the lines. The sound must *seem* an echo to the sense, Pope says: the poet must make the reader or listener *feel* he or she hears the stream or the surge or the laboring of Ajax. Whether Pope has really imitated the sounds or speed of his subject or only tricked us into thinking so is not obvious. The sibilants in the couplet about Zephyr and the stream are meant to evoke the rustling of a breeze or quiet flowing of a brook, but sibilants dominate the next couplet as well, and the alliterating l- sounds and r- sounds in that couplet are usually thought to be soft and, well, liquid. Surely we are invited to whisper softly the first set of sibilants and to hiss or spit out the second set, and it is the sense of the words that invites us to do so, not their sound alone. More objective is the second couplet's metrical pattern, which makes us read more slowly: the three neighboring stresses in "loud Surges lash" and "hoarse, rough Verse" do delay us a little. As for Ajax, the same trick of successive stresses, deployed three times ("Rock's vast Weight," "Line too labours," and "Words move slow"), slows down his couplet and conveys the sense of striving, even though "strives" itself is no more laborious a sound than "strain" and "stream" in the Zephyr couplet. Is the line about Camilla really swift? "Swift Camilla" goes nicely with "skims" in the next line, but "swift Camilla scours" is something of a mouthful and a speed bump. The next line, which is metrically longer (an alexandrine), seems to go just as fast, or faster. Pope is a wizard, no question, but his effects, insofar as they are separable from the suggestions implanted by the sense, have more to do with alterations of meter than a word's sonic expression of a thing's nature.

In the nineteenth century, it was still a widely held view that languages begin in onomatopoeia, and that ancient languages, and especially the supposed proto-languages of each family, such as "Aryan" (then used for "Proto-Indo-European"), show a closer connection to their natural sources. The German philologist Max Müller believed that "There is a law which runs through nearly the whole of nature, that everything which is struck rings. Each substance has its peculiar ring."[17] To the extent that this mysterious "ring" is auditory, and the speakers of primordial languages were attuned to it, these languages would be onomatopoeic. The poet Gerard Manley Hopkins, whose idiosyncratic poems are brilliant touch-stones of sheer sound-effects, was interested in this theory, and made up a verb, "to selve," for Müller's "ring." In his great sonnet "As kingfishers catch fire" he has these lines:

> Each mortal thing does one thing and the same:
> Deals out that being indoors each one dwells;
> Selves—goes itself; *myself* it speaks and spells,
> Crying *What I do is me: for that I came.*   (5–8)

With his alliteration on d- in line 6 and on s- and sp- in line 7, and especially in the way he places the rhyme-words "dwells" and "spells" around the strange but central word "selves," Hopkins enacts what he is talking about: he makes the whole idea of the selving of the thing seem natural, or ring true. It's not exactly evidence of the truth of the idea, but it conveys something of what it must feel like to believe it.

A more extreme but not unique claim about sound symbolism is found in Rimbaud's sonnet "Voyelles" ("Vowels"), which opens with a list of equations between vowels and colors: "A noir, E blanc, I rouge, U vert, O bleu: voyelles, / Je dirai quelque jour vos naissances latentes" ("A black, E white, I red, I green, O blue: vowels, / I shall tell one day of your hidden origins"). He goes on to give examples of each color, ending with "O the Omega, violet ray of Her Eyes!" Rimbaud never did tell of their hidden origins, and no scholar has come up with a convincing theory, but the poem has haunted poetry-readers since it first appeared in the 1870s by raising the possibility of a mysterious connection between sights and sounds. Another French poet, Mallarmé, found the French language perverse in making *jour* ("day") sound dark and *nuit* ("night") sound light (*Divagations* 205) – in contrast to Latin *dies* and *nox*, presumably – but it is no more perverse than, say, German *Tag* ("day") and *Nacht* ("night"), with identical "dark" vowels.

If Mallarmé thought vowels have inherent meanings, Galway Kinnell, among others, seems to relish words for their consonant clusters. In his sonnet "Blackberry Eating," he celebrates "certain peculiar words / like *strengths* or *squinched*, / many-lettered, one-syllable lumps" which belong to the "black language" of the berries. If the berries could speak, they might speak in such lumps; in any case, they taste and feel like these words in our mouths.

Something of the power of poetry to capture the truth of things through sounds occupies the thoughts of Stephen Dedalus in Joyce's *Portrait of the Artist as a Young Man* (1916). A phrase from a poem has entered his mind:

> —A day of dappled seaborne clouds.
>   The phrase and the day and the scene harmonized in a chord. Was it their colours? He allowed them to glow and fade, hue after hue: sunrise gold, the russet and green of apple orchards, azure of waves, the greyfringed fleece of clouds. No, it was not their colours: it was the poise and balance of the period itself.

Stephen uses "period" in its metrical sense, as a "line" of verse, not in its grammatical sense, as a complete clause. Later, thinking of another line, "Darkness falls from the air," he will note "its black vowels" (253), but in this earlier moment, after a little more reflection, Stephen seems to reject the usual naturalistic thesis that a language (or a poem) reflects "the glowing sensible world" in favor of an interiorized version, where "an inner world of individualized emotions" is "mirrored perfectly in a lucid supple periodic prose" (180–81). With this idea, we have abandoned the usual concept of sound symbolism for a more subtle relationship between emotions and what we normally call style. It is needless to repeat that Joyce was the greatest master of English style – and of every English style – in the twentieth century, and that his novels are a master class in what a sentence can do, but they are novels in "periodic prose," not verse periods, and this book is about verse. When we turn to style later in this book, we will consider to what extent it has an iconic or imitative character, a kind of onomatopoeia of the order and pace of events.

Is there visual onomatopoeia? By this phrase I am not referring to sign languages used by the deaf, which linguists have shown to be no less complete languages than any spoken one: a great many of their signs are obviously iconic, for hands can shape themselves and move about in ways that imitate objects and actions to a far greater extent than the mouth can make iconic sounds. I am referring to writing systems of spoken languages: is there something in the shape of the characters of a writing system that reflects the meanings they represent? Some scholars think that Rimbaud was referring not to the sounds of the vowels but to the shapes of the letters, an idea no less obscure than sound-colors and rather less interesting. Though it is true that the original Phoenician alphabet was derived from pictograms, even in Phoenician writing the signs must have largely lost whatever pictorial character they had and become conventional, and by the time they were recycled and tinkered with in the Greek and Etruscan

alphabets and then reprocessed again in the Roman system they had
become simply a set of random symbols. There are graphic links between
some pairs with similar sounds (C and G, P and B, M and N, maybe S and
Z), but they do not amount to links to meanings or referents.

The Chinese written characters are a more interesting case. When
western scholars first learned about them, they seemed to be an ideal
writing system, where each of its thousands of characters stood for one
thing or idea; they were originally pictures of the things or ideas, and later
squared off and stylized when brushes replaced pointed tools. The simpler
ones combined to make more complicated ones. "Sun" (日) behind "tree"
(木) denotes "east" (東), for example, though it's not obvious why it
doesn't mean "west," while "rice paddy" (田) combines with "power"
(力) to make "man" (男) – presumably "man" as counted by a lord who
had quite a few of them working in his rice fields. The earliest speculations
in the west about these characters, and indeed about the origin of language
itself, dwelled on nouns, as if there could be a language entirely of nouns.
In the late nineteenth century, the American scholar Ernest Fenollosa took
the view that Chinese characters were mainly verbs, and expressed action.
Chinese notation, he wrote, "is based upon a vivid short-hand picture of
the operations of nature."[18] Both theories assumed that a pictographic or
ideographic principle underlay the characters, but that turns out to be true
of only a few hundred, if even that many, of the thousands of characters in
common use. In fact, each character represents not a thing but a sound, a
single syllable, and since virtually all Chinese words have one syllable, each
character corresponds to one (spoken) word. Even though standard
Mandarin has nineteen consonant phonemes and five (or perhaps six)
vowels, as well as four tones (and a neutral one) that multiply the number
of distinguishable vowel sounds, there are still inevitably a lot of homophones in this monosyllabic language. No two homophones – that is, no
two words that sound alike but have different meanings are represented by
the same character; there are no Chinese homonyms (like English "grave"
or "lie," for instance, each representing two unrelated words). To distinguish among several homophones, characters may combine two radicals
derived from other characters, one to indicate the general semantic domain
and the other to indicate the sound. Geoffrey Sampson gives an interesting
example. The character for "foundation" includes a root for "earth," which
points to the semantic domain, and a root for "winnowing basket," which
has nothing to do with the meaning but once had a sound identical to the
word for "foundation."[19] To assume that pictures underlie the characters
will breed absurd "etymologies," such as that winnowing is the foundation

of life, or that the earth is some sort of basket. Moreover, the sound-similarities have been lost: "foundation" and "winnowing basket" were homophones around 1000 BCE (reconstructed as *kjəg), but the words for them today sound very different.

A careful look at the whole range of characters, then, shows a development not unlike the path of onomatopoeia. It seems that a couple of hundred pictures served as the original basis of the system, which then got stylized and somewhat abstracted (rather like the "phonemization" of imitative sounds), and then expanded vastly by means of character-radicals that referred to homophones with unrelated meanings, with the result that, though this secondary expansion was not entirely arbitrary, the result even 2,000 years ago was a system predominantly conventional and "unnatural," its pictorial connection to the real world largely broken.

Though Chinese poetry has a deep connection to music, and the phonemic tones were sometimes made the basis of meter, it would be surprising if Chinese poets, when they planned to write down their poems, did not sometimes exploit the pictorial dimension still traceable in some of the characters, perhaps in the way western poets might bring out the normally neglected etymology of words. The long and refined tradition of calligraphy might enhance this effect. Whatever the case in Chinese poetry itself, the pictorial aspect of the Chinese characters, however misinterpreted, reinforced the Imagist movement and its sequels in English poetry. Ezra Pound, who gathered Fenollosa's notes and published them as *The Chinese Written Character as a Medium for Poetry* (1918), tried to establish a norm of poetry in which several images combine to make an implicit emergent or composite meaning.[20] Many of his *Cantos* consist of quotations from disparate works from disparate times, along with words in Greek, French, or even Chinese (both in characters and in phonetic transcriptions), with little if any connecting commentary in his own voice. In the space of a dozen lines, we might find a reference to the hanging of Benito Mussolini, the death of the founder of Manichaeanism, the god Dionysus, T. S. Eliot's "The Hollow Men," the ancient city of Dioce, two rivers in China, and a few words in Greek from Homer. Eliot's own "The Waste Land" (1922) sets a contemporary conversation in a pub among allusions to Wagner, St. Augustine, the *Aeneid*, the *Metamorphoses, The Tempest*, Sanskrit literature, and many other sources. Somehow, we are expected to intuit the commonalities among these segments and grasp the whole as a kind of giant ideal character, a character as imagined by Pound and Fenollosa as a complex visible onomatopoeia.

Notes

1. Abrams and Harpham, *Glossary of Literary Terms*, 236.
2. It is true we readily speak of "coining" a new word or phrase, and say words "circulate," as coins do; money is "currency" and words are current or not; words and money wear out; and so on. But none of this is implied by the word *pepoiēmenon* or its root.
3. See Bredin, "Onomatopoeia," 555–56.
4. Translation by Benjamin Jowett, in Plato, *Collected Dialogues of Plato*, ed. Hamilton and Cairns. For interesting comments on the *Cratylus*, see Anderson, *Grammar of Iconism*, 46–54.
5. Saussure, *Course in General Linguistics*, 67.
6. Saussure, *Course in General Linguistics*, 69.
7. As indices of how things stand, a major textbook in phonetics and phonology (Clark, Yallop, and Fletcher, *Introduction to Phonetics and Phonology*) does not mention onomatopoeia or sound symbolism even once in its 450 pages, and a major textbook on semantics (Saeed, *Semantics*) mentions onomatopoeia only once in a brief footnote (p. 21).
8. Sadler, "Onomatopoeia," 176.
9. It would be interesting to know whether speakers of !Xuun, in Namibia, Botswana, and South Africa, which has 141 phonemes, are a lot better at onomatopeia than speakers of Rotokas, in Papua New Guinea, which has 11 phonemes. One would think so, but maybe !Xuun speakers find imitating nature too easy to bother with.
10. A point made extensively by Anderson, *Grammar of Iconism*.
11. There was a difference of opinion among professed Tagalog speakers (from the Philippines) on the website www.bootstrappin.com/2008/10/cock-a-doodle-doo-dialects-of-the-rooster. Is it a coincidence, by the way, that we call the bird a "cock" (or *coq* in French)? The etymology of "cock" is disputed, but if it is "echoic" like the cry itself, then we have another example of onomatopoeia radiating through the language, e.g., "cocky" (meaning arrogant or conceited), "cocktail," perhaps "cocksure," etc.
12. Leech, *Linguistic Guide*, 96.
13. Add the terms "near" and "far." English used to have three deictic positions, as many languages still do (some have more): "this," "that," and "yon." I have not found the same vowel pattern in other languages: Italian *questo, codesto, quello*; Japanese *kono, sono, ano*.
14. Anderson, *Grammar of Iconism*, 77–86.
15. For much more on the debate over onomatopoeia and sound symbolism, see Jespersen, *Language*, Ch. 22; Jespersen, "Symbolic Value"; Jakobson and Waugh, *Sound Shape of Language*, Ch. 4; Anderson, *Grammar of Iconism*, Chs. 3 and 5; and Bredin, "Onomatopoeia." Needless to say, there are many words beginning with these consonant clusters that have nothing to do with the meanings of these "sets."

16. An "autonym" would be a word or phrase that is a member of the class it names, such as "word," "noun," "two words," "nominalization," and "derivative."
17. Quoted in Sprinker, "Hopkins on the Origin of Language," 125, and Anderson, *Grammar of Iconism*, 41.
18. Fenellosa, *Chinese Written Character*, 80.
19. Sampson, *Writing Systems*, 153.
20. For more on this, see Kenner, *Pound Era*, 223–29.

CHAPTER FIVE

Unusual Word Order and Other Syntactic Quirks in Poetry

A striking feature of most western poetry until recently, and one that confuses many readers, has been its peculiarities of word order. In Greek and Latin, grammatical endings or inflections usually made clear what case a noun or adjective was in, so poets could shuffle them around in the wildest ways, as we will see later, and still make sense to their sophisticated audience. English and most modern European languages are far less inflected than their ancient ancestors – English least of all – so it is word order that tells us which noun is the subject, which the object, and which adjective goes with which noun. Nonetheless, poets in these languages have taken many liberties with syntax, sometimes to emphasize certain words or phrases, sometimes to withhold a word for dramatic effect, and sometimes just to make it easier to fit words into the meter or rhyme scheme. Because spoken Greek, despite the freedom its inflections gave it, still had normal patterns of phrases and clauses, these dislocations were given a generic name by the Greeks, ὑπέρβατον (*hyperbaton*), meaning "overstepping," and there were several other terms for particular kinds of overstepping. When we read English poetry, it is not always clear, however, if what sounds to our 21st-century ears like a transposition or postponement is a poet's artificial hyperbaton or a feature of the spoken language of the poet's time. Very often, it will be an archaism, a feature of the spoken language of an earlier time that poetry had preserved, though for our purposes we need not distinguish between the two. Most of the kinds of dislocations discussed in this chapter, at any rate, are traceable to normal patterns in earlier spoken English, even if some of them became fossilized in the special language of the poets.

The Verb-Final Rule

Like its Proto-Indo-European ancestor, English was once a mainly verb-final language – that is, the verb usually came at the end of the clause; if the verb took an object, the object preceded it. This pattern was especially strict in subordinate (or dependent) clauses: clauses that cannot stand alone and are often related to the main clause as an adverbial addition. To put it another way, Proto-Indo-European was mainly an S-O-V language, that is, subject-object-verb (for instance, "The poet a bad poem wrote"); occasionally O-S-V ("A bad poem the poet wrote"). Old English inherited the S-O-V pattern, though not very rigidly; the predominant or default order in English now is S-V-O ("The poet wrote a bad poem").

In subordinate clauses, the Old English order tended to be S-O-V-aux, where "aux" stands for "auxiliary verb" (be, have, shall, will, must, etc.). For example, using modern English words:

$$\text{S} \qquad \text{O} \quad \text{V} \quad \text{aux}$$
because the hunter the bear killed has

Here we have assumed "the hunter" is the subject and "the bear" the object, though of course the clause could be taken the other way round. You might also find S-aux-O-V ("the hunter has the bear killed") in both main and subordinate clauses. (In German and Dutch, the closest relatives of English, main clauses with an auxiliary verb are still S-aux-O-V and subordinate clauses are S-O-V-aux.)

There was also a verb-second rule: after an initial subject, object, adverbial phrase, or prepositional phrase, the verb follows, whether it is a main verb ("Yesterday killed he the bear") or an auxiliary verb ("Yesterday has he the bear killed"). In modern English, such phrases as "So goes the nation" or "Scarcely had he heard the thunder . . ." are remnants of the verb-second rule, which still governs German and Dutch. We will return to this rule later.

English poetry, at least before the twentieth century, preserved verb-final constructions much longer than everyday speech did; because of the demands of meter and rhyme, moreover, poets wanted more options in word order, so they could vary it from S-O-V to S-V-O and sometimes to other orders.

Here is a passage from the second stanza of Book 1 Canto 1 of Spenser's *Faerie Queene*. The verbs are in boldface:

> And on his brest a bloodie Crosse he **bore**,
> The deare remembrance of his dying Lord,
> For whose sweete sake that glorious badge he **wore**,
> And dead, as living, ever him **ador'd**.

The past-tense verbs "bore," "wore," and "ador'd" are all transitive verbs, that is, they take an object: "Crosse," "badge," and "him." Three times in four lines, then, a verb is postponed until after its object, and twice the subject ("he") is also postponed (O-S-V), in order to place the verb at the end of the line.

Spenser's contemporary Sidney is less archaic, but still routinely delays his verbs.

> You that poor Petrarch's long-deceased woes
> With new-born sighs and denizen'd wit do sing[.]
> (Astrophel and Stella 15.7–8)

The verb phrase "do sing" would normally come after "You that" but here it is put off until after its object ("woes") and a long prepositional phrase. As for the meaningless "do," that too we will take up later in this chapter.

The tradition continued for centuries.

> The people, which what most they fear esteem,
> Death when more horrid, so more noble deem[.]
> (Marvell, "Upon the Death of the Lord Protector" 7–8)

In these lines, easy to misread, the noun phrase "what most they fear" is the object of the verb "esteem," and "Death" is the object of "deem."

> Know then thyself, presume not God to scan[.]
> (Pope, Essay on Man 2.1)

Here the infinitive "to scan" follows its object, "God."

Even among the Romantics, who in many ways modernized English poetry, you will often find postponed verbs:

> In Xanadu did Kubla Khan
> A stately pleasure dome decree[.]   (Coleridge, "Kubla Khan" 1–2)

> Thus mellowed to that tender light
> Which heaven to gaudy day denies.
> (Byron, "She Walks in Beauty" 5–6)

> . . . its sculptor well those passions read[.]
> (Shelley, "Ozymandias" 6)

These passages are not difficult to interpret, and when you have read a fair amount of poetry from about 1900 or earlier you hardly notice the postponed verbs. The motive for postponing them is sometimes to make rhymes, but it is also usually true that the verb is the central or most energetic position syntactically – it is certainly the only part of speech that a sentence must contain – and poets have usually felt that the final position of a line is the most emphatic.

Here is an example from Thomas Gray:

> In vain to me the smiling mornings **shine**,
> And reddening Phoebus **lifts** his golden fire:
> The birds in vain their amorous descant **join**,
> Or cheerful fields **resume** their green attire[.]
> ("Sonnet on the Death of Mr Richard West" 1–4)

This quatrain is composed of two parallel couplets, linked by "in vain." One of their parallel features is that lines 1 and 3 are alike in that their verbs end their lines (which rhyme with each other), though only line 3 postpones the verb so it follows its object, while lines 2 and 4 are alike in the normal position of the verbs, which each precede their objects, rhyming nouns. Wordsworth disliked these lines, and several others from the same sonnet, as we will see in Chapter 6.

Here is an unusual couplet from the colonial American poet Anne Bradstreet:

> My pleasant things in ashes lie,

So far so good: a postponed verb. But then:

> And them behold no more shall I.

This second line is O-V-S in form, rather rare and artificial even in poetry. To be more exact, its form is O-V-adverb-aux-S, whereas the normal order (or one normal order) would be the exact reverse: S-aux-adverb-V-O, i.e., "I shall no more behold them."

A line from Milton's "Lycidas" –

> But the fair Guerdon when we hope to find,

– is a clause in O-S-V form. (The V refers to a verb phrase, "hope to find.") Rearranged to normal order, it would read:

> But when we hope to find the fair Guerdon,

"Guerdon" is not a girl's name, as you might think at first, but an old word for "reward."

From Milton's Sonnet IX:

> The better part with Mary and with Ruth
> Chosen thou hast[.]

This is unusually complicated in structure. It is more or less O-S-V, but the verb phrase is ordered: V (participle) – subject – auxiliary verb.

Here Milton speaks like Yoda in *Star Wars*. The normal order, of course, would be "Thou hast chosen the better part," etc., while also normal – if archaic – would be "Thou hast the better part chosen with Mary and Ruth" (S-aux-O-V-PP) (PP = prepositional phrase). Happily such constructions as this and the Bradstreet example grew rare by the eighteenth century.

Here is Gray again:

> Full many a gem of purest ray serene
> The dark unfathomed caves of ocean bear[.]
>
> ("Elegy Written in a Country Churchyard" 53–54)

This is structured O-S-V: it is the caves, of course, that bear the gems.

Sometimes in a verb-final clause, however, it is hard to determine which is the subject and which the object. Take this famous opening line by Wordsworth:

> A slumber did my spirit seal[.]

We might wonder whether the slumber sealed the spirit or the spirit sealed the slumber. Cases have been made for both possibilities, but it seems less of a strain semantically to take "slumber" as the subject, and more probable syntactically since S-O-V (here S-aux-O-V) is the normal or default order in poetry, as it once was in speech. Note, incidentally, the function of "did": it holds the place of the verb as if it were S-V-O, and allows the poet to have an uninflected form (the infinitive) at the end to rhyme with "feel" – useful here since the past tenses do not rhyme ("sealed" vs. "felt"). It also provides a syllable where the meter needs it. Or one could say that the auxiliary "did" serves as the past-tense marker of the main verb; hence we could notate it S-t-O-V, where t = tense. Something similar takes place in the lines from "Kubla Khan" quoted earlier.

Compare these lines by Blake (from "London"):

> How the Chimney-sweepers cry
> Every blackning Church appals[.]

What appals what? If we take S-O-V as the norm, then the cry appals every church, but you might make an argument for the reverse. It is hard to settle the question, but if you get a grasp of what "appal" meant in 1794 (roughly, "make pale with fear or guilt"), the case for S-O-V seems stronger, though you must still sort out what "black'ning" means. (For starters, is it transitive or intransitive?) It is also relevant to look at the next couplet, which seems exactly parallel:

> And the hapless soldier's sigh
> Runs in blood down palace walls.

In each couplet, we have a young male victim, the sound he makes, and some sort of impact on an oppressive institution. The syntax of the latter couplet is clear, so we may read its meaning back onto the former.

Verb-final constructions, then, create ambiguities not always easy to resolve. In some cases, it may not matter whether we can resolve them or not, as both readings may be acceptable and congruent with each other. Beardsley, in *Aesthetics* (1958), cites Gray's line "And all the air a solemn stillness holds" ("Elegy" 6) and comments, "we do not need to make a choice; the ambiguity suggests that it is hard to distinguish between the air and the solemn stillness" (145). Lonsdale, however, in his heavily annotated edition *The Poems of Gray*, notes "The subject of 'holds' is 'stillness,' the object 'air'" (119) and cites other poems where the air is the object of an action. Even though the default pattern is S-O-V, in Lonsdale's view this line is O-S-V.

Other Kinds of Postponements

A participle may be postponed:

> Some frail memorial still erected nigh,
> With uncouth rhymes and shapeless sculpture decked[.]
>
> (Gray, "Elegy" 78–79)

> Like a pale flower by some sad maiden cherished[.]
>
> (Shelley, "Adonais" 48)

>   . . . a love
> That had no need of a remoter charm
> By thought supplied[.]   (Wordsworth, "Tintern Abbey" 81–83)

> He went like one that hath been stunned
> And is of sense forlorn[.]
>
> (Coleridge, "Rime of the Ancyent Marinere" [1798] 656)

An adverbial or prepositional phrase may interrupt verb and object:

> Never did sun more beautifully steep
> In his first splendour valley, rock, or hill[.]
>
> (Wordsworth, "Westminster Bridge")

For a moment you might mistake the noun "splendour" as part of the series with "valley, rock, or hill," or perhaps as a noun modifying "valley," but

"In his first splendour" is a prepositional phrase inserted between the verb ("steep") and its threefold object.

French poetry had a fondness for placing a prepositional phrase before the noun it modifies, as in this passage from Racine's *Phèdre* (17–18):

> Qui sait si le Roi votre père
>
> Who knows if the King your father
>
> Veut que de son absence on sache le mystère?
>
> Wishes that of his absence one may know the mystery?

Or this, a little later in the same opening scene (67–68):

> Des sentiments d'un coeur si fier, si dédaigneux,
>
> Of the feelings of a heart so fierce, so disdainful,
>
> Peux-tu me demander le désaveu honteux?
>
> Can you ask of me the shameful disavowal?

Often an adjective will follow the noun it modifies:

> The forward youth that would appear
> Must now forsake his Muses dear[.]   (Marvell, "Horatian Ode" 1–2)
>
> . . . of aspect more sublime[.]   (Wordsworth, "Tintern Abbey" 38)
>
> Thou from whose unseen presence the leaves dead
> Are driven, like ghosts from an enchanter fleeing[.]
> (Shelley, "Ode to the West Wind" 2–3)

"Dead leaves" is so common a phrase that we hardly think of it as a metaphor; by reversing the normal order, Shelley defamiliarizes the phrase just enough to make us notice it, and see that, like ghosts, they are really dead. Note also the postponement of the participle "fleeing."

English has two kinds of participles, both forms of the verb: e.g., "speaking" and "spoken." They are often called the present participle and the past participle, but those terms are misleading. "He was speaking" is in the past tense, so it is odd to say "speaking" is a present form; and "He has spoken" is in the present perfect. It is better to call the V+ing form the progressive participle ("speaking") and the V+en form the perfect participle ("spoken"). The progressive and perfect are *aspects*, not tenses, of the verb. The term "aspect" is deployed in different ways by different linguists, but roughly speaking it has to do with the relationship of an action or state to a period of time, as opposed to where on the time-line (past, present, or future) it falls. We will take a closer look at aspects shortly, where examples will make the distinction clearer.

Sometimes a noun will come between two adjectives, a habit of Milton's, as in these phrases, all from *Paradise Lost*: "dismal Situation waste and wild" (1.60), "ever-burning Sulphur unconsum'd" (1.69), "human face divine" (3.44), and "vast profundity obscure" (7.229). In "L'Allegro," Milton famously describes Shakespeare as warbling "his native Wood-notes wild" (136); in "Lycidas," it is "sad occasion dear" that compels the poet to write (6).

Both Blake and Wordsworth virtually quote Milton. Blake writes "And Love, the human form divine" ("The Divine Image" 11), while Wordsworth has "their human form divine" (*Excursion* 9.151). Wordsworth was especially fond of this adjective-noun-adjective construction, which he liked to arrange as a wrap or enjambment around the line:

the fretful stir / Unprofitable[.]	("Tintern Abbey" 53–54)
wise restraint / Voluptuous[.]	("Nutting" 23–24)
strong desire / Resistless[.]	(*Two-Part Prelude* 42–43)
murmuring cities vast[.]	(*Excursion* 3.104)

Days of sweet leisure, taxed with patient thought
Abstruse, not wanting punctual service high[.](1850 *Prelude* 1.44–45)

Shelley has "deep bosom fairest" ("Ode to Liberty" 91), and Keats has "gold clouds metropolitan" (*Hyperion* 129).

Occasionally a quantifier (such a word as "many" or "some"), which normally precedes adjectives in noun phrases, is postponed to the end of a clause, for emphasis or dramatic effect. Milton, again, provides an example:

other creature here
Beast, bird, insect, or worm durst enter none[.]   (*PL* 4.703–04)

Normal order would be "none other creature here . . . durst enter."

Perhaps oddest to our ears, occasionally a preposition will be postponed:

All breathing human passion far above[.] (Keats, "Grecian Urn" 28)

The normal order would be: "far above all breathing human passion." Gray, speaking of the grove, lawn, and mead of Eton:

> Whose turf, whose shade, whose flowers among
> Wanders the hoary Thames[.]
>
> ("Ode on a Distant Prospect of Eton College" 8–9)

Blake has this:

> Now like a mighty wind they raise to heaven the voice of song,
> Or like harmonious thunderings the seats of heaven among[.]
>
> ("Holy Thursday" (*Innocence*) 9–10)

The normal order would be: "among the seats of heaven." Here are a few more of these "postpositions," taken from the Romantic poets:

> something night and day between,
> Like moonshine[.]   (Wordsworth, "Eclipse of the Sun" 25–26)

> Soft went the music the soft air along[.]   (Keats, *Lamia* 2.199)

> Beams fall from high those depths upon[.]
>
> (Shelley, *Prometheus Unbound* 2.2.17)

Also strange to our ears is the placing of a prepositional phrase before the verb that would ordinarily precede it:

> Into these Loves who but for Passion looks
>
> (Drayton, "To the Reader of These Sonnets" 1)

We would expect: "Who looks but for Passion into these Loves" (i.e., "Whoever looks only for passion into these loves").

One of the most striking dislocations of syntax is Milton's clause "Him who disobeys / Me disobeys" (*PL* 5.611–12). This is spoken by God himself, so it must be correct. ("Him" refers to the Son.) It means "who[ever] disobeys him disobeys me." The first three words make up a clause in the order O-S-V, and that clause is the subject of the main clause, in the order S-O-V. It is effective as verse, if you can figure out the grammar, but Ezra Pound had a point when he complained that Milton was "doing wrong to his mother tongue."

Do

One of the peculiarities of English is its frequent use, for many centuries now, of the verb "do" as an auxiliary verb. Today, we use it mainly for: (1) emphasis ("You may doubt it, but I do love poetry"); (2) questions ("Do you like Milton?"); (3) negation ("He doesn't read poetry"); and (4) ellipsis ("Do you like Milton?" "Yes, I do"). Some of these functions have existed for centuries, but before about 1750 "do" also had a "pleonastic" or "periphrastic" use in positive, non-emphatic sentences – that is, it was superfluous: it added no meaning. There was little if any felt difference between "I love thee" and "I do love thee," or between "How like you this poem?" and "How do you like this poem?" The origin of this auxiliary "do" is obscure: in Old English, it may once have had a causative sense (still visible in such expressions as "It did me a great deal of good"), which then became vaguely "aspectual" (perhaps by setting off the main verb to focus attention on it) before its meaning bleached out. We can at least surmise a motive for its use in questions: once the S-V-O order got well established, sometime during the early Middle-English period, putting a "do"-form at the front preserved that word order. Instead of "Lovest thou me?" (V-S-O) people said "Dost thou love me?" (do + S-V-O). Something similar was afoot in the French use of "est-ce que" ("is it that") at the beginning of a question: instead of "Aimez-vous Baudelaire?" (V-S-O), the French usually say "Est-ce que vous aimez Baudelaire?" (Est-ce que + S-V-O) – if they don't drop the "est-ce que" altogether and just say "Vous aimez Baudelaire?"

However it arose, the "pleonastic" use of "do" survived in poetry much longer than in everyday speech, or written prose, not only because poetry tended to be conservative in diction and syntax but also because it was a great boon to poets to have an alternative way of deploying verbs. Since the beginning of the fifteenth century, Otto Jespersen writes, "it served chiefly to fill up the line and to make it possible to place the infinitive at the end as a convenient rime-word."[1]

As a filler, however, it is semantically null, and can weaken a poetic line. When Hamlet begins a soliloquy with "How all occasions do inform against me" (4.4.32), we hardly notice the "do," but it certainly has little purpose but to fill a stressed metrical position in the line. Wordsworth, I think, gets away with it in "A slumber did my spirit seal" because the rest of the line is dense with not quite certain meanings, not to mention the insistent alliteration. Coleridge's lines "In Xanadu did Kubla Khan / A stately pleasure dome decree" so dazzle us with exotic and euphonious names and images that we hardly care about the "did." Wordsworth's "Never did sun more beautifully steep" also succeeds, perhaps because "steep" is a striking verb to be governed by "sun," and perhaps because of the old verb-second tendency (as in Coleridge's lines as well).

It is hard to see such justification, on the other hand, for the four instances of "did" in the opening stanza of Spenser's *Faerie Queene*:

> A gentle Knight was pricking on the plaine,
> Ycladd in mightie armes and silver shielde,
> Wherein old dints of deepe woundes **did** remaine,
> The cruell markes of many a bloody fielde;
> Yet armes till that time **did** he never wield:
> His angry steede **did** chide his foming bitt,
> As much disdayning to the curbe to yield:
> Full jolly knight he seemed, and faire **did** sitt,
> As one for knightly giusts and fierce encounters fitt.

Three times "did" lets him put the infinitive at the end and thereby avoid the past tense, no doubt to help with the rhyme, as Jespersen suggests, and once it is just metrical filler.

These lines of Blake's seem weak:

> The sun does arise
> And make happy the skies;
> . . . .
> Old John with white hair
> Does laugh away care,
> . . . .
> The sun does descend
> And our sports have an end[.]

Their justification, perhaps, is that they are meant to sound naïve and folksy. Shelley does not have that excuse in "Hymn to Intellectual Beauty," a poem at a much higher register:

> Spirit of Beauty, that dost consecrate
> With thine own hues all thou dost shine upon[.]

Each "dost" here seems mere metrical filler, while the one in the first line is also a maneuver to avoid "consecratest," which would be much harder to find rhymes for (Shelley has the noun "state" and the adjective "desolate" as rhymes in the following lines). We see one of the costs of addressing Intellectual Beauty as "thou" instead of "you" – not that Shelley had much choice, as the decorum of an ode required the archaic singular (and intimate) form: note "Thou still unravished bride of quietness," the opening line of Keats's "Ode on a Grecian Urn."

The Verb-Second Rule

Earlier, we mentioned the verb-second rule (V2), according to which the verb (the finite verb) must come second, whatever else comes first (the subject, the object, a prepositional phrase, an adverbial phrase, etc.). (A finite verb can stand alone in a simple declarative sentence, as opposed to the infinitive or participle; in many languages, it is de*fined* by person, number, and tense.) In German, Dutch, and the Scandinavian languages, the V2 rule holds for main clauses, but in subordinate clauses the verb comes later (in German and Dutch, it must come at the end of the clause by the verb-final rule).

In German, "Tomorrow I am going downtown" would be "Morgen **gehe** ich in die Stadt" (literally, "Tomorrow **go** I into the city"). Or you could say "Ich **gehe** morgen in die Stadt" ("I **go** tomorrow into the city"). Or even "In die Stadt **gehe** ich morgen" ("into the city **go** I tomorrow"). In all three instances, the verb (**gehe**) must come in second position. "Second position," as the examples show, does not mean "second word," but "second phrase," with the understanding that a phrase may consist of a single word.

The verb-second rule prevailed in Old English and was still frequently followed in Middle English.

> On þis gær **wolde** þe king Stephne tæcen Rodbert.

> During this year **wanted** King Stephen to seize Robert.

Note that this sentence neglects the verb-final rule (by which "tæcen" would come at the end) while obeying the verb-second rule.

> No thing **dorst** he seye.

> Nothing **dared** he say.

And it is frequently found in poetry.

> Thanne **longen** folk to goon on pilgrimages[.]

> Then **long** people to go on pilgrimages[.]
> > (Chaucer, "General Prologue" to *The Canterbury Tales* 12)

> Forth **fly** the tepid airs[.]   (Thomson, "Spring" 32)

> Now **fades** the glimmering landscape on the sight[.]
> > (Gray, "Elegy Written in a Country Churchyard" 5)

> Then **felt** I like some watcher of the skies
> When a new planet swims into his ken[.]   (Keats, "Chapman's Homer" 9)

> This **saw** that Goddess, and with sacred hand
> Parted the veils. Then **saw** I a wan face[.]   (Keats, *Fall of Hyperion* 255–56)

In the first line above, "This" is the object of "saw" (O V S).

> While **glow** the heavens with the last steps of day[.]
>> (Bryant, "To a Waterfowl" 2)

> And after many a summer **dies** the swan.   (Tennyson, "Tithonus" 4)

> I saw in Louisiana a live-oak growing,
> All alone **stood** it and the moss hung down from the branches[.]
>> (Walt Whitman, "I saw in Louisiana a live-oak
>> growing," from *Leaves of Grass*)

The Clausal Brace

Historical linguists have identified a syntactic pattern in West Germanic languages called the "clausal brace," which may have arisen in tandem with the verb-second rule. In a main clause, if there is a finite auxiliary verb and a non-finite main verb (participle or infinitive), the auxiliary verb comes second (following the verb-second rule) and the main verb comes last in the clause. This is the pattern described at the beginning of this chapter as S-aux-O-V. Modern German still obeys this pattern:

Ich **werde** das Gedicht so schnell wie möglich **schreiben.**
I   **will**   the poem   as quickly as   possible **write.**
I will write the poem as quickly as possible.

Here, **werde** is the finite auxiliary verb (it is marked for person, number, and tense) and **schreiben** is the infinitive. The pattern is S-aux-O-adv-V (where "adv" stands for "adverbial phrase").

Ich **habe** das Gedicht so schnell wie möglich **geschrieben.**
I   **have** the poem as quickly as possible **written.**
I wrote the poem as quickly as possible.

Here, **habe** is the finite auxiliary verb and **geschrieben** is the perfect participle. (What looks like the present perfect in German now functions as the past tense.)

The famous opening soliloquy of Goethe's *Faust* is a fine example of an extended clausal brace:

> **Habe** nun, ach! Philosophie,
>
> (I) **have** now, alas, philosophy,
>
> Juristerei und Medizin,

Jurisprudence and medicine,

Und leider auch Theologie

And sadly also theology

Durchaus **studiert**, mit heißem Bemühn.

Thoroughly **studied**, with hot effort.

This pattern was common in Old English. In Middle English it survived in poetry.

> ... and the yonge sonne
> **Hath** in the Ram his halve cours **yronne**[.]

> ... and the young sun
> **Has** in the Ram its half-course **run**[.]
> (Chaucer, "General Prologue" to *The Canterbury Tales* 7–8)

Hath is the finite auxiliary and **yronne** is the perfect participle. Note, by the way, the prefix y- in **yronne** – it marks perfect participles; it corresponds exactly to the German prefix ge- in **geschrieben**.

> Ful ofte tyme he hadde the bord bigonne[.]

> Very often he had the board begun[.]
> Very often he had sat at the head of the table[.] (52)

Chaucer freely departs from the pattern quite often, and then sounds quite modern:

> So **hadde** I **spoken** with hem everichon[.]

> So **had** I **spoken** with them everyone[.] (31)

Had he embraced the clausal brace here, **spoken** would have fallen at the end of the clause (and line).[2]

Absolute Clauses

An absolute clause is a subordinate clause not linked by a conjunction or in any other explicit way to the main clause. For example: "All things considered, we would rather stay here"; "The classroom having emptied, he ended his lecture half an hour early"; "Off we went, he remaining behind." As a rule, these constructions use a participle ("considered," "having emptied," "remaining"), though it might be implicit: "Tom, his head upon the desk, fell asleep." The term comes from Latin *absolutus*, meaning "unfettered" or "unlinked." These clauses are not absolutely unfettered, of course, because we can easily infer the words that would link them (e.g., "After considering all things, we would rather stay here"), but they are only loosely tethered.

In some fellow Indo-European languages, absolute clauses are (or were) marked by a particular case. In Latin, the noun or pronoun and the participle or adjective fell into the ablative case. At least one such Latin clause has entered English, *ceteris paribus*, "other things being equal"; philosophers, lawyers, and economists may state laws that apply *ceteris paribus* – that is, the laws govern events if nothing else intervenes. Sanskrit put such clauses in the instrumental case, Greek put them in either the genitive or the accusative, and modern German uses the accusative. English, having long discarded most of these cases, uses the nominative (or subject) case, though we only mark subject and object cases in our pronouns, as we see in the example above, "he remaining behind." Older English sometimes used the object case. Curme quotes a passage from Milton's *Paradise Lost*: "and him destroyed, / Or won to what may work his utter loss, / For whom all this was made, all this will soon / follow" (9.130–33). Modern English would prefer "and he destroyed" (for "and he being destroyed"), or perhaps "with him destroyed."[3]

These clauses seldom cause trouble in everyday speech or in written prose. In verse, as we see in the Milton example, they are sometimes a little difficult to sort out; it is helpful to have the concept of absolute clauses in mind, lest you get stuck searching for the missing link. Here is a passage from Wordsworth, with the absolute clause in italics:

> ... that serene and blessed mood,
> In which the affections gently lead us on,
> Until, *the breath of this corporeal frame*,
> *And even the motion of our human blood*
> *Almost suspended*, we are laid asleep
> In body, and become a living soul[.]   ("Tintern Abbey" 42–47)

Once we see that it is an absolute clause, we can appreciate its placement within the long sentence, where it indeed almost suspends the sentence, as our breath and blood are almost suspended by the serene and blessed mood.

Yeats has placed an absolute clause near the beginning of a very complicated sentence that occupies a whole ottava rima stanza of "Among School Children":

> What youthful mother, *a shape upon her lap*
> *Honey of generation had betrayed,*
> *And that must sleep, shriek, struggle to escape*
> *As recollection or the drug decide,*
> Would think her son, did she but see that shape
> With sixty or more winters on its head,
> A compensation for the pang of his birth,
> Or the uncertainty of his setting forth? (33–40)

It is worth studying this tour de force of a stanza. On first reading it, we might easily come to a halt not only in the absolute clause but at the preposed auxiliary verb of the contrary-to-fact subjunctive ("did she but see" = "if she but saw"). Notice that there is no participle in the main part of the absolute clause; we might mentally insert one ("a shape sitting upon her lap") but there is no need for one, and Yeats by this point in his career had learned to cut everything unneeded. The interrogative sentence, "What youthful mother ... would think her son ... a compensation," is interrupted for three and a half lines by the absolute clause and for one and a half lines by the subjunctive if-clause, before ending with one and a half lines of explanation as to what the son might be a compensation for. The two interruptions describe the "shape" sixty years apart: the first right after its birth, but evoking its prenatal existence (it has been betrayed into being born, it shrieks and struggles as it recollects its former life, and it sleeps only when drugged); the second in its old age, its hair whitened by sixty winters, and perhaps with failings and sins "on its head" as well. It is a heartbreaking rhetorical question with its implied negative answer, poignant enough if we think of an individual youthful mother with her baby but bleak and wintry when we take in that it is a well-nigh universal case; its unillusioned stoicism is aptly embodied in the strict control of the complicated syntax and the formal rhyme scheme.

Yeats had a penchant for absolute clauses. A famous one concludes his best known poem, "The Second Coming":

> And what rough beast, its hour come round at last,
> Slouches towards Bethlehem to be born?

By putting the hour in an absolute construction, Yeats leaves it unclear who or what has sent the hour round or how the rough beast knows it is time to begin its slouch; it all just somehow happens as it is destined to. But perhaps his most brilliant, and charming, instance is this, from the opening of "Politics":

> How can I, *that girl standing there,*
> My attention fix
> On Roman or on Russian
> Or on Spanish politics[.]

By dropping that girl into the first line, Yeats makes sure we can no more our attention fix (note the postponed verb) on politics than he can. In her absolute clause, she absolutely forbids it. The speaker goes on to think about politics for a moment, "But O that I were young again," he concludes, "And held her in my arms."

The Subjunctive Mood

In English, the verb has several "moods" (sometimes called "modes"): indicative, interrogative, imperative, and subjunctive; some traditional grammars include the infinitive; some languages have others, such as the optative (in Greek and Sanskrit) and the precative (in Sanskrit). The subjunctive mood is no longer used as much as it was even a century ago, and much less than in Old English, but it is still normal under many circumstances.

> If I **were** you . . .
> I wish I **were** a bird.

This form, sometimes called the contrary-to-fact conditional, is the subjunctive corresponding to the indicative **am**. Though it may look like one, it is not a past tense (though it has been miscalled the past subjunctive), and it is not a plural. It is more or less by accident that the distinctive subjunctive forms evolved to be identical to some indicative forms. In our cousin language German, the forms remain distinct, usually with an umlaut over the vowel in the subjunctive forms:

> Wir **waren** jung.   We were young. (indicative)
> Wenn wir nur jung **wären**.   If only we were young. (subjunctive)

In English, the convergence of forms must be one reason the subjunctive is dying out, and many speakers, shying from using what seems to them a plural verb for a singular subject, say "If only I was young." Some baseball announcers, *after* a play, say, "If he fields that ball cleanly, he has a double play," resorting to the simple present, and shrinking from the apparently daunting complexities of "If he had fielded that ball cleanly, he would have had a double play."

The subjunctive form often precedes (though it may also follow) a clause with the conditional **would:**

> If I **were** you I **would**n't do that.
> I **would**n't do that if I **were** you.
> I wish I **were** a bird. Then I **would** fly to Cancun.

The if-clause ("If I were a bird") can be restated without the "if" by placing the verb first ("Were I a bird").

> **Had** you only listened to me!
> **Were** I in your shoes, I would stay home.

This kind of subjunctive is still common and should cause no confusion when you meet it in a poem, as in Shelley's "Ode to the West Wind":

> If I **were** a dead leaf thou mightest bear;
> If I **were** a swift cloud to fly with thee;
> . . . .
> . . . I **would** ne'er have striven
> As thus with thee in prayer in my sore need.

But sometimes the subjunctive form of the verb replaces the **would**, as in these lines from Shakespeare's *Macbeth* (1.7.1–2):

> If it **were** done, when 'tis done, then 'twere well
> It **were** done quickly[.]

That means "If it were (really) done when it is done, then it **would be** well if it were done quickly."

There is a similar example in Shelley's "Hymn to Intellectual Beauty":

> Man **were** immortal, and omnipotent,
> **Didst** thou, unknown and awful as thou art,
> Keep with thy glorious train firm state within his heart.

The first line means "Man **would be** immortal, and omnipotent." The inversion of the subjunctive verb **didst** in the second line restates the if-clause: "If thou didst." Yeats does the same thing in the passage from "Among School Children" we quoted earlier ("**did** she but see that shape").

From Wordsworth:

> She has a baby on her arm,
> Or else she **were** alone.

That means "Or else [if she had no baby on her arm] she **would be** alone."

From Blake:

> Then **had** America been lost, o'erwhelm'd by the Atlantic,
> And Earth **had** lost another portion of the Infinite,
> But all rush'd together in the night in wrath and raging fire[.]

For the two instances of "had," we say "would have." But it is important to see, in both the Blake passage and the second Shelley passage, that the verbs are not in the past tense of the indicative mood. They do not assert that something happened, but entertain the possibility that something might have happened but did not. And note the first line seems to be governed by the old verb-second rule, for we would expect "Then America **had** been lost."

From Coleridge:

> A delight
> Comes sudden on my heart, and I am glad
> As I myself **were** there!

The second clause means "and I am as glad as I would be if I were there myself."

> . . . the strings of this Aeolian lute,
> Which better far **were** mute.

Or "which would be far better mute."

Another example from Coleridge illustrates the subjunctive (twice) and a reliance on the do-form to get the rhyme right:

> Swans sing before they die—'**twere** no bad thing
> **Did** certain persons die before they sing.

That is, "It would be no bad thing / If certain persons died before they sang." Yeats's line quoted earlier, "But O that I were young again," is a good example of the subjunctive of wishing.

There are other forms of the subjunctive, sometimes misleadingly called the "present subjunctive," where the possibility of something is more likely, not contrary to fact, and sometimes hoped for or even proposed:

> I move he **be** appointed secretary.
> God **bless** you.
> God **forbid**.
> Long **live** the king.
> We must obey the king however wicked he **be.**
> Glory **be** to God.
> **Be** it ever so humble, there's no place like home.

Send him a note, lest he **forget** to come.
He will be appointed if he **come** on time.

For the last sentence, today we would probably say "if he **comes** on time," but with the subjunctive **come** you get a slightly greater sense of doubt; this usage is probably extinct in America. But notice it is somewhat more hopeful than the "past" subjunctive would be: "He **would be** appointed if he **came** on time." And for "however wicked he be," we would now be more likely to say "however wicked he **may** be."

Note too that "God bless you" and "God forbid" are not imperatives. English does not have a third-person imperative (as Greek and Latin did), and, besides, we are not in a position to give commands to God.

Here are some examples from poetry.

From Shakespeare:
So shaken as we are, so wan with care,
Find we a time for frighted peace to pant. (= **Let** us **find**)
(*1 Henry 4* 1.1.1–2)

From Scott:
Part we in friendship from your land. (= **Let** us **part**)
(*Marmion* 6.13.17)

From Wordsworth:
If this / **Be** but a vain belief . . .   ("Tintern Abbey" 50–51)

Then, though too weak to tread the ways of truth,
This age **fall** back to old idolatry[.]   (1805 *Prelude* 13.431–32)

And here is an interesting example from prose: "It looked as though the war were going on for a long time" (Hemingway, *A Farewell to Arms* 2.19).

Poetry in Inflected Languages

We noted at the outset that in languages with grammatical endings or inflections, such as Greek and Latin, poets have been free to arrange words in almost any order they pleased as long as they made clear, through unambiguous endings, which nouns, pronouns, and adjectives were in which gender, number, and case, so that their audiences could sort them out and stick them together.

In English, nouns and adjectives no longer have gender; gender is only noted in third-person singular pronouns ("he, she, it"). French, Italian, and Spanish have two genders, masculine and feminine; all nouns must be one or the other, and pronouns referring to them must correspond.

Old English had three genders, as our kindred languages German, Icelandic, and some dialects of Dutch still do: masculine, feminine, and neuter. Even articles must be coordinated with the nouns they precede; thus, in German: **der** Mann ("the man"), **die** Frau ("the woman"), **das** Haus ("the house"). Greek and Latin had the same three genders, as did Sanskrit, inherited from the Proto-Indo-European mother language.

English still indicates number by marking plurals differently from singulars, mainly by adding an -s or -z sound, or a little syllable -əz, but with a few archaic exceptions such as "man/men," "mouse/mice," and "child/children." Old English had a third number, the dual, with distinct endings, mainly used for pairs of things, such as shoes or hands. Sanskrit and Homeric Greek also had a dual, while Latin had lost it except for a few traces. You can see that, with three genders and three numbers, some languages had nine possibilities for nouns, pronouns, and adjectives, with nine different endings.

And then there is case. Case is a grammatical category of nouns and pronouns, and of adjectives and determiners (such as articles) because they are attached to nouns; it indicates the function of the noun or pronoun or its grammatical relationship to other words – that is, its place in the syntax of the clause. In English, we mark the difference between subject and object only on the first-person and most of the third-person pronouns: I/me, we/us, he/him, she/her, who/whom, they/them; we use "you" and "it" for both cases, but we used to have the pair thou/thee. (On "thou" and "you," see Chapter 6.) But we do mark nouns in the possessive or genitive case with the same -s sound we use for plurals (leading to confusions over plural possessives): the cat's pajamas, the dog's tail, the children's playground, John's book, the girls' party, and so on. Pronouns have their own forms (I/my, we/our, etc.), though the -s in "his" is originally the same possessive marker as the one for the nouns.

And that's all we do in English to "mark" case – that is, to add something or change the form. All other distinctions, including the crucial one between subject and object in nouns, and the difference between direct and indirect object in nouns and pronouns, we do by word order. We say "The boy loves the girl" and we know that "the boy" is the subject and "the girl" is the object. In "The girl loves the boy" we know "the girl" is the subject and "the boy" is the object. In "I bought the boy the dog," "the boy" is the indirect object and "the dog" the direct object (inflected languages would give them different case-endings); if we want the objects in the opposite order we either create a new and odd meaning ("I bought the dog the boy") or preserve the original meaning by inserting a preposition ("I bought the dog for the boy"). Word order is decisive.

In Latin, where every case is marked on the noun, word order is not a factor in settling who loves whom, or who bought what for whom; it is used for more subtle purposes, such as emphasis or contrast. Compare these sentences:

> puer puellam amat
> boy girl   loves

> puellam puer amat
> girl   boy loves

These sentences mean the same thing: "The boy loves the girl." (Latin lacked definite and indefinite articles.) In both sentences, "boy" (*puer*) is in the subject (or nominative) case, and "girl" (*puellam*) is in the direct object (or accusative) case. By putting one or the other first in the sentence, we emphasize it; in English, we might do this by raising our voice. If we want to say "The girl loves the boy" in Latin, however, we must change the endings on both nouns, but we may put them in either order:

> puerum puella amat
> boy   girl loves

> puella puerum amat
> girl   boy   loves

We could also fidget with the placement of the verb – putting it first, perhaps, for emphasis or contrast with another verb, though the default pattern was verb-final.

You may feel grateful that English no longer has an extensive set of endings for nouns, but boys and girls in ancient Rome had no trouble learning them before they fell in love. And it allowed Latin to be flexible and creative in word order, especially in poetry. Latin in fact had six cases. Greek had five of them (with traces of several others), Sanskrit had eight, Polish still has seven, Lithuanian has seven or eight, depending on the dialect; Proto-Indo-European had eight, or possibly nine. Latin poets, with three genders, two numbers, and six cases, could indicate thirty-six different distinctions, while Greek poets, with three, three, and five, could distinguish forty-five kinds. And what fun they could have with them!

Here are two and a half lines from Euripides' *Medea*, spoken by the heroine after she has vowed to take revenge on her husband, Jason, and his new bride (386–88). In a word-for-word gloss, I have attached case markers on all the nouns, adjectives, and pronouns, here needing only two cases, nominative (subject) and accusative (direct object):

> τίς με δέξεται πόλις;
> tis me dexetai polis?
> What-*nom* me-*acc* will receive city-*nom*?

> τίς γῆν ἄσυλον καὶ δόμους ἐχεγγύους
> tis gēn asylon kai domous exenguous
> What-*nom* land-*acc* asylum-*acc* and house-*acc* secure-*acc*

> ξένος παρασχὼν ῥύσεται τοὐμὸν δέμας;
> xenos paraskhōn rhysetai t'oumon demas?
> host-*nom* granting-*nom* will save the-my-*acc* person-*acc*?

"What city will receive me? What host, granting a land of asylum and a secure home, will save my person?"

It may seem perverse in the first line that "what" is separated from "city" by two other words, but by putting "city" at the end Euripides emphasizes it. *Tis* can also mean "who," so we have a complete clause ("Who will receive me") before we get to "city," the arrival of which causes us to reinterpret the "who" as "what" in order to include "city" in the now longer clause. The next line begins with *tis* again, but we don't get the noun it modifies until the beginning of the line after that one (ξένος, *xenos* ["host, guest-friend"]). If this were an uninflected language like English, we would take the word after *tis* as the word it modifies, namely *gēn* ("land, earth"), but this is Greek and *gēn* is in the accusative case: it cannot mean "What land [will be my] asylum?" or the like. The whole rest of the line, two nouns, each followed by its adjective, is in the accusative case, so it must be the object of some verb yet to appear. Euripides wanted the object of Medea's desire to come first, before she speculates on who or what might provide it, and, when she does, it occupies a prominent position at the beginning of the following line.

The hypothetical host is in the nominative case, followed by a participle (*paraskhōn* ["granting"]), also nominative and masculine to fit *xenos*, and this is the verbal form, at last, that governs the two accusative noun phrases. Then comes the main verb (*rhysetai* ["will save"]), in the third-person singular to match the subject *xenos*, and then comes *its* object in normal order. Euripides may have wanted to place the participle "granting" next to the verb "save," since it is by granting that the host would save, another reason to place the objects of "granting" before it. All of the little adjustments we make in our minds as we parse and reparse this syntax came more easily to the Greeks, of course, who knew the endings well and were used to the manipulations of poetry, but it is still impressive, all the more so because very few Greeks ever *read* this play: they would have heard it chanted in the theatre of Dionysus amid a crowd of many thousands. No backtracking, no reruns; they had to get it on one hearing. And this passage is not especially intricate: there are many passages more complicated than this in Greek, and even more of them in Latin.

As for Latin, here are the opening three lines of Ovid's elegy for his fellow poet Tibullus (*Amores* 3.9), a couplet of which we discussed in Chapter 3.

> Memnona si mater, mater ploravit Achillem,
> et tangunt magnas tristia fata deas,
> flebilis indignos, Elegeia, solve capillos!

Here it is again with an English gloss with grammatical attachments, fuller than the ones for the Greek example:

Memnona si mater, mater ploravit Achillem,
Memnon-*acc* if mother-*nom*, mother-*nom* bewept-*3pers-sing* Achilles-*acc*,

et tangunt magnas tristia fata deas,
and touch-*3pers-plur* great-*fem-plur-acc* sad-*neut-plur-nom*
    fates-*neut-plur-nom* goddesses-*fem-plur-acc*

flebilis indignos, Elegeia, solve capillos!
tearful-*fem-sing-voc* unworthy-*masc-plur-acc*, Elegeia-*fem-sing-voc*,
    loose-*sing-imp* hair-*masc-plur-acc*!

In plainer English, this would be: "If a mother bewept Memnon, if a mother bewept Achilles, / and sad fates touch great goddesses, / [then] tearful Elegy, loose your unworthy hair!" But the original is organized in ways impossible to capture in sensible English, and very far from ordinary Latin.

The first line is about two mothers, and the two sons they lamented. Ovid wanted a special effect, the placing of the two mothers side by side in the center of the line, taking up two feet with four long syllables (*mātēr mātēr*), almost like a cry from a dying son; and that placement allowed him, indeed compelled him, to put the two sons at the beginning and the end of the line. So he creates the structure called a chiasm, from the Greek letter chi (X); if you break the line in half and connect the parallel parts, you get a chi (see Figure 5.1).

Figure 5.1 Example of a chiasm

In order to make this pattern come out right, Ovid had to distribute the remaining two words, *si* and *ploravit*, one to each clause, with the understanding that both words belong in both clauses. In English you might manage not to repeat them ("If a mother bewailed Memnon, a mother Achilles"), but it is impossible to distribute them the same way ("If a mother Memnon, a mother bewailed Achilles"). It is also impossible, I think, to put "Memnon" first, unless you also put the verb in the passive voice and thereby ruin the parallelism; and "if" cannot go second in an if-clause, in English or Latin – at least not normal Latin. It is all very artificial and elegant, and Ovid's sophisticated audience must have relished it. And that's just line 1.

The second line, after *et*, begins with a plural verb, *tangunt*, so *mater* cannot be its subject, even though there are two of them; their verb, *ploravit*, was singular, and in a different tense. So we await the subject of "touch," but with the next word we get the beginning of its object instead, the adjective *magnas*, in the accusative case, which means "great" (feminine plural). We now know something touches more than one feminine entity. We've had two feminine beings in line 1, so we can plausibly guess the mothers will be the object: will it be "great mothers"? But the noun is postponed, interrupted by another adjective, *tristia*, and the noun *it* modifies, *fata*, both neuter plurals. Now it happens that in Latin (as in Greek) neuter plural nouns have the same ending in the nominative and the accusative, so at first this noun phrase might seem another object of the verb, or part of the object, but it cannot mean "great sad fates," fitting though that might be, as *magnas* must attach to a feminine noun, not a neuter one. The sad fates, it turns out, are the subject of the verb. At last the missing object-noun shows up, *deas*, and we realize, if we had not already realized, that both the mother of Memnon (Aurora, or Eos in Greek) and the mother of Achilles (Thetis, the sea-nymph) were goddesses, and they were certainly deeply touched by their sons' deaths. But still a little doubt may linger: as goddesses go, these were not great goddesses, such as Juno or Venus or Minerva, so possibly line 1 does not just restate line 2 but enlarges it to include the great goddesses, and indeed, in lines 15–16, Ovid tells us Venus was no less distraught over the dying Tibullus than she was over her beloved Adonis.

As for the strange chain *magnas tristia fata deas*, its pattern is adjective¹-adjective²-noun²-noun¹, an impossible construction in English and weird enough in Latin, but not uncommon in Latin poetry. This pattern is another chiasm, or nested structure, and it sounds good, with four long a- sounds and two short ones, and three t- sounds. The Romans went in for this sort of grammatical pattern. If the verb had come in the middle, dividing the two adjectives from the two nouns, it would be an instance of the "silver line." Even more admired was the "golden line," where the pattern is adjective¹-adjective²-verb-noun¹-noun², as found in this line from Virgil: *aurea purpuream subnectit fibula vestem* ("gold purple bound clasp cloak," or "A gold clasp bound [her] purple cloak") (*Aeneid* 4.139).

Finally, after the two-line if-clause, comes a one-line then-clause. It is addressed to Elegy, as if she too is a goddess like the great or lesser goddesses already cited, and the verb is in the imperative mood (*solve* ["loose" or "loosen"]). "Elegy" is the very form of this poem, the elegiac couplet (like those we discussed in chapter 2), which Tibullus used for his love poems and Ovid for not only love poems but this mournful elegy. Ovid had personified her before, even saying she has a charming limp because one of her legs is shorter than the other; here she is the "mother" of Tibullus, his Muse, his very fame as a poet. What is she to do? Loosen her hair and weep. As in line 2, the adjectives come in another clump: *flebilis* in the feminine singular vocative (the direct-address case), followed by *indignos* in the masculine plural accusative. We know that two different nouns are involved, one tearful, the other unworthy. Elegy comes first, the tearful one, then the imperative verb, and then finally the noun *capillos*. If we had wondered what would be unworthy, we might still wonder why her *hair* should be unworthy, and it's not obvious. Some translators think *indignos* can mean "undeserving," on the assumption that Elegy did not deserve such suffering, and that may be so, but it is more likely a way of saying that no elegiac poem can do justice to Tibullus. It might also be a gesture of modesty on Ovid's part, since he is not only personifying Elegy as a character mourning Tibullus but embodying her in a mournful elegy of his own, which he concedes is loose and unkempt and unworthy. We might respectfully disagree with him, after working our way through all sixty-eight lines of this masterpiece of elegant and elaborate verse in a demanding meter. We might think it would be more authentic or sincere, more elegiac, if it were *more* unworthy, more ragged, less artificial, for how can real grief express itself in highly wrought silver lines and chiasms? Two of its English successors in the elegiac tradition, Milton's "Lycidas" and Shelley's "Adonais," faced similar criticisms. To give an adequate reply to these strictures is beyond the scope of this book, but we should take note of their assumption that real grief must find proper relief in something artless and raw, like a howl. Not all the grief-stricken have felt this way, or felt this way for long: highly stylized ritual laments have offered them greater solace.

Whatever we think about sincerity in poetry, what we have from Ovid, and many other Greek and Latin poets, are brilliant examples of what can be done with the resources of inflected languages. Some English poets may have longed to have the same means at their disposal, and did what they could to import certain features into English, which, combined with archaic features of English itself, helped create the special language of poetry that prevailed until the early twentieth century and even beyond.

Verbal Aspects and the Lyric Present

We often use the word "tense" very loosely to categorize any finite form of the verb (that is, anything but the infinitive or participles), but it is important to distinguish tense from another feature having to do with time, called "aspect." Linguists differ on just where to draw the line between tense and aspect, and on how many aspects English has; I will offer one way to think about them, and if it differs from other approaches, it will still serve to make clear certain distinctive usages in poetry.

English distinguishes between a habitual present and an ongoing or progressive present: "I eat pizza" and "I am eating pizza," for example, are both in the present tense but in different aspects, and their meanings are very different. Spanish makes a distinction much like this one, but French, and Italian, and German cannot, or rather they must use some round-about phrase, such as *je suis en train de manger du pizza* ("I am in the process of eating pizza"). The simple form has a habitual sense ("I eat pizza on Tuesdays" or "I eat pizza but never with pineapple"), while the progressive form does not: it sounds odd to say "I am eating pizza on Tuesdays."

Then there is the perfect aspect: "I have eaten the whole pizza." That is really in the present tense as well, though it has a past dimension: it implies a completed act that has a bearing on the present. Some authorities would call the perfect a tense rather than an aspect, but if it is a tense, it is a tense that has tenses, and it seems neater, with regard to the forms if not the meanings, to call it an aspect.

And then there is the combined perfect progressive aspect ("I have been eating pizza all day"), also in the present tense. That's four present tenses, and they make trouble for foreigners learning English. The habitual present is the simple form, while the other three make use of one or both of two auxiliary verbs, "be" and "have."

There is another present form, which most linguists would not call an aspect but which is very common: "I do eat pizza." We might call it the emphatic. As we saw earlier, the do + infinitive form was pleonastic or meaningless for some centuries, but it became the basis for questions ("Do you eat pizza?") and negation ("I don't eat pizza"), and now the positive form is used mainly for emphasis or insistence. The emphatic cannot be added to the other aspects, at least in "standard" English – that is, we cannot say "*I do be eating pizza" or "*He does have eaten pizza."

The past tense is even more complicated. The simple past form of the verb is not habitual, like the present, as it is perfectly normal to say "I ate pizza yesterday at noon." If we want to make a habitual past, we normally say "I used to eat pizza"; it is in fact so well established that "used to" has become a new verb – "usta" or "yusta" – pronounced with a voiceless s and not the voiced z found in "The screwdriver is used to turn a screw." It is almost a new modal auxiliary, like "gotta" for "have/has got to." We also have past tenses of the other aspects: "I was eating," "I had eaten," "I had been eating," and "I did eat." That makes six past tenses. French and German speakers no longer distinguish between the simple past and the present perfect in speaking (though it is still found in narrative literature): "j'ai mangé" looks like a present perfect but it means "I ate." In French, too, a single form, the "imperfect" ("je mangeais") can mean both "I was eating" and "I used to eat."

English also has a variety of futures, which use other auxiliary verbs. "I will eat" and "I shall eat" have different nuances, while in common speech "I'm gonna eat" (for "I'm going to eat") has largely displaced both of those modal forms. Those forms can both take the other three aspects ("I will have eaten," "I will be eating," "I will have been eating"), but to some ears it is a little strange to deploy "be + gonna" in the same positions, as in "I'm gonna have been eating pizza." No future forms can combine with the emphatic "do."

Those who say English is easy because it lacks word-endings forget this proliferation of aspects. Some verbs, moreover, called "stative" verbs, sound weird in the progressive aspect of any tense – verbs that refer to states rather than actions, such as "appear, believe, hate, include, like, love, mean, need, promise, see, understand, wish," and quite a few others. We say "I believe in Santa Claus," not "I'm believing in Santa Claus," because believing is a state, not an action. Any of these verbs, needless to say, can be wrenched into a progressive form for certain effects, just as mass-nouns can be recruited into count-nouns, and vice versa. When MacDonald's restaurants and then Justin Timberlake put the slogan "I'm lovin' it" into circulation, they forced the stative verb "love" into a progressive aspect, as if to turn love into a deed rather than a feeling or state of mind. Its catchiness was due to its strangeness, and though it has grown moldy by now, it has not fully infected other uses: we still say "I love you" rather than "I'm loving you," though no doubt there are occasions when the latter is apt enough.

The subtleties of meaning this multitude of forms conveys, which we seldom think about, can be deployed in poetry just as readily as in prose or speech. Sometimes there are unusual uses, however, that require us to consider whether some special shade of meaning is in play. The Keats who liked to make count-nouns out of gerunds also sometimes used the progressive aspect where the simple (habitual) aspect would seem more normal. In the opening of "Endymion" he writes: "Therefore, on every morrow, are we wreathing / A flowery band to bind us to the earth" (6– 7). Surely, if he does it every morrow, this is a habitual action, and it should read "we wreathe a flowery band," etc. He evidently wanted a rhyme with "breathing" in the preceding line (another of his gerunds), but it comes at the price of strangeness, almost as if he is not a native speaker of English with its many aspects. If we stop to ponder the passage, we may get the idea that this wreathing is taking place now (in the progressive) even as it takes place every day (habitual), a fair enough point when we remember that wreathing a flowery band is an ancient metaphor for making poetry – the very poetry we are now reading. But the price may be too high.

In English lyric poetry, several literary critics have noticed something they call the "lyric present," the use of the simple present where the progressive would be the more natural in everyday speech. George T. Wright gives some well-known examples:

> I wander thro' each charter'd street   (Blake)
> I fall upon the thorns of life! I bleed!   (Shelley)
> Darkling I listen   (Keats)

I walk through the long schoolroom questioning (Yeats)
I sit in one of the dives
On Fifty-second Street (Auden)

These are not stative verbs, but verbs of action. Poetry has not kept pace with the increasing use of the progressive aspect in spoken English over the centuries; the proportion of progressive forms in poetry has grown, but not as steadily or as much, and, as these examples show, the simple forms still seem at home in modern poetry. Wright suggests that these instances borrow meaning from contexts in speech or in earlier poems where the simple is normal, from the "historical present" used to narrate past actions, and from its use for habitual or repeated actions – as if to suggest that Blake wanders through the streets more than once, or that his wandering is somehow permanent. "The actions described seem suspended, removed from the successiveness of our ordinary time levels, neither past, present, nor future, neither single nor repeated, but of a different dimension entirely" (Wright, *The Lyric Present*, 565). Jonathan Culler prefers to describe the effect as "the time of enunciation, which is both that of a speaker/poet and that of the reader"; it is the attempt by the poem "to be itself an event rather than the representation of an event," and not timeless but a repeated moment every time a reader reads it (*Theory of the Lyric* 294–95). This subtle lyric phenomenon in English, difficult to describe and explain, cannot be captured in languages that lack the simple/progressive distinction, but it is distinctive of our poetry, and part of its allure. It is not unique to poetry, of course, for it often turns up in prose fiction; it would be interesting to see statistics on the frequency of the simple forms in the different genres.

Really Strange Syntax

We will conclude this discussion of syntax by noting some of the poetic distortions of it that bear little or no connection with archaic patterns once normal in the language. Milton's "Him who disobeys me disobeys" may echo a pattern in Latin, but it seems alien to English. Gerard Manley Hopkins watches a bird "in his riding / Of the rolling level underneath him steady air" ("The Windhover"), a long prepositional phrase which we might want to rewrite as "in his riding / Of the rolling, level air steady underneath him," though we would sacrifice the steady rolling effect. The compound adjective "underneath-him-steady" resembles a once common construction in German, but it has been rare in English.

Dylan Thomas presses syntax to the breaking point in a twenty-line sentence that takes up the first half of "After the Funeral." It begins:

> After the funeral, mule praises, brays,
> Windshake of sailshaped ears, muffle-toed tap
> Tap happily of one peg in the thick
> Grave's foot, blinds down the lids, the teeth in black[.]

We cannot tell at first if "praises" and "brays" are nouns or verbs. Since "Windshake" seems to be a noun, we might then assimilate "praises" and "brays" to nounness as something like a list of nouns and noun phrases gets going. That intuition seems confirmed with the first "tap," as that seems to be a noun. But then there is a second "Tap": Is it the second half of an enjambed sound ("tap tap") and hence a noun phrase, or is it a verb governed by the first "tap," as the adverb "happily" suggests (but then it should be "Taps")? And is "blinds" a verb or noun? The incantatory sound-effects distract us from sorting all this out, which may be just as well. Thomas in this very poem calls himself a "bard," and like some of his Welsh precursors he seems more interested in mesmerizing us than making himself clear.

Cummings, to take a last example, delighted in playing with grammar. The opening line of one of his best-known poems – "What if a much of a which of a wind" – forces two words into noun status that do not readily take to it. The *OED* says that "much" "never completely assumes the character of a noun," but it does so here; and "which" as a noun seems even less likely. We can understand why there have been attempts to construct the syntactic rules of Cummings's poetry as if they were written in a separate language. In Cumminglish, accordingly, "much" and "which" are nouns with supposedly determinate meanings. Yet surely his poetry only works within and against standard English, and a great part of his effect is due to the surprise and disorientation (and sometimes laughter) that his syntactic shenanigans induce. Reading it, we must find our way anew each time by setting out from normal English and taking the measure of the departures from it – departures being part of the point.

Unusual Words

Poets like to make up words. Though the syntactic relations these words enter into may not be unusual, a discussion of unusual word formation belongs well enough to this chapter. Probably the two main types of word-making, at least in the Indo-European languages, are: (1)

compounding, the connecting of two or more independent words; and (2) affixing, the attaching of prefixes or suffixes to a word.[4] Another set of types is: (3) making nouns into verbs or verbs into nouns, and making mass-nouns into count-nouns, or the opposite. Whether these types are a matter of inventing new words or of pressing existing words of one grammatical kind into service as another is not important here; the *OED* has separate entries for the noun and verb functions of what we might call one word, while it collects the two kinds of noun under the same entry. For our purposes, the point is simply to take a look at the sorts of innovations poets go in for.

Word formation, or the study of it, is called morphology, a branch of linguistics with deep ties to the other branches, especially syntax, but which has grown recently into a rich area of its own. One of its fundamental concepts is the "morpheme," the smallest meaningful part of a word, a concept parallel to "phoneme," the smallest meaningful sound, though "meaningful" in the case of the phoneme, as we saw, refers to the change in the meaning of a word (or indeed of a morpheme) that a change in phonemes brings about, as disclosed by "minimal pairs." A word may consist of one morpheme, or *be* one morpheme (such as "child" or "elephant"); it may be composed of two morphemes, through plural endings ("children" or "elephants"), for example, or another kind of suffix ("childish" or "elephantine"); it may have three morphemes ("childishly" or "quasi-elephantine"); it may have many more. English words with many morphemes are usually derived from Latin or Greek, languages that liked to add prefixes and suffixes to their words. So the putatively longest word in English has at least seven morphemes: *anti-dis-establish-ment-ari-an-ism*. One might argue for an eighth one here, for *-ish-* is historically a suffix to certain verbs of French origin, such as "finish," though it is no longer felt to be a possible addition – if it ever was – in English. Some languages, particularly those called "agglutinative" and "polysynthetic," pack together lots of little morphemes into one "word," which to translate into English would demand several words or phrases, maybe even a sentence. Over time, morphemes can be eroded and lost, or merged with others; so "king," as we noted earlier, which now has one morpheme, used to have two, when it was *cyn-ing*. And sometimes the form before affixing can die out, leaving only the secondary form, such as "uncouth": the original "couth," meaning "known," dropped out of usage in the seventeenth century, and is now ready for recoinage. So is "plussed," which might mean "unfazed," but, alas, "nonplussed" is now circulating in that sense among the ignorant. And how about "combobulated"?

English is good at compounding, as in "daredevil" and "drugstore," and there are rules, usually easily understood by native speakers, that tell you which half is the "head" of the word: the element that determines the category it belongs to. For example, a "drugstore" is a kind of store, not a kind of drug; its head is "store." The head of the verb "download" is "load" because downloading is a kind of loading. (There are some compounds that lack a head, such as the verb–noun compounds "scarecrow," "pick-pocket," and their like, because a scarecrow is not a crow but something that scares one.) In a triple compound such as "plainclothesman," there is a hierarchy of compounding: first plain+clothes, then plainclothes+man. If it were the other way round, we would have the concept of "clothesmen" (men who wear clothes?), of which some are plain (and others, it would seem, fancy).

German is really good at compounding. *Die Unabhängigkeitserklärung* means "the declaration of independence" or, more closely, "independence's declaration." But English can do the same thing, more or less; we just keep spaces between the words when we write them. "Emergency subway evacuation route map" would presumably be glued together as one German word typographically.

Morphology is about formations of this sort.[5] In this section, we will take up just a few examples of word coinages by poets – that is, of "onomatopoeia" in the original Greek sense of "name-making."

There are many compound words in Homer which he may or may not have invented personally (assuming he really existed) but which are distinctive of Homeric diction and were doubtless created by one or another bard in the long oral tradition of epic. A great many of them are adjectives, though in form they are indistinguishable from nouns:

rhododaktylos ("rose-fingered"), the epithet of "Dawn"
nephelēgereta ("cloud-gathering"), a frequent epithet of "Zeus"
khaliphrōn ("loose-minded")
thumoleōn ("lion-hearted")
hippodamos ("horse-tamer")

The playwright Aeschylus seems to have loved these compounds, and he was admired, and laughed at, for his own grand creations, such as *strophodinountai* ("circle-eddy," a verb) and *thesphatēlogos* ("god-ordained-worded" or "prophetic"), both in the *Agamemnon*.

Aristophanes took delight in concocting absurd polysyllabic words, and in the *Frogs* he let it rip in mockery of Aeschylus, who is a character in it. Here are four:

pompholugopaphlasma ("bubble-splashifications," according to W. B.
 Stanford, *Sound of Greek*, commenting on line 249)
kompophakelorrhēmōn ("boast-bundle-worded")
salpingolonkhupēnadai ("lancer-whiskered-trumpeters")
sarkasmopituokamptai ("flesh-tearing-pinetree-benders")

These last two make up a single line of iambic tetrameter (966).

Sprinkled throughout Old English and Old Norse poetry we find
compound nouns called kennings, often both formulaic and metaphorical,
even riddle-like. Here are five from Old English poetry[6] followed by two
from Old Norse poetry:

banhus ("bone-house") = body
wordhord ("word hoard") = book
heofoncandel ("heaven candle") = sun, moon, or star
brimhengest ("sea horse") = ship
hwælweg ("whale way") = sea
unnsvín ("wave-swine") = ship
bengrefill ("wound-hoe") = sword

Seamus Heaney's translation of *Beowulf* (2000), rich in such compounds,
is well known and much admired, but he had been coining compounds of
the Old English sort since his earliest poetry: waterweed, haunter-son,
hedge-hop, oxter-sweat, oak-bone, brain-firkin (these last two together
composing one line), drowned-mouse fibres, rain-flirt leaves. Geoffrey
Hill, in his poems about King Offa of Mercia, talks in similar ways,
appropriate to his subject: underkingdom, rune-stone, hammer-pond,
trout-fry, toy-shards, lime-splodges. No doubt the most extreme and
persistent case, however, is Gerard Manley Hopkins, who has made
many memorable compounds, often alliterative: wanwood, leafmeal
(adjacent to each other in "Spring and Fall"), fire-folk, circle-citadels,
quickgold (based on "quicksilver"), wind-beat, flake-doves, May-mess,
March-bloom.

One of Hopkins's most striking words is not a compound but what
seems a simple prefixing of a common verb. The opening couplet of
"Spring and Fall" begins

> Margaret, are you grieving
> Over Goldengrove unleaving?

We might think he has taken the participle of the verb "to leave" and
attached the negative prefix, and since the most common meaning of

"to leave" is "to depart" or "to go away," we might first think Hopkins's word means "not departing." We quickly see that that makes little sense in itself, and because the next line begins "Leaves, like the things of man," where "leaves" must be a noun, we reconstruct "unleaving" as having to do with leaves of a tree: Margaret is grieving because the golden leaves in the grove are falling from their trees. So then we wonder whether Hopkins has postulated a non-existent verb "to leave," meaning "to grow leaves" or "to come into leaf," before attaching the prefix. As it happens, there was such a verb, or two verbs: "to leave" (from the thirteenth century) and "to leaf" (from the seventeenth), both with participles ("leaving" and "leafing"), and current in Hopkins's day, though unusual now. So Hopkins did not create a verb and then negate it, or reverse it, but he did something similar by taking a somewhat rare verb that is a homonym of a much more frequent verb and negating that one. But, in fact, "to unleave" had also existed, barely, from the sixteenth century to Hopkins's day, usually in the transitive sense "to strip of leaves," so what he really did was revive that verb while making it intransitive. Note, finally, the curious little effect of the meaning of the better-known verb "leave" (= "depart") that rises up briefly: while the trees are unleaving, the leaves are actually leaving their trees!

Wallace Stevens (in "Reality is an Activity . . .") seems to invent a new word with the Latinate negative prefix in this line:

> There was an insolid billowing of the solid.

The *OED* cites two instances of "insolid" from the seventeenth century, so Stevens is reintroducing a lost word, but it feels new and interesting. I think it must be pronounced with the stress on the opening syllable, making the line a set of three dactyls and two trochees.

Lewis Carroll's "Jabberwocky" is too well known to need analyzing here. Some of its coinages have entered the language: "chortle," for instance ("He chortled in his joy"), began appearing in print within five years of the publication of *Alice in Wonderland* (1871). Others look like coinages but were already in use for centuries: "gyre," for example ("Did gyre and gimble in the wabe"), has been around since at least the sixteenth century. (It is pronounced /dʒaɪər/. Yeats was very fond of the word, which became a technical term in his esoteric theory of history and culture; he pronounced it /gaɪər/.) Whatever their past and future, the Jabberwocky words are sometimes cited by linguists as examples of *English*, because they are formed according to English "phonotactic" rules: they are all possible words in English. Carroll wrote "All mimsy were the borogoves, / And the mome raths out-grabe," and English speakers have no trouble pronouncing them, whatever they might mean. Had he written "All msimy were the gbovrsovo, / And the mome thsar gtoeutbr," it might still be pro-nounceable in some language or other, but not English.

All nouns in English and many other languages are either count-nouns or mass-nouns. All of them may in principle be both, and many are comfortable being both, but most are normally one or the other. Count-nouns are countable, can be made plural, and can take the indefinite article, certain quantifiers (such as "many"), or a number. We can say "a house" and "two houses," "a boy" and "several boys," "a sin" and "the seven deadly sins." Mass-nouns are not countable or pluralizable and cannot take the indefinite article or a number; to count such nouns, some unit has to be deployed, such as "cups (of coffee)." For example, "music," "poetry," "happiness," "water," "coffee," "butter," and "fish" all sound strange to varying degrees, or at least archaic, if forced into plurals; it seems very odd to say "He listened to three musics," though it has probably been said, and more or less understood. In the Bible, we find "the waters of Babylon" and "all the fishes of the sea," and it used to be the custom to "take the waters" at a spa, while today at a school cafeteria a student might take two "butters" (i.e., pats of butter), and in that context it sounds fine. Pressing a count-noun into service as a mass-noun is also possible, though less common: "She got a lot of house for her money" (using "a lot" as the countable unit), or "There was porcupine all over the road."

Normally the suffix "-ness" creates an abstract noun out of an adjective, such as "goodness," "happiness," "greatness," and "weakness," and nor-mally the result is a mass-noun. The same is normally true of the suffix "-ity," which yields such nouns as "theatricality," "specificity," "normal-ity," and "rectangularity." It would be odd to make most of them into count-nouns, and when we find "Three Happinesses Soup" on a Chinese restaurant menu we know the menu-writer is not a native speaker of English. (Chinese does not distinguish between the two kinds of nouns and has no marker for plurals.) As with the more concrete nouns (such as "butter" and "water"), sometimes such derived abstract nouns can be pressed into service as count-nouns by native speakers to good effect, as in "He compensates well for his weaknesses" or "I am grateful for your many kindnesses." These seem normal, or at least not striking. Poets, on the other hand, like to be striking.

Keats in his early poems had a penchant for nouns with the -ness suffix. In "I stood tip-toe upon a little hill" (1817), he has "dewiness" (53), "clearness" (173) and its rhyme "nearness" (174), "silkiness" (196), and "faintness" (196); in "Sleep and Poetry" (also 1817), he gives us "leafiness" (7) and "cragginess" (126). These at least remain mass-nouns, but when he describes the flowing water of a little stream as "hurrying freshnesses" ("Tip-Toe" 70) – which is an attempt, indeed, at freshness of expression – it sounds forced and precious. If "water" itself can be made a count-noun, he might have thought, why not a noun made of an adjective that describes it? He also makes a count-noun out of an -ity noun: seeking fame as a poet, he hopes to sprout "Wings to find out an immortality" ("Sleep" 84).

More pervasive in the early Keats is his tendency to take a progressive participle of a verb and make it into a noun – that is, a gerund – and a count-noun at that. He does it about twenty times in the 404 lines of "Sleep and Poetry," and several of them are count-nouns: "The very archings of her eye-lids" (238), "the shiftings of the mighty winds" (286), "the trippings of a little child" (369). We may grow tired of these gerundizings (Keats would like that word) and attribute them to his immaturity as a poet, but we find it, strikingly, in "The Eve of St. Agnes" (1819), where Madeline is told she might receive "soft adorings" from her beloved (48), and in one of his last poems, the justly admired "To Autumn" (1820), in which he seats the figure of Autumn beside a cider press, where "Thou watchest the last oozings hours by hours" (22).[7]

A short, dense poem in a very different mode is *Schlachtfeld* ("Battlefield"), by August Stramm (1915), a German Expressionist poet who was killed on the Eastern Front shortly after he wrote it. Much of its grim power lies in its distorting of mass-nouns into count-nouns. Here are the three middle lines:

Blute filzen Sickerflecke	bloods clot ooze-stains
Roste krummen	rusts crumble
Fleische schleimen	fleshes slime

In each line a mass-noun is made plural and the subject of a plural verb. To have put these lines in proper German, with the equivalent of "pools of blood" or "pieces of flesh," would have been effective enough, but not nearly as ghastly. Adding to the horror is the transformation of the noun *Schleim* into a verb. It is as if the language breaks or turns inside out in order to convey the sights of the battlefield after the battle; it is as if the language is another victim of the *Schlacht*.

Notes

1. Jespersen, *Growth*, 219.
2. For more on the V2 rule and the clausal brace, see Lass, *Old English*, 224–28, and (more technical and demanding) Ringe and Taylor, *Development of Old English*, 399–406.
3. Curme, *English Grammar*, 151.
4. There are more exact definitions, but we needn't deal with them here.
5. Rochelle Lieber has written an excellent introduction to morphology that shows the great range of topics it may include: *Introducing Morphology*.
6. For a fairly full list of Old English kennings, see Gardner, "The Old English Kenning."
7. Possibly Keats found "oozings" in an article in the *London Magazine* in the same year (*OED* under "oozing, n."). The adverbial phrase "hours by hours" sounds odd, as if the plural ending of "oozings" oozed over to the phrase.

CHAPTER SIX

The Meaning of a Poem

A poem means what the poet meant. That is the briefest way to state a widely held belief, taken as indisputable common sense by most ordinary readers and many literary critics. We understand and interpret a poem by inferring the intention of the poet who wrote it. That is how we understand ordinary speech-acts – people communicate what is in their minds to other people – and that is how we understand the speech-act we call a poem. Without the anchor of the poet's intention, we go adrift, subject to any passing wind or wave, and there is no other anchor. It is true that we often have no external evidence of a poet's purposes. We know little of any consequence about William Shakespeare, for example – so little that many otherwise intelligent scholars have convinced themselves that somebody else wrote his works. About Homer, we know nothing at all: he may not even have existed, being only a name attached to a long tradition of oral bards. In these cases, the anchor is merely notional, and its chain weak, but when we meet difficult passages, we nonetheless do our best to imagine what Shakespeare and "Homer" must have intended in order to rule out our own subjective associations and limit our susceptibility to the currents and tides of voguish literary theory.

A poem, in this light, is a kind of utterance, spoken by a real person. In everyday conversation, we must often infer the intention of a speaker in order to make clear to ourselves what an utterance means. When a speaker misspeaks, saying, for instance, "Would you mind closing the door?" while pointing to a window, courtesy demands we close the window because we know that is what the distracted speaker meant, and meant to say. So, the argument goes, when a poet tells us what she meant by an ambiguous passage, we learn from her how we must read it.

I believe this "intentionalist" theory of interpretation is fundamentally mistaken, and that we should not refer or defer to the intention of a poet even where it is explicitly stated. It sometimes does no harm to say that Wordsworth "meant" something or other in a poem, but if we go outside the poem to find this, perhaps in the notebooks of his sister Dorothy, we may impose a meaning on a passage that it does not really mean, and that would never have occurred to us had we not found that meaning elsewhere. After all, in our example, the speaker really did say "door" when he meant "window," and "door" has a different meaning. A poet might correct a misprint, but once a poem is in our hands we are entitled to read the words as they stand and not guess what the poet ought to have written, or what the poet "had in mind." Poems are interpretable by educated readers who understand the language they are written in; such readers do not need, and should not seek, clues from the poets.

Authors are not oracles, in any case. Sometimes they are manifestly mistaken about their own works: they may have meant to say one thing, but in fact said (or rather wrote and published) something else. When they talk about their intentions, they sometimes lie. Feeling embarrassed later when their opinions have changed, they may deny they meant what they said, as when Wordsworth denied he had been a "worshipper of Nature" even though he said so in "Tintern Abbey." Sometimes they throw out "critic bait" and enjoy the resulting frenzy. To take a notorious example from prose, James Joyce concocted schemata or outlines of the symbolism and Homeric parallels to be found in his daunting masterpiece, *Ulysses.* These schemata certainly look like his intentions, and in a letter accompanying one of them he spoke of "My intention."[1] It is likely, too, that, without them, readers would have taken a long time to discover some of the patterns that are indeed present in the book. But are all of them really there? Some early critics took the schemata as gospel, but many later ones have had serious doubts. There are two of these outlines, moreover – the Linati plan and the Gorman-Gilbert plan, named after those who acquired them – and they are not the same. For chapter 2 of *Ulysses*, Linati lists as symbols "Ulster, Woman, common Sense," whereas Gorman-Gilbert has "Horse"; for chapter 3, Linati has the color blue and Gorman-Gilbert has green. Was Joyce pulling our leg? I think so. It was a violation of his own ideal even to issue a schema, let alone two of them, or at least it was a violation of his character Stephen Dedalus's ideal in *Portrait of the Artist*: "The artist, like the God of the creation, remains within or behind or beyond or above his handiwork, invisible, refined out of existence, indifferent, paring his fingernails" (chapter 5). He does not issue authoritative guides to his creation. And even if Joyce was sincerely trying to help his befuddled early readers, he didn't help them much by issuing two inconsistent plans. Samuel Beckett, more consistent than Joyce, was notorious for refusing to help readers come to grips with his enigmatic plays; if they got headaches over them, as he famously put it, he would not provide the aspirin.

Poems, moreover, and all other forms of artistic literature, are not ordinary speech-acts; they are not "utterances" of the poet or author in any normal sense of the word. When W. H. Auden writes, in a poem, that when they get to Hades, "Poets must utter their Collected Works, / Including Juvenilia" ("Letter to Byron" III), he is using "utter" in an odd and amusing way. We do not say that T. S. Eliot uttered "The Waste Land" in public, but that he read it or recited it or even performed it. If "utter" really is an appropriate word for such speech-acts, then it has gained so broad a sense that it is utterly useless; we must make distinctions. Poems are artistic constructions – Auden called them "contraptions" – more like paintings or piano sonatas than everyday speech. Poems are public: they are published, and to publish is not to utter or speak in any useful sense of those words. It is a special act with its own meaning and implications, chief of which is to cut the work off from the normal or practical kind of speaking that we do every day. Delivered to its readers, the work has its own internal utterer, if you like, which we call the speaker or *persona* (Latin for "mask") of the dramatized speech in the poem. We call a poem a "work" or a "text," but it would be very strange to use either of these words for the utterance "Would you mind closing the door?" If the real John Keats came upon a Greek urn in the British Museum and said, "Thou still unravished bride of quietness," we might in a pinch call it an utterance, but we would be more likely to call it a snatch of a poem he is rehearsing and not a conversational gambit with a piece of marble. When "Ode on a Grecian Urn" was published, readers could enter into it quite fully without knowing anything about what real urn Keats may have seen, if he really saw one, or even imagining that any real person would ever talk to one.

The claim that poems are utterances of a poet and that we are bound to find out what the poet had in mind when he or she uttered them is sometimes attributed to the Romantics, who were given to such pronouncements as that a poem is the spontaneous overflow of powerful feelings or that it must come as naturally as leaves to a tree. If we believe them, we may then grow concerned with the "sincerity" or "authenticity" of a poem, or turn our attention to the "life" of the poet who revealed some of it in a poem, as if the life were the more important or more interesting thing. But we also find in the Romantics quite a different viewpoint. Shelley wrote to a friend, "The poet & the man are two different natures: though they exist together they may be unconscious of each other, & incapable of deciding upon each other's powers & effects by any reflex act."[2] Byron agreed: "A man's poetry is a distinct faculty, or soul, and has no more to do with the every-day individual than the Inspiration with the Pythoness when removed from her tripod" – that is, the priestess of Apollo at Delphi who went into a trance as she uttered her oracles.[3] Friedrich Schlegel, the main theorist of German Romanticism, claimed, "The question of what the author intends can be settled; not, however, the question of what the work is."[4] Said Victor Hugo: "As a person, one is sometimes a stranger to what one writes as a poet."[5] And finally, Emily Dickinson wrote: "When I state myself, as the Representative of the Verse—it does not mean—me—but a supposed person."[6] Faced with assertions like these, intentionalist interpreters are drawn into a paradox – or nearly so – for, if we are to be guided by a poet's intentions, what are we to do with the poet's intention that his or her work should stand by itself, or the poet's conviction that someone else, not his or her everyday self, wrote it? I think Virginia Woolf is right: "once a book is printed and published it ceases to be the property of the author; he commits it to the care of other people" (Preface to *Mrs Dalloway*).

In a conversation among five American poets in 1999, Paul Muldoon said, "I'm not interested in what the poet intends. I'm only interested in what the poem intends." "I agree," Charles Simic responded, "God, in his infinite mercy, made poetry far smarter than poets."[7]

Against those who would assimilate literature to ordinary speech, and then insist we must appeal to the intentions of the writer just as we must refer to those of the ordinary speaker, we could turn the tables and argue that even ordinary conversation is more like composing a poem than spontaneously transmitting what is in our minds. We compose ourselves, we play roles, we have no authentic self or life to express or reveal – only *personae*. For our purposes, we need not pursue this line of thought; I only want to establish that there are well-considered theories of meaning and semantics that do not rely at all on intentions or on what speakers "mean."

Many critics and scholars still routinely invoke what a writer intended or "had in mind" as if William Wimsatt and Monroe Beardsley never published their famous article "The Intentional Fallacy" in 1946. There they argued that "the design or intention of the author is neither available nor desirable as a standard for judging the success of a work of literary art." (The emphasis in this article was on quality or aesthetic value ["success"], but Beardsley later clarified the matter, distinguishing between interpretation and evaluation and rejecting intention as a factor in either one.) "Judging a poem is like judging a pudding or a machine. One demands that it work." We do not care about the intentions of our cook or mechanic. If a poem seems to express something in the poet, nonetheless "We ought to impute the thoughts and attitudes of the poem immediately to the dramatic *speaker*, and if to the author at all, only by an act of biographical inference." We do not read the poet's mind, gleaning private information: "The poem belongs to the public. It is embodied in language, the peculiar possession of the public, and it is about the human being, an object of public knowledge." The article concludes, "Critical inquiries are not settled by consulting the oracle."

We should also note that even attributing the poem to a dramatic speaker or persona and taking it as a representation of a fictional speech-act does not do justice to many lyrics. As Jonathan Culler has forcefully argued, such an approach takes all lyric poems as dramatic monologues, like those of Robert Browning, whereas there are many poems that seem not to correspond to any imaginable speech-act;[8] some, such as E. E. Cummings's more typographically inventive ones, cannot even be recited aloud. That approach also ignores such prominent features as rhyme, lineation, and meter, often the very things that attract us to a poem in the first place. If we wanted to preserve the concept of the persona or voice on the grounds that "meaning" is unintelligible without it, we would be driven to extreme lengths, assuming, perhaps, that a certain poem was spoken by a stoned typewriter.

Needless to say, the "intentional fallacy" article ignited controversy for many years, and occasionally still does, though it has largely burned out, partly from exhaustion and partly because it was subsumed under later waves of literary theory, such as the "death of the author" promoted by Roland Barthes and Michel Foucault, or the "intertextuality" of a text, whereby texts are seen to respond to other texts – interesting ideas that we cannot go into here. Today many critics, as I have said, seem to have reverted to positions normal before 1946, but I think most teachers in classrooms have made a point of distinguishing the author from the speaker and of concentrating on how a poem "works." Though historical and context-oriented approaches are prevalent today, even these do not usually rely on authorial intention in any strict sense. There are a few gray areas, of course. There is "coterie" literature, for instance – poems written for circulation among an in-group. Wimsatt and Beardsley mention such a thing in passing, and try to assimilate it to the history of the language, which is in principle public knowledge. We might say these groups speak a dialect or slang, which must still be "public" within the group or it couldn't be understood by members of it, and if these poems are eventually "published" to a larger public, footnotes will be necessary, just as they are for Robert Burns's Scots English poems, which are only partly understood by most Anglophone readers. An extreme case might be the "prophetic books" of William Blake, who seems to have been the only person on earth to speak a dialect that included many odd names of people, places, and states of mind, such as Urizen and Golgonooza – most of them never defined.

It is interesting, too, that when editors try to establish a reliable or authoritative text of a work, they usually seek the "final intention" of the author, meticulously comparing published editions with manuscripts and corrected proofs in order to do so. That seems right, if only as a courtesy to the (usually dead) author, but, if it seems to contradict the argument against relying on intention to interpret or evaluate a work, it does not really do so. We try to establish the text that the author intended, but we need not try, even if it is possible, to find out what the author intended by the text. There may be gray areas here as well, but the distinction is clear enough.

I have brought up these debates about the author's intention, even though they have little to do directly with linguistics, to make clear my own assumptions and to prepare the way for the topics that follow in this and the next chapter, such as poetic diction, style, and figurative language, on which linguistics may shed light. I believe they can be objectively analyzed, as indeed some of them have been since at least Aristotle, without the distraction of wondering what a poet intended by them or what it is about the poet's soul that they express.

Meaning in General

"Meaning" is notoriously difficult to define. Some textbooks on semantics don't even try to define it, and, even though meaning is the main focus of most critical essays and university classes on poetry, it is absent as an entry in all the handbooks of literary terms that I have consulted. It seems either too obvious – we all know what "meaning" means – or too amorphous as a general term to warrant discussion. In some places, it is implicitly defined as "sense" or "significance," but then "sense" and "significance" get defined as "meaning." Sometimes meaning is taken as the object that semantics, or semiotics, or hermeneutics, or interpretation pursues, but they in turn are defined as various pursuits of meaning. Even if we fall back on intention, to what the poet "means" or "meant" by his or her poem, we are not close to a definition of "meaning" but only to a place where we might find it if we know what we are looking for.

To put it mildly, philosophers have not agreed on a general theory of the meaning of words and sentences in ordinary use. For centuries, the dominant view tied meaning to reference: words and sentences referred to, or pointed to, or were derived from, objects and situations in the world. Thus, "dog" meant an instance of the four-legged furry mammal that barks and wags its tail, etc., and "There is a dog in the yard" referred to a real yard with a dog in it and was a true proposition if there was a dog in the yard. This theory seems plausible for nouns, or certain nouns, for we do learn (or teach children) many names of things "ostensively" by pointing to them and naming them. For such things as colors, which are difficult to define in words, ostensive definition may be the only way to proceed. The theory seems less plausible for some other parts of speech, however, such as adverbs, conjunctions, prepositions, and determiners. How do you refer to an instance of "however" or "such" or "of" in the real world? It may be that such words can be accounted for in a theory that considers sentences as a whole, which refer to situations and events, and which can be compared with other sentences referring to other situations and events, but the argument is complicated and has not convinced many philosophers of language. There is a fundamental disagreement, for example, as to whether the meaning of a sentence derives from the meaning of the words in it or vice versa. And theories of sentence meaning tend to take declarative sentences in the indicative mood as the norm, thereby neglecting the many other kinds of possible sentences (and non-sentences) we use in everyday speech, and in poetry.

As we saw in Chapter 4, Saussure distinguished between the "concept" and the "referent." In his definition of the sign, the signifier /dɔg/ is bound to the signified DOG, where DOG is the concept, not the referent, not a real dog. In some languages, the equivalent of /dɔg/ might signify a broader category than it does in English (including the wolf, perhaps) or a narrower one (excluding lapdogs, which are really noisy cats). In fact, the word "dog," the source of which is unknown, once meant a particular kind of dog; "hound" was the original generic term. Saussure's distinction is somewhat like the one Gottlob Frege drew at about the same time between *Sinn* ("sense") and *Bedeutung* ("reference"). To repeat Frege's famous example, Hesperus (the Evening Star) and Phosphorus (the Morning Star) have different senses but the same referent (the planet Venus). Some nouns or noun phrases may have sense but no referent at all, such as "unicorn" or (to take Bertrand Russell's example) "the present king of France."

Extensive debates, needless to say, have swirled around this distinction, which has roots in ancient and medieval philosophy. For our purposes, we may note that it opens the door to what we might call "virtual reference," or reference to things that might exist in conceivable worlds. Literary theorists concerned with the status of fiction have taken up this idea. While reading a work of fiction, they say, we suspend our disbelief and temporarily lend credence to an imaginary world where there really are unicorns or dragons and people named Lancelot or Dumbledore, and where words really refer to them. Not all poetry is fictional, of course, and quite a bit that we take as fictional now (such as the *Iliad*) was once taken as true. But a lot of poetry is a kind of fiction; in Marianne Moore's phrase, such poems are "imaginary gardens with real toads in them."

Ludwig Wittgenstein argued that meaning is not dependent on a mental representation or an external referent but is simply use, and his standpoint has influenced many later philosophers. The meaning of words or sentences, he said, is a function of how people use them in different situations or contexts, and they don't always use them to refer to things or make propositions about the world. There are many different "language-games" that we take part in, and a natural language is a family of such games, which range from making statements about the world to asking questions, giving commands, performing ceremonies, telling jokes, and reciting poetry. The title of J. L. Austin's book *How to do Things with Words* (1962) expresses Wittgenstein's standpoint very well, and in it Austin distinguishes among various speech-acts, such as giving verdicts, voting, promising, apologizing, congratulating, and cursing. In this approach, "meaning" more or less evaporates as a general idea, as does "truth," for they are inapplicable to many of these speech-performances.

Semiotics, inspired by Saussure and distinctive-feature theory in phonology, tries to show that meaning emerges through systems of differences, whereby "down" might be "negative-up," and "male" might be "negative-female," and so on. We will take a closer look at the application of this approach to poetry at the end of this chapter, but we can note here that it is susceptible to Wittgenstein's critique if it purports to be a universal theory of meaning, and even in the narrower domain of defining nouns it cannot account for a number of things in the world, such as colors, which are not plausibly reducible to a set of binary oppositions.

To return to Wimsatt and Beardsley, finally, their case for separating the meaning of a poem from the intention of the poet does not depend on a general theory of meaning in ordinary speech, if there is one to be found, for composing a poem – and especially publishing one – is arguably a special sort of speech-act that cuts the work free from the context of its composition. It might create a new virtual context for it, and a virtual *persona* who speaks the poem, but it will probably also have features that do not resemble those of any possible speech-act in ordinary life, such as meter, rhyme, and weird word order. Moreover, some philosophers have argued against the idea that intention, or one's state of mind, determines the meaning of any utterance, or at least any utterance that refers to things. As Hilary Putnam has said, "meanings are not in the head." They are not psychological but social phenomena.[9]

Happily for us, we do not need to settle on a general theory of meaning before we can consider some of the ways poetry means what it means. A vague common-sense intuition about it or, if Wittgenstein is right, a familiarity with the way "meaning" is used in our speech-community will be enough. In what follows, I will not try to elaborate a theory even of poetic meaning, but examine instead a few aspects of it, starting with the importance of getting straight the language the poem is composed in, and perhaps departs from – that is, "historical" meaning; followed by poetic diction, which is partly historical; and then style, which includes the interaction of syntax with the verse-line (notably enjambment) and rhyme. I will conclude with an account of structuralist semiotics and a briefer look at "pragmatics."

Historical Meaning

One aspect of the debate over the poet's intention does have to do with linguistics, for it turns on what a language is, and here Wimsatt and Beardsley make a mistake. In a footnote to their notorious article, they say: "the history of words *after* a poem is written may contribute meanings which if relevant to the original pattern should not be ruled out by a scruple about intention." Walter Benjamin made a similar argument in his famous (though opaque) essay "The Task of the Translator" (1923). "For in its afterlife," he writes, "the original undergoes a change. Even words with fixed meaning can undergo a maturing process ... the tenor and the significance of the great works of literature undergo a complete transformation over the centuries" (73). Benjamin gives no examples, but Beardsley does. In his textbook, *Aesthetics*, Beardsley writes (156):

> Since a literary work exists, so to speak, in the habit patterns of people who belong to a certain speech-community, it may be said to change as the meanings of its words change. If we ask for the meaning of a certain Shakespeare sonnet, we can ask what it meant in 1650, in 1750, in 1950; this does not involve an appeal to intention but only ... to usage at a given time. Some discourses probably gain new richness of meaning with age, as their words are used in notable contexts by other writers: the King James version of the Bible is an example.

In a later set of lectures he gives an example:

> I cite these lines from Mark Akenside, *The Pleasures of Imagination* (II, 311–13), referring to "the Sovereign Spirit of the world":
>
>> Yet, by immense benignity inclin'd
>> To spread about him that primeval joy
>> Which fill'd himself, he rais'd his plastic arm.
>
> "Plastic arm" has acquired a new meaning in the twentieth century, and this is now its dominant one (though the older one has not disappeared). Consequently the line in which it occurs has also acquired a new meaning.[10]

It is not surprising that many scholars balked at this argument, and that its obvious absurdity backfired against the whole anti-intentionalist stance. Akenside's lines cannot possibly mean that God had an arm made out of synthetic organic polymers invented by German scientists, and the reason many scholars would give is that Akenside could not possibly have had that idea in mind in 1744. Under Beardsley's theory of evolving meanings, hilarious anachronistic readings crop up everywhere. Here is Edmund Spenser in *Epithalamion* 48–51:

> And let the ground whereas her foot shall tread,
> For feare the stones her tender foot should wrong
> Be strewed with fragrant flowers all along,
> And diapred lyke the discolored mead.

Quite a lot has happened to the word "diaper" (noun and verb) since Spenser's day. When he published these lines (1595), the verb meant "adorn with diversely coloured details" or "variegate," an extension of an older sense, "diversify the surface of something with a small uniform pattern." It had nothing to do with baby diapers or (in British English) nappies, but that is the first sense that will come to mind today to someone who knows little about the history of the word.[11] When Keats, to take a later example, writes in "Ode to a Nightingale" that "The voice I hear this passing night was heard / In ancient days by emperor and clown" (63–64), he is not claiming that the bird sang to Bozo in the circus. "Clown" meant "peasant" or "countryman," and though a more modern sense as "jester" or "fool" (as in Shakespeare's characters) was also available to him, Keats was free to use the word without any condescension. Emperor and clown are simply the highest and lowest ranks of the social order; in other words, the nightingale was heard by everyone.

E. D. Hirsch's distinction, in *Validity in Interpretation*, between "meaning," which is what an author willed or intended, and which cannot change, and "significance," which is not fixed but open, and depends on what readers make of the meaning, struck many scholars as a reasonable response to Wimsatt and Beardsley, but while it might draw a circle around "plastic" and "diaper" and "clown," it does not deal adequately with the other arguments they mounted against intentionalism. There is a way to exclude the proliferating clowns without relying on the intention of the poet, however, and that is to look more carefully at what is meant by "language" and "speech-community." When a language changes, even by a little, in strict terms it is no longer the same language. When "plastic" in the modern sense entered English around 1910, it began to dislodge an older sense, which went back to the Greeks; today that older sense has practically vanished, and the new meaning has engendered yet another meaning, "credit card." We call the pre-1910 language "English" and we call our language today "English," but they are different Englishes, and they are not mutually intelligible without a little effort. (We might not have much trouble reading a book written in 1909, but that is because we know a good deal about older English from reading other books, but if a person from 1909 were transported here, he or she would face a steep learning curve.) The "speech-community" that Akenside belonged to no longer exists, except insofar as that community is the tribe of poets who also wrote in the same poetic register of English that he did and that some devoted readers of old poetry are fluent in today. To read Akenside or Spenser we must first learn their languages, which are not the one(s) we now speak or write.

Beardsley's and Wimsatt's mistake, then, rests on equivocal uses of "English" or "language." It might be called "the fallacy of insufficient specification." They seem to think that anything that was ever called "English" is one language, or that we can somehow speak the vast assemblage of words, phrases, and sentences contained in the *OED*, which really ought to be called the *Oxford Dictionary of Every English on Record* (*ODEER*, for short). They do not keep in mind Saussure's distinction between the "synchronic" and "diachronic" aspects of language – that is, between language considered as a system of sound, syntax, and meaning at one moment of time, and a language considered over time, historically, as a series of evolving stages. I think they would not make the mistake of thinking that a word in Chaucer, "ferme," the ancestor of modern "farm," actually means what "farm" means today, in the line about the begging friar who "yaf a certeyn ferme for the graunt" ("gave a certain farm for the grant") ("General Prologue" to *Canterbury Tales* 252a). The *OED* makes clear that the friar gave a "fixed yearly sum in lieu of taxes," not a "farm" in the modern sense, where cows and cornfields may be found. But I suspect the reason they would not make that mistake is that Chaucer's language is called "Middle English" and by its strange pronunciation and spelling it shows itself as obviously foreign to us. In fact, Wimsatt and Beardsley were exceptional scholars with a thorough understanding of the history of English, and, were they to meet this sentence in Laurence Sterne's *Sentimental Journey* (1768), "You have been making love to me all this while," they would certainly not think it is about sexual intercourse, a meaning that emerged only in twentieth-century America. But why wouldn't they? By their own theory, they have no basis for ruling it out. The point is that every historical phase of "English" is foreign to a degree, not to mention its myriad dialects in myriad places at any one time. Today, it is routine among sociolinguists to speak of "Englishes," as a count-noun, and for good reason.

It is not that readers of older poetry or any other kind of literature must become historical linguists, but they must acquire some sense of the history of the language if they are to understand fully what they read. In textbooks, poems will be annotated by the editor – old words and old meanings of current words will be flagged – but the notes are usually brief and minimal, and a reader who wants to follow the nuances of the words and phrases will have to repair to the *OED*, which has made itself essential to the serious study of literature in English by its sheer size and by presenting its definitions in historical order with dates for all its quotations.

Here is a simple example, chosen almost at random from Shakespeare's *Sonnets*. Sonnet 12 begins, "When I do count the clock that tells the time, / And see the brave day sunk in hideous night." The primary sense of "brave" today feels odd here, but if there were no note to correct us we might decide, despite its oddness, that Shakespeare is saying that the day is courageously entering into a losing combat with night, a plausible segment of some myth or other, though the idea would come to a dead end as we took in the rest of the sonnet. A major student anthology glosses "brave" as "splendid," and that is helpful as far as it goes; in fact, the *OED* tells us that a dictionary of 1570 defines "brave" as Latin *splendidus*. The other quotations it gives from Shakespeare's day or earlier can mean "splendid" but with the connotation, or secondary sense, of "finely dressed," and if we are alert to that nuance we would get the sense that the day is only temporarily dressed in finery – that its very nature is brief and superficial, no match for hideous night. That sense suits the three other images in the octave, all plants that flourish and die or lose their leaves as time makes its demands:

When I do count the clock that tells the time,
And see the brave day sunk in hideous night;
When I behold the violet past prime,
And sable curls all silver'd o'er with white;
When lofty trees I see barren of leaves
Which erst from heat did canopy the herd,
And summer's green all girded up in sheaves
Borne on the bier with white and bristly beard,
Then of thy beauty do I question make,
That thou among the wastes of time must go,
Since sweets and beauties do themselves forsake
And die as fast as they see others grow;
   And nothing 'gainst Time's scythe can make defence
  Save breed, to brave him when he takes thee hence.

The sonnet is one of several that appeal to the speaker's friend to marry and produce an heir, for that is the way to achieve a kind of immortality in the face of time's relentless course. The word "brave" returns, this time as a verb, in the final line, and again it sounds a little quaint to our modern ears, though the phrase "to brave it out" is still current. The anthology glosses this "brave" as "defy," and probably no other single word would capture it better, but again the *OED* takes us a little further. It tells us that our most recent sense, "to meet or face (danger) with bravery," is anachronistic for 1600, the first attested example dating from 1776. In Shakespeare's day, courage was secondary or only inferred; what was in play, says the *OED*, was "bravado," a word taken from Spanish in Shakespeare's time and meaning an ostentatious display of boldness. Do we have a hint here too that when the friend braves Time's scythe, he will be a little showy and superficial? Will his bravery before death connote what "bravery" also meant, "ostentation," "finery," or "decoration"? Perhaps not, but by repeating "brave" as a verb in the final line, Shakespeare evokes its sense as an adjective in the second line, and thus invites us to read the words backward and forward: in retrospect, perhaps the day does show some defiance as it sets; while in prospect, perhaps the friend, by leaving an heir behind, may not pose as deep a challenge to death as it first seems he will.

The word "bravado" should make us take a look at the etymology of "brave" and "bravery," and what we learn is interesting. (The etymologies in the *OED* are usually quite thorough.) The two words are borrowed from French, and attested in English for the first time only a generation before Shakespeare's day; from the many quotations in the *OED* we get the feeling that the words still seemed a little showy or slangy, or that people in that era, including Shakespeare himself, were playing with them as new toys.

"Brave" occurs scores of times in Shakespeare's plays, once even in French (in *Henry V*), and though it usually means "courageous," it often shades into the other senses we have noticed. It was a brave new word. The French got *brave*, we learn, from Italian *bravo*, and that fact reminds us that those of us who go to classical concerts and operas may shout "Bravo!" after a well-sung aria ("Brava!" if the singer is a woman); it does not mean "courageous," of course, but "splendid" or "terrific."

This example is more subtle than "plastic," "diapered," "clown," or "make love," the oddness of which in their contexts is striking, and amusing. As you read more poetry from various times, and acquire the habit of looking up words regularly in the *OED*, you also acquire a nose for detecting such subtleties. A word might even seem perfectly appropriate in its current sense but mean something else, or something else in addition, that you might not suspect, so sometimes you ought to look up prominent words at random just to see what turns up. Be a geek! David Foster Wallace read the entire first edition of the *OED* when he was a teenager, and went on to become one of the most exciting and innovative essayists and novelists of his generation. (He is now quoted seventy-two times in the current electronic edition.) We lesser mortals can at least discover the esoteric pleasures of English in all its diachronic bravery.

Thou, Thee, Ye, and You

Perhaps the most important, or at least the most pervasive, feature of older poetry to get right is the set of different words for "you," so I will go into the matter at some length; it will serve as an example of the kind of systematic changes English has gone through. Today, we use "you" as both the singular and the plural form, and both the subject and the object form, of the second-person pronoun. Long after they had died out in common speech, however, and even into the twentieth century, poets often kept the older forms (see Figure 6.1).

	singular	plural
subject	thou	ye
object	thee	you

Figure 6.1 Second-person pronouns in English

Thus, three different words have given way to "you," which was originally the plural object form. Because it covers much more ground today, "you" no longer has the meaning it had in speech 300 or 400 years ago, or in poetry much more recently. It was a loss of semantic specificity, of the sort most European languages preserve. In fact, we still feel the need to distinguish plural from singular, if not object from subject, so we generate new plural forms, such as "you all" (or "y'all"), "you ones" (or "y'uns," or "yinz" in Pittsburgh), "you guys," "you lot" (mainly British), or even "youse" or "youse guys."

Today, "ye" survives only in such "fossilized" expressions as "Ye gods!" and in archaic churchly speech and song, such as "O ye of little faith" and "O come all ye faithful." It is *not* the "Ye" seen on fake old signs such as "Ye Olde Shoppe"; the "Y" there is not really a Y but the old runic letter "thorn" (usually printed Þ) for a th- sound (I think both voiced and voiceless); so it is just "The Olde Shoppe."

"Thou" and its kindred forms seem extinct outside of church and the King James Bible, though they may linger on in some dialects in Britain; "thee" persists among Quakers, but not "thou."

There are also possessive forms (see Figure 6.2).

If you have studied any other European language, ancient or modern, you will have learned several different words for "you" that are not synonyms. French has one of the simpler sets – just four forms, not counting the possessives (see Figure 6.3) – but with the complication that *tu, te,* and *toi* are considered intimate (used for close friends, family, children, and God), and *vous* polite (in the singular). German has more

singular	plural
thy, thine	your

Figure 6.2 Second-person pronouns in the possessive case

	singular	plural
subject	Tu	vous
object	te, toi	vous

Figure 6.3 Second-person pronouns in French

forms, with a polite form (*Sie*, derived from *sie*, "they") distinct from botl the singular intimate (*du*) and the plural intimate (*ihr*), plus several objecι forms. Spanish distinguishes gender in the plural forms (*vosotros, vosotras*). If you have learned to use such forms in a foreign language, you will understand the differences among the four forms in English. Treat the poetic register of English, then, as a foreign language, especially with respect to the "you" forms.

Old English, of course, really is a foreign language to us, and one of the features that makes it strange is that it not only had different forms of "you" for the singular and the plural, and for subject and object (and more than one kind of object at that), but it had forms for a third number, the dual. The word *git* (pronounced /jɪt/) meant "ye two" (the -t may go back to the t- in the ancestor of "two"), and *inc* meant "you two." This was not a quirk of the Anglo-Saxons, for the dual goes back to Proto-Indo-European: Greek and Sanskrit had not only dual pronouns but a set of dual endings for all nouns and verbs. Traces of the dual/plural distinction linger in modern English in the contrast between "both" (of two) and "all" (of three or more), between "either" and "any," and between "between" and "among."

In poetry since the Middle English period, by which time dual pronouns had disappeared, it is sometimes crucial to grasp the difference between singular and plural pronouns. Keats's "Ode on a Grecian Urn," for instance, concludes with these famous lines:

> Thou shalt remain, in midst of other woe
> Than ours, a friend to man, to whom thou say'st,
> Beauty is truth, truth beauty, —that is all
> Ye know on earth, and all ye need to know.

Some critics have argued that the final line and a half (from "that is all" to the end) are spoken by the same speaker who has been speaking the poem all along, but if that is true he cannot be addressing the urn any longer, for he has been calling it "thou" from the poem's first word. "Ye" is plural, so the addressee must be "man," understood as plural, and it seems simpler to take the urn as speaking the whole of the last two lines than to have the original speaker step in to comment (to us) on the urn's maxim about beauty and truth. There is more to be said about this question, but it cannot be usefully discussed before the pronouns are sorted out.

Poets are usually careful to maintain the distinctions, though occasionally they are casual about it, as when Keats himself switches between "thy" and "your" for the same addressee in "Ode on Melancholy." By the fifteenth century, "ye" sometimes substituted for "you" as the object:

> Thus I . . . shall . . . bring ye to the place[.]   (Milton, *PL* 2.840)

And sometimes poets are inconsistent within the same sentence:

> I call upon ye by the written charm
> Which gives me power upon you.   (Byron, *Manfred* 1.1.35–36)

The second-person singular (thou) form of the verb in both present and past tenses ended in -st or -est. For example:

> That time of year thou mayst in me behold . . .   (Shakespeare, Sonnet 73.1)

> Thou preparest a table before me in the presence of mine enemies.
>   (King James Bible, Psalm 23.5)

> For those whom thou think'st thou dost overthrow
> Die not, poor death, nor yet canst thou kill me.(Donne, Holy Sonnet 10.3–4)

>   From the heart
> Of London, and from cloisters there, thou camest,
> And didst sit down in temperance and peace,
> A rigorous student.   (Wordsworth, 1805 *Prelude* 6.278–81)

> O THOU! meek Orb! that stealing o'er the dale
> Cheer'st with thy modest beams the noon of night!
>   (Robinson, *Sappho and Phaon* 24.1–2)

A few verbs (mainly "be" and the modals) are exceptions, and take only -t:

> Grant if thou wilt, thou art beloved of many   (Shakespeare, Sonnet 10.3)

> Death, thou shalt die   (Donne, Holy Sonnet 14)

> O rose thou art sick   (Blake, "The Sick Rose" 1)

> Bird thou never wert   (Shelley, "To a Sky-Lark" 2)

Keats disagrees with Shelley, incidentally, on the past tense of "art," at least when you address a bird:

> Thou wast not born for death, immortal Bird!
>   (Keats, "Ode to a Nightingale" 61)

An odd contraction is occasionally found, as in this from Wordsworth's "To a Sky-Lark" (20–21):

> Thou wouldn'st be loth
> To be such a Traveller as I.

It seems a mistake to contract "wouldst not" into "wouldn'st," as if it were
from "would notst," but perhaps this was common enough in the spoken
language of Wordsworth's Lake District. The "correct" contraction,
"wouldstn't," after all, is unpronounceable.

The third-person singular (he, she, it) form of the verb ended in -th or
-eth (again with exceptions):

> What availeth me to moan?
>
> > (Wyatt, "The Lover Complaineth his Estate" 9)

> He maketh me to lie down in green pastures; he leadeth me beside
> the still waters.   (King James Bible, Psalm 23.2)

> He that hath clean hands, and a pure heart . . .   (Psalm 24.4)

The -th and -eth endings changed to -s and -es before the -st and -est
endings dropped out; the King James translation was somewhat archaic in
its own day (1611).

Poets of the Romantic period sometimes switched back and forth
between the modern and archaic verb-endings when they needed to add
or subtract an unstressed syllable to make the meter come out right, or just
to make a line sound better. In Coleridge's "The Rime of the Ancyent
Marinere" (1798 version), we find these lines about the Hermit (543–44):

> He singeth loud his godly hymns
> That he makes in the wood.

The archaic endings have dominated the poem, so "singeth" is routine;
without the syllable -eth, the first line would not be perfect iambic
tetrameter. But the second line inconsistently abandons the -eth ending
and modernizes "maketh" to the one-syllable "makes." Why? Coleridge
wanted a line of six syllables here, of the sort he writes throughout the
poem, and "maketh" would make seven. The resulting line is a little
hard to scan: we are tempted to turn it into two anapests ("That
he **makes** in the **wood**") but I think it is more consistent with the
prevailing meter to make it three iambs ("That **he** makes **in** the
wood"), though it sounds somewhat artificial. (If Coleridge had
dropped the "That" and retained the -eth ending he would have had
a perfect iambic trimeter.)

Another inconsistent practice is visible in Wordsworth's sonnet
"Composed upon Westminster Bridge." It begins

> Earth has not anything to shew more fair

but reverts to the archaic forms in the remainder, with "doth" in line 4, and then this line (12):

> The river glideth at his own sweet will:

Without the -eth ending, this line would not glide at all. But why not use "hath" in the opening line? Probably because "Earth hath" is a bit of a tongue-twister, and with another th- sound four syllables later the line would sound like a lisp.

And here is Byron, pretending to wonder where Childe Harold is:

> Methinks he cometh late and tarries long.
> (*Childe Harold's Pilgrimage* 4.1470)

Poetic Diction

"Thou," "thee," "ye," and the verb-endings are prime examples of a larger set of features collected under the general name "poetic diction." The word "diction" here means the choice of words and the manner or style of arranging them; it does not have the more recent meaning of "enunciation" in speaking or singing. In most – if not all – cultures, and for as long as we can trace it back, poetry (or song) has spoken a language of its own, overlapping with but distinct from the language of everyday speech. It has usually felt more elevated, more evocative, more profound, and, in any case, tinged with its ties to special occasions such as rituals and festivals. In churches, synagogues, mosques, and shrines all over the world today, the language of liturgy is very different from the spoken language of the worshippers. It might even be a completely different language – Latin, Hebrew, Classical Arabic, Sanskrit – but even if it is the "same" language, it is not really the same. Many churches in the English-speaking world, for instance, still use the King James (or Authorized) version of the Bible in their services, and while there have been countless retranslations since 1611, many parishioners resist modernization. Poetic diction is like liturgical language in this respect, and indeed quite a lot of liturgical language is in verse to begin with. Though it may have lacked religious sanction, poetic diction – until the last two centuries, at least – still garnered a great deal of respect; it had its own sanction of tradition and the example of great poets in the past. It was conservative and archaic, as we have seen with respect to the syntactic structure of sentences in Chapter 5 and with "thou and thee" in this one. Many words lingered on, preserved in the amber of poetry, long after they died out in contemporary speech.

The best-known and most influential critique of "what is usually called poetic diction" in English is that of William Wordsworth in the "Preface" to the second edition of *Lyrical Ballads* (1800). He has written his poems, he says, in "the very language of men," and in particular those from "low and rustic life," because they "speak a plainer and more emphatic language." His readers will find "no personifications of abstract ideas in these volumes," and no difference in vocabulary from what might be found in good prose. His use of meter and rhyme does not require him to use the "phrases and figures of speech which from father to son have long been regarded as the common inheritance of Poets." He quotes an entire sonnet by the estimable Thomas Gray, "Sonnet on the Death of Mr. Richard West" (1768) – Gray's only sonnet, as it happens – and prints five lines of its fourteen in italics: these five, Wordsworth says, are the only ones "of any value," because they do not differ in their language from that of prose. Among those of no value are the opening quatrain which we discussed earlier:

> In vain to me the smiling mornings shine,
> And reddening Phoebus lifts his golden fire:
> The birds in vain their amorous descant join,
> Or chearful fields resume their green attire[.]

He does not take the trouble to analyze these or any other lines, assuming it as obvious to his readers that they are valueless, but it is worth trying to infer what he thinks is wrong with them. There is "Phoebus," first of all, another name for Apollo, god of the sun, but here pretty much just a synonym for "sun." If it is a personification, it is not a personification of an abstract idea, but a kind of imposition of a mythical personage on a concrete object. We are given a brief glimpse of something interesting, Apollo lifting his golden fire, which might have come out of the *Iliad*, but it goes nowhere: Phoebus just lifts himself – that is, the sun rises. It is as if Gray thinks the word "sun" is too prosaic to be admitted into a poem. And yet something might be said for it: Gray is so grief-stricken over the death of his friend that even the arrival of the great Apollo, the god of poetry as well as light, fails to touch him.

At least three of the other words belong to a different register from the rest: "amorous," "descant," and "attire," and perhaps also "resume." As pure sound the phrase "amorous descant" is pretty, but it is an absurdly grandiose way of saying "love song," and it is part of Gray's inheritance as a poet, taken as it is from Milton's *Paradise Lost* (4.603). That it is taken *from* Milton might make it an allusion *to* Milton that Gray thought his readers would recognize (it is from the description of paradise before the Fall), and thus import some meaning beneath its lofty aura (that the death of West, perhaps, has brought about the loss of Gray's innocent happiness), but Wordsworth says nothing of this possibility, and we are trying to guess what he disliked about these lines, not what subtleties they might contain. To "resume their green attire" is to "put on their green clothes again," and Wordsworth probably objected not only to two of Gray's words but to the over-used metaphor of clothing for green leaves and grass. Perhaps, too, Wordsworth disliked the clichéd pairing of dawn (lines 1 and 2) with spring (3 and 4), though if you are going to write an elegy it is almost a rule that you must note the returning of life and the sad contrast with your unreturning friend.

He might also have scorned Gray's submission to the rule that every noun must have an adjective, as if nouns look common or vulgar without the decent dress a good adjective provides. Of the seven nouns in this quatrain, only one is naked, "birds," and they at least get an amorous descant to sing. Some of these adjectives, too, are nearly epithets – that is, the standard adjectives that frequently go with names and some common nouns in the epic tradition, such as "swift-footed Achilles" and "rose-fingered dawn." That Phoebus is "reddening," in fact, owes something to Homer's dawn, as well as to phrases in Virgil, Ovid, and other Latin poets. Gray did not invent the smiling morning or the shining morning, either; both are found several times in Milton, and many times elsewhere. At least Gray did not replace "birds" with "feathered tribe," as some of his contemporaries did.

Whether or not Wordsworth is altogether fair to Gray, whether or not one or two of the italicized lines can be redeemed, Wordsworth has carried the day. He was not alone, but he gave voice to what has become the prevalent contempt today of poetic diction, especially that of the eighteenth century. The high registers and circumlocutions, classical personifications, well-dressed nouns, and the sheer repetition of stock phrases – these defined everything that poets increasingly vowed to get away from as they strove for originality, freshness, or novelty.

Wordsworth returned to the question of poetic diction in an appendix to the third edition of *Lyrical Ballads* (1802), in which he assumes as beyond question a certain history of it.

> The earliest poets of all nations generally wrote from passion excited by real events; they wrote naturally, and as men: feeling powerfully as they did, their language was daring, and figurative. In succeeding times, Poets, and Men ambitious of the fame of Poets, perceiving the influence of such

language, and desirous of producing the same effect without being animated by the same passion, set themselves to a mechanical adoption of these figures of speech, and made use of them, sometimes with propriety, but much more frequently applied them to feelings and thoughts with which they had no natural connexion whatsoever. A language was thus insensibly produced, differing materially from the real language of men in *any situation.*

This theory is attractive and may even seem obvious, but its then commonplace primitivism and Romanticism, such as the contrast between the "natural," a good thing, and the "mechanical," a bad, should put us on our guard. "It was standard procedure in Wordsworth's day," M. H. Abrams writes in his classic study of Romantic literary theory, "when characterizing poetry, to refer to its conjectured origin in the passionate, and therefore, naturally rhythmical and figurative, outcries of primitive men."[12] Such a view of poetry may have some basis with respect to oral folk-ballads and songs, as Abrams notes, but it is quite mistaken with respect to the oldest poetry we have, at least in the west: Homer and Hesiod. It is also odd that Wordsworth says the earliest poets *wrote* naturally, for he must have been aware that poetry long preceded writing, and still flourished in the illiterate cultures of his day. But even if we confine the question to oral poetry, we have to concede that the epic, at least, was permeated by the kind of poetic diction Wordsworth scorned.

As we noted in Chapter 2, there is little question now that Homer was an oral poet. It is possible that he was the first of such poets to adopt the new alphabet, but certainly the *Iliad* and the *Odyssey* are a kind of poetry that bears every hallmark of oral composition, not least the heavy use of repetition of phrases, whole lines, and even groups of lines, the famous "formulas" that have been so thoroughly studied since Milman Parry.[13] We have good reason to believe that not only the stories they tell, but many of the epithets and other formulas, and the dactylic hexameter line, go back centuries before the epics were first written down, perhaps to about 700 BCE, not long after the alphabet arrived in Greece. Some metrical anomalies point back to the Mycenaean era (*circa* 1400 BCE) for their explanation. And the diction of the Homeric epics as we have them, and very likely for centuries during their entirely oral transmission and development, is highly artificial, very much the "inheritance" of the guild of bards. No one ever spoke Homeric Greek "in any situation" except during the recitation of an epic poem, accompanied by a lyre. It is a composite of dialects from different parts of Greece and from different periods, making it "pan-Hellenic" in some respects, but still very different from anything spoken in any part of Greece; it is laced with archaic or esoteric words, some of

them perhaps intra-epic coinages, which puzzled even the Greeks not long
after the epics were written down, and with many words whose vowels are
lengthened or shortened to make them fit into the demanding dactylic
meter, not the most "natural" meter for normal Greek of any dialect. There
are five different forms of the infinitive "to be," for example, each with a
different metrical form – very useful for composing on the spot in dactylic
hexameter, but remote from the actual usage of any Greek community. It is
what the Germans call a *Kunstsprache*, or art-language.

   In the *Iliad* there are almost 1,100 ἅπαξ λεγόμενα (*hapax legomena*),
which means "once-said things" – that is, words that occur only once; the
Odyssey has over 800. Many of these words recur in later Greek texts, but
between the two epics there are about 500 "absolute" *hapax legomena*,
words that recur nowhere else in extant Greek literature. We have lost the
great bulk of written Greek literature and, of course, all oral poetry that
remained only oral, so we can only guess how esoteric and distinctly epic
some of these words were, but it is safe to say that Homer, even in the
eighth century BCE, at times sounded obscure and strange.

   Many words have unknown etymologies, and even if they occur more
than once we can only infer their meaning from their contexts. It wouldn't
be so difficult to do so if the context varied, but sometimes these words are
epithets that modify the same noun each time they appear. The word
ēlibatos, for example, occurs six times in Homer, but always as an epithet of
petrē, which seems to mean "rock" or "rocky cliff"; that suggests *ēlibatos*
means "steep" or "lofty" or maybe "enormous," but it is hard to be sure.
Some words, too, were probably generated through mistakes in interpret-
ing the lines. "Asphodel," for example, the flower of the underworld, and
the source of our word "daffodil," may not have been a flower at all at first.
The word may have arisen from hearers' mistaking the phrase *kata sphodelon leimona* as *kat' asphodelon leimona* ("down the asphodel meadow,"
three times in the *Odyssey*); *sphodelon* may have been an old and unfamiliar
word, not understood by later generations of Greeks; it may be akin to the
noun *spodos*, meaning "ashes," and "ashen" is surely a more likely epithet
for a meadow in Hades than something flowery. Once the pseudo-word
asphodelon got accidentally generated, people took it for a flower of some
kind, and it both entered into the common inheritance of poets and got
attached to various real flowers.[14] So we can thank the artificial and archaic
poetic diction of Homer, if this conjecture is right, for one of our most
poetic flowers.

   The first epics in Greek, then, were prime perpetrators of poetic diction,
and they were the model for all subsequent epics in Greek and Latin, and

then in the modern languages until well into the nineteenth century and even the twentieth. Recent translators of Homer invariably try for some sort of normal – if dignified – English, and some go very far toward casual and idiomatic diction in order to capture what they take to be his vigor and speed. Such an approach is no doubt needed for producing a version people will enjoy reading today, but the results give a very misleading impression of the effect Homer had on his original audience.

With lyric poetry, the situation is similar, for Homer's influence was great on Sappho, Pindar, and many other Greek lyricists; they in turn were models for Roman poets; and so it went among the tribes of vernacular poets up to recent times. Indeed, it was in part the inheritance of Latin poetry in all genres that defined the peculiar diction of English poetry in certain of its phases. Milton has been berated for his Latinisms, such as, to take a notorious example, his description of a bush "with frizzled hair implicit" (*PL* 7.323). "Implicit" here evokes its Latin etymology more vividly than does its usual meaning ("implied, tacit"): *implicitus* comes from *implicatus*, the participle of *implicare* ("to enfold, entangle, entwine"); Catullus uses it of a vine on a tree (61.35, 103–04). It is easy to smile at instances like this one, but Milton is not notably more Latinate than many other poets, as Sherbo has shown,[15] and, in any case, his uses of Latin roots are often interesting and effective, unless you insist that poets are obliged to speak the real language of men. Milton may have smiled over "implicit" himself, as he realized that he was making explicit the sense that is implicit in "implicit." For thousands of years, audiences were happy to listen to a special sort of language, not only metered and (later) rhymed, but filled with archaic or esoteric words and phrases. There were revolts from time to time against this language even among the ancients, and satires of it in verse, but it kept drawing new audiences down to very recent times. This "language within a language" in the poet Paul Valéry's phrase (*Art of Poetry* 64), makes demands on to   eaders who are not used to it, but if modern poetry has abandoned this special diction it has more than made up for it with its notorious difficulties – in allusion, density of imagery, disruptions of syntax, shifts of tone and register, abrupt changes of subject, and so on – as found in Eliot, Pound, Ashbery, Muldoon, and many others.

Style

A common exercise in literature classes is the writing of a "précis" of a poem or another literary work, which is a summary or abstract of it. It is often an excellent thing to do in preparation for writing a critical essay, even if you don't make use of it explicitly in the end. To boil down Wordsworth's "Tintern Abbey," a poem of 160 lines, into a précis of, say, 160 words, forces you to think hard about the argument, the structure, the dramatic situation, the dominant image(s), the point or moral – in short, the poem as a whole, as if seen from a middle distance where the details recede. If you have done this well, when you return to the details – the exact wording, the tone, the pacing, the syntactic quirks, the figures of speech, the varying emphases the meter creates, and so on – you will be much better able to show how these things fit together and elaborate or "express" the whole. As the word "précis" (taken from French) suggests, it is an exercise in precision as well as reduction; it is to get things precisely right, and thereby clear up whatever vague ideas have been floating through your mind as you were distracted by the details in your first few readings of the poem.

That said, the process of distilling a poem into its essence or core lures you into thinking that the rest of the poem is secondary, mere elaboration, so much poetic decoration or fluff. Perhaps some poems, some routine products of the eighteenth century, for instance, with their predictable "feathered tribes" and the like, or the Hallmark greeting-card factory, might seem to fall into these two halves: a commonplace thought about virtue or marriage dressed up in conventional clichés. Even the Homeric epics, because of their formulaic character, may tempt us to see the verbal details as quite secondary to the story. But with all poems, even bad or unoriginal ones, the division between *what* is said and *how* it is said, between body and dress, between message and medium, between content and form, is misleading, and may be fatal to understanding and appreciating them. Dryden's comment that "Words are the colouring of the work" ("Preface" to *Fables*), and Pope's famous line "What oft was thought but ne'er so well express'd" ("Essay on Criticism" 298), both assume the same dichotomy, implying that the same "work" might be verbally "colored" in many different hues, or that for every thought there are many expressions of it, some better than others. That dichotomy might be true of a certain kind of work or a certain kind of "thought," such as a proverbial truth or nugget of wisdom, but it is a travesty of thinking to reduce it to a set of separable truisms of this kind, and it is a travesty of a poem to consider it an outline or structure with words painted on it.

This dichotomy was one of the targets of the New Critics of the mid twentieth century. Cleanth Brooks called it "the heresy of paraphrase." If we try to make an adequate paraphrase of a poem, the closer we come to adequacy the more nuance, complexity, ambiguity, or irony we will have to accommodate, until we have composed something much longer than the poem itself and not nearly as impressive. The texture of a poem – or at least the texture of a rich and interesting poem – is so interwoven with its structure and argument that to separate them is to unravel the poem. To think otherwise, Brooks suggests, is crude, reductive, and even "heretical."

Still, the effort is worth making. To try for a good précis of a poem is both to lay bare something of its structural features and overall "point," and to come to a recognition of the disparity between what is revealed this way and the poem's richness of detail, and especially the felt experience of living through the poem. That recognition should make us rethink and regroup in a fruitful way. It is useful to do this, I have found, in preparation for translating a poem into another language: the translated poem may lose most of the sound and many of the nuances of meaning of the original, but it had better preserve the larger features or it will hardly be a translation at all.

I would add that some reductive travesties earn their keep by being funny, such as this version of Keats's "Ode on a Grecian Urn" in monometer couplets by Desmond Skirrow:

> Gods chase
> Round vase.
> What say?
> What play?
> Don't know.
> Nice, though.

Skirrow's travesty – not even half a "tweet" in length – leaves out quite a bit of the ode, to put it mildly, but it also lets the air out of Keats's sometimes windy and repetitive rhetoric. Perhaps that rhetoric can be defended and integrated into an adequate interpretation of the whole poem, but it is nonetheless bracing to see this cheeky twelve-word deflation of a poem usually approached with reverence.

Under the label "style," I hope to pull together a few ideas already raised in this book and to investigate a few new ones having to do with nuances of poetry. "Style" is a questionable word to use here, I admit, and for two reasons. It is much more often used to refer to prose than poetry, perhaps because of the sheer variety of poetic modes today. More important, it seems to have fallen prey to the dichotomy I have been discussing, and to confine itself to the superficial or external side of it. The style section of newspapers is all about clothing, hair-dos, accessories, and maybe home furnishings, while "stylist," which used to mean someone who wrote distinctively and well, now means someone who works in a hair salon or on a movie set. The etymology of the word nudges its meaning toward this secondary terrain: it comes from Latin *stilus* (not *stylus*), the writing implement, and when a man's *stilus* was discussed, it might first have meant his handwriting or penmanship before it meant his mode or manner of writing, or of speaking. As one's "hand" does not alter the meaning of the letters or words one writes, "style" in this sense is decorative only. In English, it never meant handwriting, but it often bore the comparable "inessential" sense summed up in Lord Chesterfield's dictum, "Style is the dress of thoughts," quoted in the *OED*.

There is a much more interesting and useful definition of style that the New Critics developed, though with many partial precedents. William Wimsatt notes that ancient rhetoricians, when they analyzed the meaning of a speech, found that "there remains an irreducible something that is superficial, a kind of scum—which they call style."[16] On the contrary, "That which has for centuries been called style differs from the rest of writing only in that it is one plane or level of the organization of meaning; it would not be happy to call it the outer cover or the last layer; rather it is the furthest elaboration of the one concept that is the center" (11). That definition assumes that the work has a pervasive unity across its levels, with one concept at its center, whereas we might want to use style in Wimsatt's sense even of works that are poorly unified. As Monroe Beardsley puts it, "the style of a literary work consists of the recurrent features of its texture of meaning," and "style is detail of meaning or small-scale meaning."[17] These two kindred definitions may seem counter-intuitive because we have imbibed the familiar dichotomy between message (meaning) and decoration (style), and perhaps in part also because in an early phase of generative linguistics, in the 1960s, when it was just becoming well known, there was an effort to keep syntax and semantics distinct and independent of one another, and, as we saw, some linguists assumed the meaning of a sentence will remain constant when the sentence is transformed from active to passive, or vice versa.

If we take Beardsley's definition of "style" seriously, we find that no two sentences have exactly the same meaning, and no two words are synonymous. And surely such shades of meaning are the life of poetry. Meaning goes all the way down, or all the way up: everything is meaningful. In the end, it may be that we are drawn to a poem for more than its meaning – we find it mesmerizing or fun for its rhythms and rhymes, for instance – but a concept of style as an affair of meaning is still crucial, I would argue, for a thorough understanding of it.

Style is partly a matter of diction – what Aristotle called *lexis*; it can often be described by studying word choices among possible near-synonyms.

Diction here is not the "poetic diction" we have been discussing, which is a narrower category, but rather the selection of a word (or phrase) among the field of possible candidates, "poetic" or otherwise, to fill a position in a sentence. Keats begins his "Ode to a Nightingale" this way: "My heart aches, and a drowsy numbness pains / My sense." The seeming contradiction here – numbness causing pain – tempts us to speculate about what other words Keats might have used, and what meaning or effect is created by just the words he chose. We might try:

> my [soul, spirit, core] aches
> my heart [hurts, throbs, smarts, yearns]

We would have twenty possible combinations if we add just these options, only one of which Keats chose. Some of these we might rule out as awkward, funny-sounding ("heart smarts"), or whatever, but we should be on our guard against assuming that the Great Poet made unerring choices and all these others are inadequate. If the only version we knew began "My soul throbs," I suspect many readers would take it as definitive and unimprovable. But, of course, each phrase is at least somewhat different from the others, and will bring a different meaning into the poem it launches. For "drowsy numbness" we might have "[sleepy, lazy, weary] [dullness, deadness, coldness]" – using examples that preserve the meter – and each of these phrases has distinct nuances. For "pains my sense" we could try "[hurts, wounds, stings] my [feeling, mind, body, limbs]": the difficulty of finding even a distant synonym for "sense" here tells us something about Keats's sometimes unusual choices.

We can usefully consider such alternatives in any poem. I riffled through an anthology at random and put my finger on one by Gary Snyder, which begins:

> I went into the Maverick Bar
> In Farmington, New Mexico.
> And drank double shots of bourbon
> backed with beer.

What can we say about this style? The last phrase has an air of inevitability about it, alliterating nicely with "bourbon" and making a frame rhyme, "beer" and "Bar." But "backed" seems a tad overdone, and we might wonder why bourbon, which is much stronger than beer, needs beer's backing. Alternatives suggest themselves. Why not "between beers"? Or "after every beer"? Or "broken up by beers"? By coming up with reasons to eliminate these possibilities, we gain a better understanding of what

Snyder in fact wrote, whether or not we think it was inevitable in this context. These alternatives would not change the poem's blunt and informal register, but they would change its style, its details of meaning, a little. As they stand, the lines hint, perhaps, that the Maverick Bar is a little menacing, a place where one might need to prove one's manhood, and that double shots of bourbon by themselves won't quite cut it, so they must be backed, or the drinker must be backed, by a more down-to-earth drink, as a knight or bishop on the chessboard had better be backed by pawns.

A set of words or phrases like "drowsy," "sleepy," "somnolent," and so on, which are in paradigmatic or "vertical" relationship to a comparable word in a sentence, composes a "semantic field" or "domain." Under the label "color," for example, the words "red," "orange," "yellow," and so on would belong to the same field – that is, they are "hyponyms" (Greek for "undernames") of "color." Under the domain "red," we have quite a few hyponyms, such as "carmine," "crimson," "magenta," "scarlet," and "vermilion." Most domains are more complicated than colors, such as "meal," which might range from "eats," "chow," and "mess" to "picnic," "luncheon," and "fine dining." Such fields are criss-crossed with registers or levels of politeness, social ideologies, and regional or dialectal associations. Sets of words or phrases that share a denotation or primary meaning may have very different registers: as in "urinate," "micturate," "pass water," "piss," and "pee." (Domains about intimate bodily parts or acts are good examples of such diversity.) Even how we pronounce a word may convey a different nuance. An old half-serious example would be "vase": if it costs less than 10 dollars, it is a /ves/; if it costs between 10 and 100 dollars, it is a /vez/; if it costs more than 100 dollars, it is a /vaz/. (This case also reveals the prestige of French in certain circles.)

Understanding a poem is a kind of reverse engineering. We are given a contraption: to find out how it works, we take it apart and look at all its springs, sprockets, and spirals until we see what everything does and how it connects with everything else. If we want to duplicate it but lack some parts, or if we want to reassemble the original but a piece has gone missing, we consider substitutes or "workarounds" or fixes. We are given a poem (which Auden calls a contraption): we take it apart and put it back together, and to enhance our grasp of it, even though we haven't lost any of its pieces, we may ponder other possibilities. Why this word, and not that?

A good way to reverse-engineer a poem, of course, is to find out how it was engineered in the first place, and sometimes poets have obliged us by leaving behind their drafts or early versions. Helen Vendler gives an

interesting account of the adjective choices Emily Dickinson mulled ov
as she wrote her poem "The Bible is an antique Volume" (#1577).[18] The
poet notes that to most boys the Bible stories are dull, "Written by faded
Men," but if they could be told in a different way they would draw the boys
back. She drafts these lines:

> Had but the Tale a _____ Teller –
> All the Boys would come –

She needs a good adjective, in trochaic form, and she makes a list of
candidates, including "thrilling," her first choice, and then thirteen
more: "typic, hearty, bonnie, breathless, spacious, tropic, warbling, ardent,
friendly, magic, pungent, winning, mellow." If we projected a semantic
field of terms meaning something like "attractive to boys" and appropriate
to both Bible stories and a preacher who retells them, we would come up
with some of these; others, such as "typic" and "tropic," having to do with
modes of biblical interpretation, might not have occurred to us. Try
substituting one – say, "breathless," which would alliterate nicely with
"Boys" – and connote the passion or enthusiasm of the teller, as if he had
just run into the pulpit or Sunday-school class with exciting news, indeed
the Good News. If she had settled on "breathless," we would no doubt
consider it *le mot juste*, the inevitable word, and find justifications for it in
the rest of the poem. As it turns out, she settled on "warbling," a little
surprising at first, as it brings a bird into the poem. Vendler thinks it must
go back to Milton's famous description of the young Shakespeare who
would "Warble his native Wood-notes wild" ("L'Allegro" 134), and
Dickinson's next lines are about the "Sermon" of the legendary bard
Orpheus, which attracted not only boys but animals and trees. But
Dickinson may also be hinting that it would be better for the boys to
skip church altogether and listen to a bird instead, as she says in poem #236:
"Some – keep the Sabbath – going to church – / I – keep it – staying at
Home – / With a Bobolink – for a Chorister." In any case, by looking at the
roads not taken, we can understand the poem's path more fully, whether
we have the poet's early versions or we conjure up a set of options hovering
paradigmatically above the final text.

Style also has much to do with syntax, with the order of words and
phrases. Here are two sentences that would seem to have the same basic
meaning:

(1)   No one ever loved him but Sarah.
(2)   Sarah was the only one who ever loved him.

But there are differences. We might say that between the first and second sentences the order of information units is reversed. In sentence (1), we first get (a) "No one ever," and for a split second, as we take in this extreme abstract negative, we wonder what no one ever did. Then we learn that it is (b) "loved him" that no one ever did, and as we take in this nugget we might feel sad for him: the sentence could end there and still be a sentence. But it doesn't: we learn (c) Sarah loved him, so our passing sorrow is checked, at least until we learn more in later sentences, or weigh it against what we have already learned about him. In sentence (2), Sarah (a) is named first and remains the focus, while we learn (b) she is the only one who ever did something. Did what? Loved him (c). Our attention is on Sarah until the end, whereas in sentence (1) it is on "no one" and then "him" until the end. If it is only the result that matters, then these sentences have the same meaning, but meaning in the fullest sense should include the path to the result, the journey and not just the arrival; if that is so, then we have been put through different experiences, very rapid of course – perhaps too rapidly for conscious consideration as we go – but nonetheless real.

The doling out of key information-bits in either sentence could be delayed with subordinate clauses:

(3)   No one ever loved him, despite his many acts of kindness, but Sarah.
(4)   Sarah, more perceptive about hidden virtues than any of her friends, was the only one who ever loved him.

But even without such insertions, the two sentences have different foci and emphases, and thus slightly different meanings.

Some linguists, notably Knud Lambrecht, would distinguish the *meaning* of a sentence from the *information* conveyed by the utterance of it, which depends on the mental states of the speaker and hearer. They treat such matters as "topic," "focus," and "givenness," which depend in part on what is presupposed between interlocutors. To take an example from Lambrecht, if I say "I finally met the woman who moved in downstairs," I presuppose that my hearer already knows that a woman moved in downstairs some time ago; what is news is that I met her.[19] Presuppositions and contexts of many kinds determine the "information structure" of sentences. In the end, it seems to me, this level of "information" can be assimilated into what Wimsatt and Beardsley mean by "meaning," though it is useful to keep in mind the subtleties of emphasis, focus, and the like that might elude semantic analysis.

Under the rubric of syntax, we might notice a great range of things poets do. Some poets are more given to the active voice, others to the passive.

Some tend to use noun phrases, others verb phrases. Some use short sentences, others long. The opening verse-paragraph of Shelley's "Mont Blanc," for example, consists of one 84-word sentence spun out over eleven lines. Wordsworth was fond of negative forms and phrases – "unripe fruits"; "uncertain notice"; "houseless woods"; "unremembered pleasure"; "no trivial influence"; "unremembered acts"; "Nor less, I trust"; "unintelligible world"; "joyless daylight"; "fretful stir / Unprofitable; no need of a remoter charm"; "Not for this / Faint I, nor mourn nor murmur" (all of these from "Tintern Abbey") – which somewhat muffle his argument, making it seem less assertive, or more tentative, perhaps more like the process of thinking as distinct from the product.

Richard Bradford reminds us that all poems, except prose poems, have a "double pattern": one based on the sentence and dependent on the rules of syntax, the other based on the line and dependent on the rules of meter and rhyme.[20] Poetic style, when it is not mainly a matter of diction, might seem to be a function more of syntax than of meter and rhyme, but in a well-made poem the nuances of meaning in a sentence will be inflected by how the sentence occupies the line, and how meter and rhyme bring out or subdue certain words.

Some poets prefer coordinated clauses, some subordinated. Shakespeare's sonnets tend toward coordination, that is, sequences of independent clauses, and they are very often arranged one to a line:

> Shall I compare thee to a summer's day?
> Thou art more lovely and more temperate.
> Rough winds do shake the darling buds of May,
> And summer's lease hath all too short a date.
> Sometime too hot the eye of heaven shines,
> And often is his gold complexion dimmed;
> And every fair from fair sometime declines,
> By chance or nature's changing course untrimmed.

Note the three instances of "and" that begin lines in this octave (from Sonnet 18), and the presence of a finite verb in every line but the last. Yeats, as we saw in Chapter 5, leaned toward complex sentences with subordinate clauses: he might devote an eight-line stanza to one intricate sentence. Here is another, from "Nineteen Hundred and Nineteen," only a little looser:

> He who can read the signs nor sink unmanned
> Into the half-deceit of some intoxicant
> From shallow wits; who knows no work can stand,
> Whether health, wealth or peace of mind were spent
> On master-work of intellect or hand,

No honour leave its mighty monument,
Has but one comfort left: all triumph would
But break upon his ghostly solitude.

Here are two parallel subordinate who-clauses, the first of which has two
coordinate parts (with the verb phrases "can read" and "sink"), and the
second of which has two parallel independent clauses as objects of the verb
"know" and each beginning with "no"; the first of these, beginning "no
work can stand," has a subordinate clause beginning with "whether" and
occupying all of lines 4 and 5, while the second (line 6) implicitly imports
the "can" from line 3. (Line 6 means something like "[And knows that] No
honorable deed can leave behind a mighty monument" – that is, such a
monument cannot stand.) The first six lines are one big noun phrase, held
together not only by its complex syntax but by the same two alternating
rhymes, and the main verb is "has" (7). The complex sentence occupies an
ottava rima stanza, and that line structure can affect how we weigh some of
the words. It gives a little extra weight, for instance, to the final word of line
7, "would," the first rhyme of the closing couplet. Had "would" appeared
elsewhere, say at the beginning of the final line, we would not dwell on it,
but placed as it is we give it a little more emphasis, taking it not merely as
the conditional auxiliary but as expressing perhaps its older sense of will
and willfulness: triumph, here almost personified, wants to break upon his
solitude, but it won't, because it can't.

Yeats's syntactic structure is a matter of style, of details and nuances of
meaning, quite apart from the hold that ottava rima has on it. We could
rearrange Yeats's intricate sentence into something more coordinated and
informal, but it would require some repetition, take more space, and
probably anticipate the main point too early. By postponing the verb
and its object to the end of the stanza, Yeats makes us dwell at length on
a kind of courageous and clear-sighted intellect while saving something
quite striking for the climax: a man with a mind like that would be
indifferent even to his own triumphs (meaning triumphal parades or
celebrations, perhaps), which would no more disturb his spiritual withdrawal than breaking waves disturb a rocky shore. We might go further: the
very complexity, concision, and elegance of the sentence, much more like
public oratory than everyday speech, conveys a sense of mastery and
detachment akin to the ghostly solitude it praises; it enacts its meaning.
It is the refined product of thought rather than, as with "Tintern Abbey,"
its process or evolution.

Sometimes the meaning of a line or set of lines depends on what
emphasis you give a word or phrase, and, since poems are not bits of real

conversation between people who share knowledge and experience, it is often difficult to know how to stress them. The meter is not always definitive. To take another case from Yeats, in "Among School Children" there is this passage (13–16):

> and it seemed that our two natures blent
> Into a sphere from youthful sympathy,
> Or else, to alter Plato's parable,
> Into the yolk and white of the one shell.

How do you recite the third line? If you stress "Plato's parable," which seems natural, since we've had nothing about Plato before, you imply that the parable, though altered, is described in the next line and has something to do with an egg. (I am referring to a stress or emphasis on top of the metrical stress.) But if you stress "alter" more, which seems less normal at first, you imply the parable is mentioned in the previous two lines and is about blending into a sphere. Passages in Plato might be cited on behalf of either reading, but surely it makes more sense to stress "alter": an egg is an altered sphere, after all.

It is often important to keep the whole poem in mind as you cast about for the right way to emphasize a line and thereby interpret it. Earlier we discussed Keats's famous lines at the end of "Ode on a Grecian Urn" and the importance of keeping the second-person pronouns straight.

> When old age shall this generation waste,
> Thou shalt remain, in midst of other woe
> Than ours, a friend to man, to whom thou say'st,
> Beauty is truth, truth beauty, —that is all
> Ye know on earth, and all ye need to know.

But how do you recite the famous five-word formula? Since this is an urn speaking, we might try to imagine what it is like to be a 2,500-year-old urn and decide to speak in a kind of slow oracular monotone, in a voice analogous to something chiseled in marble, whatever that might be, but in any case giving equal weight to all four nouns. That is how I used to recite it, and how most people still recite it. But that is to assume no context for the urn's pronouncement, no conversation with the human interlocutor who has been speaking all the poem up to the last two lines, no presupposition of "information" that they share. It's true the urn has said nothing until now, but if it is capable of speaking, we may assume it has been listening, very patiently, to the somewhat verbose fellow who has been walking all around it, and peering in and stepping back, and talking to it for almost five stanzas. Mostly the speaker has been asking it questions, ten in all, and they are questions about the facts of the matter: What legend is this? What men or gods? Where is this or that event taking place? He has been seeking the "truth" about what has been sculpted on the urn, and while he has said a few things about its beauty he is mainly obsessed with getting the story or stories straight. I would therefore argue that, having endured enough of this interrogation ("Just the facts, miss"), the urn puts the detective in his place by saying "*Beauty* is truth." You've been seeking the truth: give it up; I am beautiful; that is truth enough. Of course, the urn goes on to say "truth [is] beauty," but as that equation comes second, the urn seems to mean that the only kind of truth that matters (as opposed to the facts you've been searching for) is beautiful: it must strike your heart or imagination and carry its own conviction.[21]

Earl Anderson gives many examples of what he calls "syntactic iconism," such as the matching of word order with event-order: "He caught a cold after spending the day in the rain" is not "iconic," but "After spending the day in the rain he caught a cold" is. Another type is the repetition of words or phrases, which can imitate the passing of time because it takes more time to say them. To add my own examples to Anderson's: Macbeth bemoans the dreary meaninglessness of time by saying "tomorrow" three times in one line (5.5.19), while Wordsworth lengthens his five years away from the River Wye by beginning "Tintern Abbey" with "five" three times and two forms of "long": "Five years have past; five summers, with the length / Of five long winters!" Parataxis or coordination of clauses can be iconic of simple succession of events or perceptions:

> I was angry with my friend;
> I told my wrath, my wrath did end.
> I was angry with my foe:
> I told it not, my wrath did grow.   (Blake, "A Poison Tree")

Hypotaxis or subordination of clauses can resemble the complexity of an abstract idea or relationship, as we can see in a notoriously complex (and often misread) 47-word clause in Shelley's sonnet "Ozymandias."

> I met a traveller from an antique land,
> Who said—"Two vast and trunkless legs of stone
> Stand in the desert . . . Near them, on the sand,
> Half sunk a shattered visage lies, whose frown,
> And wrinkled lip, and sneer of cold command,   5
> Tell that its sculptor well those passions read
> Which yet survive, stamped on these lifeless things,

> The hand that mocked them, and the heart that fed;
> And on the pedestal, these words appear:
> My name is Ozymandias, King of Kings,   10
> Look on my works, ye Mighty, and despair!
> Nothing beside remains. Round the decay
> Of that colossal Wreck, boundless and bare
> The lone and level sands stretch far away."—

The clause spans five and a half lines, from 3 to 8, stopping at the octave-sestet break. The main or independent clause within it takes a little more than a line – "Near them, on the sand, / Half sunk a shattered visage lies" – and its three brief modifying phrases, two of them prepositional phrases, draw our sight in three stages from vague location to more detailed description of the visage, iconically to the way we might actually discover it if we were poking around the statue. We might note the somewhat artificial verb-final structure here, but it was common enough, as we saw in Chapter 5, and it does little to weaken the expressive force of the larger syntactic pattern. The subordinate clause, beginning with "whose," first lists three features of the visage, possibly in the order we might notice them as we drew closer to it – frown (forehead), lip, and sneer (presumably the nose) – and also in increasing phrase-length, with "frown" unadorned, "lip" with an adjective, and "sneer" modified with an alliterating phrase. That phrase, "cold command," takes us beyond visual description to surmise about what brought about the sneer, and it leads to a surmise about the sculptor.

These three features are the subject of the verb "tell," and what they tell is a that-clause, namely, "its sculptor well those passions read" (the passions expressed by the frown and sneer), with another postponed verb. The that-clause embraces another subordinate clause, a which-clause that attaches to "passions." The which-clause at first seems brief – "Which yet survive" – because we take "survive" as intransitive, but it is not; it takes two objects, "hand" and "heart," each of them with subordinate that-clauses, which together occupy the fourth rank of this nest-within-nest construction. The passions survive or outlive the hand that mocked (mimicked) them, the sculptor's, and the heart that fed them, the king's. What holds us up for a moment is the interrupting clause "stamped on these lifeless things." Shelley wanted it there, I think, to point the contrast between "survive" and "lifeless" in the same line, as well as to direct our attention a moment longer to the shattered visage lying in front of us before taking us back to the time when the king and his sculptor were still alive, an order of events plausibly like what we would go through on the site as we first examined the broken visage and then speculated on its origin, as well as the irony (brought out in the sestet) that something the sculptor did to lifeless stone is the only "life" left of this once-arrogant pharaoh.

This is a tour de force of a sentence, iconic in several ways, but mostly leaving us with the sense of an intricate thought intricately but precisely expressed. On top of all that, Shelley inserts two alliterating pairs – "cold command" and "hand/heart" – the first two of four in the poem, as well as sustaining the meter and setting up an unusual rhyme scheme, where "things" in the octave rhymes with "Kings" in the sestet, the only rhyme to cross the gap.

Meaning and Enjambment

Another feature of poetic style is the use of enjambment, which often goes with complex hypotactic sentences, or at least long ones. Enjambment is the continuation or carrying over of a syntactic unit from one line to the next; it is French for "straddling" and derives from *jambe* ("leg"), which also shows up in English "jamb," the "leg" of a door. "Ozymandias" has some examples of it. Line 2 ends with "stone," and that is the last word of the noun phrase that serves as the subject of the verb "Stand" that begins line 3. Lines 12 and 13 also end with the expectation of another phrase; the clauses are incomplete at their lines' end.

There are degrees of enjambment. For extreme cases of it, take this stanza of Timothy Steele's "Sapphics Against Anger":

> May I recall what Aristotle says of
> The subject: to give vent to rage is not to
> Release it but to be increasingly prone
> To its incursions.

It is striking to see a preposition detached from its object between lines 1 and 2, an infinitive split between 2 and 3, and the separation of the adjectival phrase "prone / To its incursions" between 3 and 4, especially in a classical stanza form. Sappho occasionally enjambed her lines, but not like this.

For a more ambiguous case, look at the first two lines of the *Iliad*:

> μῆνιν ἄειδε θεὰ Πηληϊάδεω Ἀχιλῆος
> mēnin aeide t^hea, Pēlēiadeō Ak^hilēos
> Wrath sing goddess of Peleus' son Achilles

> οὐλομένην, ἣ μυρί' Ἀχαιοῖς ἄλγε' ἔθηκε,
> oulomenēn, hē muri' Ak^haiois alge' et^hēke.
> ruinous, which on thousands of Achaeans griefs put.

Line 1 is a complete clause by itself, so there is no sense that the syntax leans forward over the line; there is nothing missing. But then an adjective shows up at the beginning of line 2, and it modifies "wrath" (both are in the feminine singular accusative), so in retrospect the line is enjambed. When we read the *Iliad* in English translation, we usually find a phrase like "ruinous wrath" in the first line, so we are unaware of how Homer separated the adjective from its noun; several recent translators, however, such as Fitzgerald and Fagles, have contrived to imitate Homer's order, with "wrath" first and "ruinous" much later. It is a feature of Homer's oral style that enjambments are loose, unperiodic, or concatenary.[22]

A similar semi-enjambment was taken seriously enough to ignite an uproar in the theatre. The opening speech of Victor Hugo's *Hernani* (1830) violated the strict classical rules against enjambments:

> Serait-ce déjà lui? C'est bien à l'escalier
> Would this be already him? It must be by the stairway
> Dérobé. Vite, ouvrons. Bonjour, beau cavalier.
> Hidden. Quick, let's open. Good day, fine cavalier.

Line 1 ends satisfactorily with *l'escalier*, and the caesura is placed in the middle where it belongs. But when conservatives heard *dérobé* in the next line, they could take it as an enjambment, and it set their teeth on edge. Hisses and hoots began.

Enjambment can have subtle effects on meaning, and a thoughtful poet will take into consideration the interaction of line and syntax. Here are three lines from the final stanza of Keats's "To Autumn":

> Then in a wailful choir the small gnats mourn
> Among the river sallows, borne aloft
> Or sinking as the light wind lives or dies[.]

If the first of these lines were end-stopped we would have a satisfactory syntactic period, but in this stanza filled with sounds Keats makes a point of locating them spatially as well (the lambs bleat on the hills, the red-breast whistles in the croft, and so on), so the mournful gnats are placed down by the river, among the sallows (willows), traditionally associated with mourning themselves. It is hard to pin down this little effect, whereby information is given to us in a certain order: we *hear* the gnats, and think about their dirge-like song for a second, and then they are taken, it seems, some distance from us, and we *see* them. And what we see is how they are moved. The second line ends with a stronger enjambed connection, for "borne aloft" leaves us expecting something to complete the period, maybe an agent ("by breezes") or direction ("to treetops") – in any case something about their upward movement. But instead we get another possibility, "sinking," a little surprise, and then in the same line the reason for the two movements: the wind "lives or dies." The third line is not enjambed, and certainly it must not be, as "lives or dies" is an arresting pair of verbs to apply to the wind; the reader needs a moment to take it in, before moving on to the other scenes that close this lovely poem.

Meaning and Rhyme

Rhyme and other sound-similarities between words seem random, discon-nected from their meanings. If, according to Saussure, any signifier can be linked to any signified (the famous "arbitrariness of the sign"), then the fact that various signifiers sound like various other signifiers is an accident of no significance. "Breath" and "death" happen to rhyme in English, and that fact has certainly seemed significant – they do belong together – to many poets and their readers, but their equivalents don't rhyme in French (*souffle* and *mort*), or German (*Hauch*, or *Atem*, and *Tod*), or Japanese (*iki* and *shibō*), and they didn't always rhyme even in English. It would be absurd to claim that their meanings are more deeply congruent, or more starkly opposite, or whatever we like, in modern English than in the great majority of other tongues. Besides, the earliest attested meaning of "breath" in Old and Middle English is "odor" or "reek." A similar inevitable pair, "womb" and "tomb," have very different origins, "womb" belonging to the Germanic heritage (and usually pronounced /wamb/ in Old English), and "tomb" taken from Anglo-Norman, which inherited it from Latin, which took it from Greek.

Meaning, as analyzed by linguists and most literary critics, is an entirely separate affair from the sounds that carry it. It is almost as if the sensuous or corporeal side of language is an embarrassment to the spiritual or intellectual side, or is at best tolerated as a kind of sideshow that draws an audience in or provides an occasional extra shiver of meaning. In professional analyses of poetry, meaning or sense almost always takes priority.[23]

If, on the other hand, onomatopoeia is a larger factor than most linguists believe, then we might make a case that it is not entirely by chance that some words rhyme or alliterate or echo each other in some way. Words sometimes sound like what they mean, and if the signifieds of two signifiers are similar, it might happen naturally that the two signifiers are similar, or grow similar over time. Perhaps, when "breath" came to be connected with "life" rather than "stink," it attracted "death" to it for the meaning but also altered the sound of "death" from a diphthong (deəθ) to a monophthong (dε̱θ) so they would rhyme. Perhaps the vowels in "womb" and "tomb" also influenced each other. Perhaps not, but words do pair up and affect each other's fortunes: "birds and bees, black and blue, each and every, house and home, pots and pans, thick and thin, right and wrong," and so on. Would we still use the word "foe" if we didn't have the phrase "friend or foe"? Or "odds" without "odds and ends"? Or "kith" detached from "kin"? Or either "spick" or "span" alone? These alliterative couples hint that sounds and meanings are not always marriages arranged by arbitrary forces, but are sometimes love matches.

Wherever we stand on the arbitrariness question, we can readily appreciate poets' uses of "semantic rhyme" – that is, rhyme that seems significant. At its simplest, that significance may lie in an emphasis of similarity of meaning. "Through the likeness [of sound]," Auden writes, "thoughts and feelings hitherto distinct in the mind are joined together. They are, in fact, sound metaphors."[24] In the opening of Milton's "Lycidas" we meet a pair of rhymes we might call semantic:

> Yet once more, O ye Laurels, and once more
> Ye myrtles brown, with Ivy never sere,
> I come to pluck your Berries harsh and crude,
> And with forc'd fingers rude,
> Shatter your leaves before the mellowing year.

The rich rhyme of "crude" and "rude" underlines the similarity between the unmellow berries and the unmellow fingers that pluck them too soon. The "sere" and "year" rhyme (which continues in four more words in this section) is somewhat more subtle, however, if we take it as "semantic" at all: perhaps in bringing out a contrast between the evergreen character of ivy, as well as laurel and myrtle, all symbols of immortal fame in poetry, and the changing seasons of the year – though if the plants were really never sere, the year would not shatter their leaves.

For an example of a rhyme that works a difference within similarity, we may return to stanza 3 of Blake's "London":

> How the Chimney-sweepers cry
> Every blackning Church appalls,
> And the hapless Soldiers sigh,
> Runs in blood down Palace walls[.]

We first notice the parallel between "cry" and "sigh," both nouns, already similar in meaning. When we met "cry," however, we probably registered its sense as "call" – that is, one of the many "street cries" of London meant to drum up business, in this case perhaps "Sweep, sweep!" But then "sigh," coming from a dying soldier, activates the other prominent sense of "cry" as a loud expression of pain, loud and terrible enough to turn the church pale, presumably with guilt, though it is also blackening, perhaps in some moral sense. Elsewhere, Blake tells us the sweeper cries "weep weep in notes of woe." The other rhymes enforce this parallel between two young victims compelled by oppressive institutions to do their bidding, each of which changes color as a result. If we were unsure just how metaphorically to take "blackning" and "appalls," the inescapably concrete meaning of "walls" implies that we are to imagine the blood, and so by extension the simultaneous paling and darkening of the church, as literal, if apocalyptic, transformations.

Pope is famous for his extremely skillful, and often very witty, rhymes.

> Whether the nymph shall break Diana's law,
> Or some frail China jar receive a flaw.

In a still influential article of 1944, Wimsatt notices the chiastic structure of this couplet: line 1 moves from breakage to fragile thing (law), while line 2 moves from fragile thing (jar) to breakage, a pattern that he finds brings out the similarity-in-contrast (Wimsatt, "One Relation" 162). We will add what might be obvious. The two rhyme-words (in fact in rich rhyme), both nouns, certainly contrast: "law" is serious, as the goddess of chastity forbids a nymph to compromise her virtue, but "flaw," the parallel comparison, implies that, well, to lose her virginity is something like clumsiness or inadvertence – not very serious, if expensive to patch up. To break this law is just a flaw, perhaps even a beauty mark. To Hamlet's anguished cry, "Frailty, thy name is woman" (1.2.146), Pope's nymphs might reply, "True enough, but please, don't make such a fuss."

Not every set of rhymes will afford such subtleties or such wit, of course; many rhymes are conventional or predictable, and if they offer the simple pleasure of sound-play, they lack what Wesling calls "cognitive eventfulness" (*The Chances of Rhyme*, 39). But rhymes might offer a kind of macro-meaning or poem-wide web of meaning not so much through their pairings or threesomes, but through the rhyme-scheme or lack of it. As a last example of rhyme's relation to meaning, then, consider Shelley's seemingly random distribution of rhymes across the 144 lines of "Mont Blanc." Here is the first, and shortest, section:

The everlasting universe of things
Flows through the mind, and rolls its rapid waves,
Now dark—now glittering—now reflecting gloom—
Now lending splendour, where from secret springs
The source of human thought its tribute brings   5
Of waters—with a sound but half its own,
Such as a feeble brook will oft assume,
In the wild woods, among the mountains lone,
Where waterfalls around it leap for ever,
Where woods and winds contend, and a vast river   10
Over its rocks ceaselessly bursts and raves.

We note right away that many lines rhyme, sometimes in pairs (we cannot call them couplets): "things," "springs," and "brings," for example – the a-rhyme. But soon we might wonder whether every line will rhyme, for the b-rhyme, "waves" (2), doesn't find a mate until the end, "raves" (11). That is a long time to wait, but it is worth waiting for, as "raves" not only goes neatly with "waves" but is a strong idea itself, the first unequivocal personification of the river Arve, whom the speaker will directly address in the next section. This is the rhyme scheme, if "scheme" is the right word: abcaadcdeeb.

The scheme of the second section, with thirty-seven lines, is even more remarkable: abbaccdefg/dfehbhbegd/giejeekjik/lleeelm. (I have arbitrarily inserted slashes every ten lines.) It starts out as if it were a traditional six-line stanza (abbacc), but then there is no discernible order: the g-rhyme at line 10 waits until line 19 to pair up, and then there is a third g-rhyme at 21; there are nine e-rhymes ("harmony," "eternity," "phantasy," etc.), but two of them are arguably distinct, "lie" (19) and "by" (45), separated by twenty-six lines. Oddest of all is that the final end-word, "there" (in "thou art there!") has no rhyme. In the next two sections, all the words but one find at least one partner. The final end-word of section 4, at line 126, is without a mate, making sections 2 and 4 alike in this odd respect. If we were keeping track of the rhymes, we might just note the parallel odd-man-out ending, shrug, and continue on, but then it might dawn on us that these two last mateless words rhyme with each other: "there" (48) and "air" (126)! And then the first end-word of section 5 is "there" (127), repeated five lines later (132). What kind of rhyme-scheme is this?

Setting aside particular pairs, or threes or fours, that might have interesting semantic implications, and setting aside as well the other sound-effects, such as the sonic kinship among "river," "rave," and the "Ravine of Arve" (12), which the speaker addresses at least through section 3, this strange and unpredictable patternless pattern of rhymes seems appropriate to the kind of poem this is, an "effusion" seemingly prompted by the grand sights of the ravine, the river, the glacier, and the summit of the mountain. Much of it sounds like blank verse, but it is not; I'd like to call it "Blanc verse." Since a major theme of this difficult poem is the mind's struggle to grasp the sublime scene before it, and its doubts as to just how real the scene would be without the mind that struggles with it, we might take the blank-verse effect as like the stark or blank thing in itself and the rhymes as like the mind's effort to make something out of it. Metaphors and similes abound in this poem, of course, but the rhyme-scheme is a kind of metaphor itself for the subject–object interaction that the poem represents – an analogy, perhaps, of the "wild thoughts" that enter the cave of Poesy, "Seeking among the shadows that pass by, / Ghosts of all things that are, some shade of thee, / Some phantom, some faint image" (45–47).

* * *

These are a few of the kinds of features that we might group under the rubric "style," understood in the broad sense of details of meaning, meaning that arises from and interacts with diction choices, syntactic structure, and rhyme. They are not the sort of thing that can be captured in a précis or summary, but neither are they detachable from it. To see how style is not just "scum" but, at least in a good poem, belongs to, expresses, or embodies what can be paraphrased in a few words is to see what makes a poem a poem.

Structuralism and Poetry

Literary scholars have repeatedly turned to theoretical linguistics, as well as to historical linguistics, for ideas or methods that might help illuminate literature, and poetry in particular. The theory we will consider here, structuralism, has fairly well run its course as an influence on literary interpretation, but it once seemed very powerful and at its best gave us insights that can usefully be absorbed into more capacious frameworks.

There have been many good accounts of the rise of structuralist linguistics and its extensions into several fields,[25] so I will just sketch a few features of it here. It begins with Saussure, who distinguished firmly between *langue* and *parole* – that is, between *language* as a "system of signs," and *speech*, or utterance. Language is not the set of all speech-acts, somehow totaled up; its sounds and meanings have their own systematic structure. A sign cannot be understood in isolation, as, say, the thing a noun refers to (where "tree" would mean that tall, leafy thing over there), for "Language is a system of interdependent terms in which the value of each term results solely from the simultaneous presence of the others" (*Course in General Linguistics* 114). What makes a phoneme a phoneme is not its positive characteristics but its distinctness from other phonemes: /b/ gains its "value" not from anything to do with lips or voice in themselves, but because it contrasts with its fellow labials /p/ in one feature (voice) and /m/ in another (nasality), and it contrasts with its fellow voiced non-nasal stops /d/ and /g/ in point of articulation, and so on. The distinctions are of the essence: "Phonemes are above all else opposing, relative, and negative entities" (119). This is true of the semantic dimension as well. Saussure sums up, "in language there are only differences" (120).

The formalization of Saussure's approach in phonology was begun by Nikolay Trubetskoy and Roman Jakobson in the 1920s. For any language, they showed, the set of all minimal meaningful sounds, or phonemes, that the language deploys can be organized by means of a small set of "distinctive features," or properties, such as voice, nasality, sonorancy (where the voice vibrates without stops or turbulence, as in the nasals and semi-vowels), stridency (where the air is turbulent, as in /v/ and /f/, or /ʒ/ and /ʃ/), and several points of articulation (labial, coronal, back, etc.).[26] At first these features were defined in acoustic terms – that is, how they sounded to a hearer; later they were redescribed in articulatory terms, according to what the speaker does. By one reckoning there are fourteen of these for English, out of which all forty-odd phonemes can be derived. Each feature – and this is the heart of the matter – has only two settings: on or off, or plus and minus. All the phonemes can be arranged in a chart or box with the phonemes running in a row across the top and the distinctive features stacked in a column on the left side; every phoneme is a column of plusses and minuses. Every phoneme, in other words, is a bundle of distinctive features. The English phoneme /m/ would be as in Figure 6.4.

Such bundles of plusses and minuses certainly represent a breakthrough in understanding phonemes: it reduces what can be a large and apparently heterogeneous group (some languages have many more than English) to a handful of settings or switches, somewhat as Mendeleev reduced the scores of chemical elements to a "periodic" pattern, or the "Standard Model" reduces the bewildering array of subatomic particles into bosons, leptons, and quarks, with features such as mass, charge, and flavor. It is easy to see why the logical and quasi-mathematical elegance of phoneme charts, though there are still disagreements over details, suggested that other components of language, such as grammar or semantics, might rest on a similar abstract basis.

$$\left[\begin{array}{l} \text{+ consonantal} \\ \text{+ anterior} \\ \text{+ labial} \\ \text{+ sonorant} \\ \text{− continuant} \\ \text{+ voice} \\ \text{+ nasal} \\ \text{etc.} \end{array} \right]$$

Figure 6.4 Distinctive features of phoneme /m/

Students of semantics made considerable use of such formalisms as they analyzed the meanings of words into conceptual components, each with two settings. Thus, the word "bachelor" might be analyzed as [-female] [+adult] [+human] [-married]. Not many words are as amenable to this sort of analysis, however, or, if they are, the number of distinctive features has to be enlarged indefinitely. The word "brother" would include two of these components, [-female] and [+human] (although we might speak of male kittens from the same litter as "brothers"), but [adult] and [married] are beside the point, and we would need at least one new category, maybe [sibling], which is irrelevant to the meaning of "bachelor." Color terminology cannot be reduced to plusses and minuses without absurd contortions, though Goethe two centuries ago tried to show that all colors are the products of light and dark. The realm of meaning, in short, is much more complicated than that of sound, if for no other reason than that the universe of things is much more complicated than the human mouth and vocal cords.

We should note, too, that even in the realm of phonology it is not obvious why certain features are posited as basic or atomic, or why they should have only two settings. The points of articulation in the mouth are virtually continuous, and in its chart of consonants the IPA recognizes twelve sites, from bilabial to glottal, where a sound can be made (several of them alien to English phonemes, such as retroflex, palatal, and uvular). It seems arbitrary to divide the mouth into two at the alveolus, calling all sounds made there and in front of it [+anterior] and the rest [-anterior]. A sound made in the middle, such as /ʃ/ and /j/, is defined as [+high], while [+back] (and not [+posterior], as that would seem to be [-anterior]) designates such sounds as the velars; there is no [+low] category for the consonants, at least in English. Expert phonologists continue to disagree over which features are primitive and which derived, which are redundant in certain contexts, and so on.[27] Some have argued that, at least for vowel height, a scale of several settings, perhaps four, would more accurately describe the phonological facts, but the attraction of binarism – the stipulation that all entities must be expressed as features with just two settings, yes or no – remains understandably strong. Binary or polar models hold such sway over so many sciences – notably information theory, cybernetics, and neuroscience – that it seems simple common sense. Digital computers are built on binary systems, and the human brain is widely assumed to be a digital computer, at least in part, with neuronal pathways open or closed, firing or dormant. To suggest that some switches might have three settings or more, that a fork in a road might have three branches or more, would be dismissed by most scientists as absurd and arbitrary, but if a switch in a phoneme feature could have several positions, it might reduce the number of features needed to account for all phonemes. That number is eleven for the English consonants, according to the current consensus – rather large, one might think, and arbitrary.

At any rate, its success in phonology and its promising start in semantics (it got nowhere in syntax) inspired researchers in many fields to see if it could be generalized and applied to other fields. Saussure himself proposed the term "semiology" for a general science of signs, of which linguistics is only the best-developed part. In anthropology, Claude Lévi-Strauss applied distinctive-feature analysis first to kinship structures and then to myths. Kinship would seem to lend itself well to such analysis, since certain key factors such as sex and consanguinity are obviously binary, but other factors might seem to have three settings, such as descendant, same-generation, and ascendant. Lévi-Strauss, in any case, surveyed a large number of kinship systems and isolated key relationships, such as maternal uncle to nephew, that set the terms for their systems. He then published several volumes about the myths of many tribes of native Americans in Brazil, extracting such binaries as "raw" versus "cooked." His best-known analysis of a myth is his reduction of the Oedipus cycle to two binaries: (1) underestimation of the kinship bond (Oedipus kills his father, his sons kill each other) versus over-estimation (Oedipus has sex with his mother, his daughter Antigone insists on funeral rites for her dead brother despite the decree against it); and (2) generation from the earth (Cadmus and the dragon teeth) versus generation by sexual intercourse (the children of Oedipus and Jocasta). The first of these pairs seems reasonable, almost unavoidable, but the second seems rather forced, though brilliant, for Lévi-Strauss tries to marshal together the monsters (Cadmus' dragon, Oedipus' sphinx) and the feet (Oedipus' name, which means "Swollen Foot," the sphinx's riddle, etc.). A set of stories, of narratives, are treated as if they are mainly a repertoire of signs with criss-crossing oppositions, signs that had impressed themselves on Aeschylus, Sophocles, and Euripides without their knowing it.[28]

That most versatile of linguists, Roman Jakobson, made quite a few detailed structuralist analyses of individual poems that are worth considering. Perhaps the most notorious of these is his essay "Shakespeare's Verbal Art in 'Th'Expense of Spirit'" (1970), written with Lawrence Jones.[29] Here is the sonnet in question, number 129:

> Th' expense of spirit in a waste of shame
> Is lust in action; and till action, lust
> Is perjured, murd'rous, bloody, full of blame,
> Savage, extreme, rude, cruel, not to trust,
> Enjoyed no sooner but despised straight,
> Past reason hunted; and, no sooner had
> Past reason hated as a swallowed bait
> On purpose laid to make the taker mad;
> Mad in pursuit and in possession so,
> Had, having, and in quest to have, extreme;
> A bliss in proof and proved, a very woe;
> Before, a joy proposed; behind, a dream.
>   All this the world well knows; yet none knows well
>   To shun the heaven that leads men to this hell.

Jakobson begins by noting rhyme patterns within its "four strophic units" (three quatrains and a couplet). Only the first pair of rhymes (*shame* / *blame*) is "grammatical," so called because the two rhyme words are the same part of speech (nouns), while the second (*lust* / *trust*) is a noun followed by "a different part of speech" (199). Right away, we might wonder why he does not call "trust" a verb rather than a non-noun. His next sentence suggests what he is up to: he is looking for a binary opposition [noun]: "The third rhyme and the last three rhymes invert this order: a non-noun is followed by a noun [*straight* / *bait*, *so* / *woe*, *extreme* / *dream*, and *well* / *hell*] whereas the fourth, the central of the seven rhymes, has no noun at all and consists of the participle *had* and the adjective *mad*." He does not provide a [noun] diagram of the rhyme pairs, but it might look like this:

1 + +
2 + −
3 − +
4 − −
5 − +
6 − +
7 − +

Is this pattern of any interest? There are seven nouns and seven non-nouns. In five of the rhyming pairs, the noun is the second of the two, and thus more prominent. Is this nouniness of rhyme-words significant? He does not say, nor does he note that the next most common part of speech is the adverb, occurring as the rhyme-word of lines 5, 9, and 13 – that is, at the outsets of all but the first strophic unit. That might seem more striking, because less usual; sonnet 130, after all, has seven noun rhyme-words, 131 has five, and 132 has nine. If you make a box of plusses and minuses for sonnet 130 you get:

```
1 + –
2 – +
3 – +
4 + –
5 – –
6 + +
7 – +
```

Is this less interesting than the pattern of sonnet 129?

He goes on to note a few other binaries, some of them involving grammatical forms, and sums up: "The numerous variables which form a salient network of binary oppositions between the four strophic units are most effective against the background of pervasive features common to all four strophes" (202). Among the pervasive features, some seem more noteworthy than others. Is it important that each strophe has one infinitive? Or even that it is the only sonnet of 154 that contains no personal pronouns? That seems more interesting – yet what is really interesting is that the sonnet consists of an abstract or general argument, applicable to everyone, and thus departs from the more or less biographical character of virtually all the others. (And what about "none" in line 13?) There are quite a few examples of "phonic affinity" (205) besides the rhymes, all carefully listed. Jakobson thinks there are enough similarities between strophes 1 and 3, and between 2 and 4, to posit a contrast between the odd strophes and the even ones – another binary opposition. The odd stanzas have a lot more nouns and adjectives than the even ones, and the odd-strophe nouns are abstract while the even-strophe nouns are concrete. There is another set of contrasts between the outer strophes and the inner ones. Though we may tire of all these contrasts, and wonder why there aren't some sets of three items, or maybe five, lurking in the poem, Jakobson hardly misses a thing as he sorts and resorts the words and phrases and lines and strophes into binary after binary.

The question is: does all this alter our understanding, our "reading," of the poem? In one sense, certainly, it does, because even if we know this poem by heart we will not have noticed everything Jakobson notices. He thinks the sonnet's "structuration" is "palpable to any responsive and unprejudiced reader" (214), but he surely overestimates us mortal readers, who are not as well equipped as he is with grammar-detecting devices and a lot of spare time. While giving him full credit for discovering dozens of patterns, then, in a larger sense his analysis not only fails to alter a more traditional attentive reading but does not really amount to a reading at all. The binary oppositions all sound equally salient, equally "palpable," perhaps because he starts with them instead of working out the general purport of the sonnet and then asking what features are enlisted to enhance it, or perhaps undermine it or ironize it. He does not fold them into a coherent argument about the sonnet as a whole.[30]

What we might generalize from this example is that structuralist analyses of poetry provide a great deal of grist for our mill, but interpretation is not just grinding out observations, no matter how subtle and thorough. The analyses are more like notes, some of which we might take up and make something out of if we deem them significant in light of our initial understanding of a poem, but it is we who confer significance on them. They do not interpret the poem themselves. They are notes, moreover, as seen through a certain optic, the same device that displays phonemes in a chart of yes-or-no distinctive features. That lens may illuminate phonemes – though doubts have been raised even there – but it is unlikely that the meaning of a poem is solely the product, or even largely the product, of binary operations on sounds, syntax, or words.

Pragmatics

Pragmatics is the name given to a branch of linguistics that deals with the meanings or functions sentences have when they are uttered in different contexts. A sentence taken out of all "real-world" contexts (except perhaps the context of being quoted in a book about linguistics) has arguably only a very general or ambiguous meaning until the context of its utterance clarifies it, or it is a bundle of potential meanings until one of them is actualized. Lambrecht's distinction between "meaning" and "information" somewhat resembles distinctions drawn in the field of pragmatics, such as that between explicit and implicit meaning. Pragmatics also studies different sorts of speech-acts, ranging from "I finally met the woman who moved in downstairs," which is an example of a "constative" utterance (it makes an assertion that may be true or false), to "I now pronounce you husband and wife" and "Play ball," which are "performative" utterances (they actually do something besides giving information). Swearing under oath, delivering a verdict, making a motion at a meeting, promising, betting, dedicating, praying, baptizing, blessing, cursing, insulting, and various sorts of verbal games are all performative speech-acts that bring something about; they may be rightly or wrongly performed, but they cannot be said to be true or false. This distinction between saying and doing, and the terms "constative" and "performative," we owe to J. L. Austin's influential book *How to Do Things with Words*, which we mentioned earlier in this chapter.[31]

An interesting example is "I love you." On the face of it, this is a declarative sentence that reports the speaker's state of mind; it might be false, so it is "constative." Yet many people find it a solemn and anxious moment when they first say it to someone they have fallen in love with, fearful that it won't be reciprocated with the same sentence; reciprocated or not, saying it brings about a change in the relationship, so it is "performative." Young people today seem more relaxed and promiscuous about saying "I love you," just as they are readier to use *tu* or *du* early in a relationship and so avoid the awkwardness of switching from the polite forms at some point, but most older speakers remember the anxiety they have felt in performing these utterances.

Publishing or reciting a poem, I argued at the outset of this chapter, is a special kind of speech-act. If so, it is certainly not a "constative" one, though the sentences found in it might seem to be, for "the poet, he nothing affirms, and therefore never lieth," as Sir Phillip Sidney notoriously put it. A poem – and in this it is no different from any other sort of literary work – is a performance. But poems, and works in prose, also imitate or represent all kinds of speech-acts, and presume all kinds of contexts, that should be intelligible to their readers who know how to speak the language. Are there any kinds of speech-acts that are distinctive of poetry? A few come to mind.

The first is the invocation to the Muse or Muses. Homer asks a nameless "goddess" in the *Iliad*, and a nameless "Muse" in the *Odyssey*, to help him sing those epics, while Hesiod boasts in the *Theogony* that all nine Muses came to him on Mount Helicon, and he names them all. Since then, it has been routine in epics and other longer forms to invoke a Muse, or some sort of creative spirit. But then these invocations are very like prayers: invoking a Muse is not very different from invoking Aphrodite, say, as Sappho does in her great ode.

Another kind is apostrophe, the direct address to someone absent or to something inanimate or abstract. (We will take up apostrophe in the next chapter.) It seems closely related to invocations and prayers to gods or goddesses; it is not an accident that Shelley addresses the West Wind as a puissant god. Jonathan Culler considers apostrophe to be distinctive of lyric poetry, and more widespread than we usually think, even "endemic" to it, though it is not unique to lyric or any kind of poetry.[32] There is a particular kind of apostrophe that lacks a name, where the speaker commands an entity to do something that it would do anyway with no regard for the speaker. Lear cries, "Blow winds and crack your cheeks! Rage, blow!" Longfellow's poetic persona directly addresses a metaphor for an abstract entity: "Thou, too, sail on, O Ship of State! / Sail on, O Union, strong and great!" An extreme example is: "Twinkle, twinkle, little star." There are no doubt a few occasions in real life where we might say something like these pseudo-commands, but they seem especially at home in poems.

Another variant of the apostrophe would be the explicit reply of the thing addressed, as when Keats's urn speaks the final two lines of the ode, or, taken a step further, the statement of a thing not even addressed, or not explicitly, as in Carl Sandberg's "Grass": "Pile the bodies high at Austerlitz and Waterloo. / Shovel them under and let me work – / I am the grass; I cover all." This kind of ventriloquism is almost a reverse-apostrophe: urn and grass address us humans, and while we are pleased to say that we personify them, from their point of view perhaps they urnify or herbify us. In any case, whether or not the utterances themselves are distinctively poetic, to attribute them to non-human subjects, in fact to make them *subjects* at all, is a hallmark of poetry.

We cannot go further into the subject of pragmatics in a book that deals mainly with the internal or intrinsic properties of language, but it is important to remember that all speech in the real world (outside, say, textbooks about language as such) is action, all sentences are utterances by someone to someone about something, at some place, at some moment, and when we read poems we bring to them our knowledge of such occasions that the poems may evoke or represent. The same is true of what we learn from the related branch called sociolinguistics, which deals with language contact, levels or registers of courtesy, class-based or race-based dialects, slang, and other aspects of the social use of language. Poetry has sometimes seemed to insulate itself from such concerns, or to speak a special dialect of its own, but of course it can absorb and reflect any of them. That, however, is a subject for another book.

Notes

1. Ellmann, *Ulysses on the Liffey*, xvii.
2. *Letters* 2:310.
3. *Letters and Journals* 9:64.
4. Behler, *German Romantic Literary Theory*, 277.
5. Robb, *Victor Hugo*, 109.
6. Vanasco, "Emily's Lists," 11.
7. Huntington *et al.*, "How to Peel a Poem."
8. Culler, *Theory of the Lyric*, 109–25.
9. Putnam, "The Meaning of 'Meaning,'" 223ff.
10. Beardsley, *Possibility of Criticism*, 19.
11. Baby diapers are so called because the cloth they are, or were, made from was diapered in the older sense. "Discolored" is also a small stumbling block today. It meant "variously colored," from Latin, whereas today it is more likely to mean "stained" or "spoiled in color," which might raise further distracting thoughts about what diapers are for.
12. Abrams, *Mirror and the Lamp*, 78. The section called "Primitive Language and Primitive Poetry" (78–84) is still essential reading on the subject; see also 110–12.
13. There are many complications, such as the possibility that "Homer" is an invented name, and that editing and emending took place quite early in the epics' early written history, but these do not affect the near-certainty that centuries of oral composition lay behind "Homer." Milman Parry (1902–35) is the scholar who established the "oral-formulaic" character of Homer both by analysis of the Homeric formulas, particularly epithets, and by comparisons with illiterate oral poets still active in Yugoslavia.
14. See Reece, *Homer's Winged Words*, Ch. 15, "Homer's Asphodel Meadow."
15. Sherbo, *English Poetic Diction*, 91–101.
16. Wimsatt, *Prose Style*, 1.
17. Beardsley, *Aesthetics*, 222–23.
18. Vendler, *Dickinson*, 491–95.
19. Lambrecht, *Information Structure*, 51.
20. Bradford, *Linguistic History of English Poetry*, especially 7–8.
21. Of course, the human speaker (and not just Keats the poet) is ventriloquizing the urn's voice and hardly expects us to believe otherwise. The urn is the "foster-child of Silence" and doesn't "really" speak. So the speaker is gently mocking himself. We might say he has taught himself through the silent urn to cease all his talking and just relish its beauty and truth.
22. Bakker, in an interesting article, "Homeric Discourse and Enjambement," would get rid of the term "enjamb(e)ment" altogether in the analysis of Homeric style.
23. On this priority, see Wimsatt, "One Relation," and Wesling, *The Chances of Rhyme*.
24. Auden, *English Auden*, 308.

25. One of the best books remains Culler's 1975 study, *Structuralist Poetics*.

26. "Coronal" includes dental, alveolar, and post-alveolar places that the "crown" of the tongue touches or approaches, though "blade" is usually preferred to "crown."

27. For some examples of the inadequacies of binarism, at least at our present state of knowledge, see Lass, *Phonology*, 102–24. See also Hall, *Distinctive Feature Theory*, 4.

28. Lévi-Strauss, "Structural Study of Myth," 209–15. For extensive criticisms of his treatment of the Oedipus cycle, see Leach, *Lévi-Strauss*, 62–82; briefer comments in Jameson, *Prison-House*, 115–17.

29. Reprinted in Jakobson, *Language in Literature*, 198–215.

30. Culler discusses this essay in a similar spirit in *Structuralist Poetics*, 71–74, and notes a mistake that Jakobson's method leads him into.

31. An excellent succinct account of Austin is in Chapter 1 of Petrey, *Speech Acts*.

32. Culler, *Theory of the Lyric*, 211–41.

CHAPTER SEVEN

Metaphor

"But by far the greatest thing is to be metaphoric." Aristotle, *Poetics* 1459a5-6

"By far the most beautiful [trope], I mean that which consists in what we call *translatio*, and the Greeks *metaphora*." Quintilian, *Institutes* 8.6.4

"It is astonishing what a different result one gets by changing the metaphor!" George Eliot, *The Mill on the Floss* 1.2.1

Metaphor seems most at home in poetry. Many would say it provides poetry's best and most distinctive furniture. Those two sentences each contain a metaphor, and the two metaphors are similar (poetry is a home, and has furniture in it), but the sentences are not parts of poems, as far as I know, and they even sound rather prosaic. So we cannot make a case that metaphor is the unique defining feature or common denominator of poetry, for there are poems without metaphors, or at least without any expressions that stand out as metaphors, and there is plenty of metaphor-rich prose. In fact, as Nietzsche insisted long ago, and Lakoff and Johnson and many other scholars have argued in detail in recent years, metaphors are pervasive in ordinary speech, and many of the ones that strike us in poetry are variants or extensions of the basic ones we use, usually without thinking about it, all the time. Still, most readers and writers would agree that metaphor counts as one of the characteristic features of poetry, one of the most salient of poetry's "family resemblances." In a "prose poem," for example, where meter, rhyme, and even line have been abandoned, what keeps it a "poem," many would say, is its density of figurative language, and especially metaphor.

What is metaphor? It is not easy to define with any precision. The two earliest discussions of it in the west are both by Aristotle: one in his *Rhetoric*, which is about public speaking, and one in his *Poetics*, which is mainly about tragic drama. The fact that he takes up metaphor in both books reminds us that poetry has no unique claim on it: public orators, Aristotle assumes, should make judicious use of metaphors to persuade their audiences to return a certain verdict or endorse a course of action.

Though speech in tragic drama, according to the *Poetics*, has a different purpose, being one of the means of imitating an action in such a way that it brings about a catharsis of pity and terror in the audience, metaphor has the same definition and structure in both contexts. Here it is in the *Poetics*: "*Metaphora* (μεταφορά) is the application of an alien name either from genus onto species or from species onto genus or from species onto species or according to analogy" (1457b6-9). The word translated here as "application" is *epiphora* (ἐπιφορά), with the same root as *metaphora*. Aristotle thus makes metaphor a kind of *epiphora*. Though it is usually translated as "application," its kindred verb (*epipherō*) can mean "impose" or "confer," so it might be translated as the "imposition" or "conferral" of an alien name (onto a familiar or "proper" name, presumably). It comes very close to meaning "substitution," and many discussions of metaphor for thousands of years have relied on that sense. In any case, it is important to see, as Paul Ricoeur argues, that the "application" is an action or a motion, a bringing of something to (or onto) something else, accomplished by a speaker who makes an assertion.[1] They are events, not inert entries in a dictionary. The poet Paul Valéry calls metaphors "those stationary movements!"[2] Greek *pherō* means "carry" or "bear," like Latin *ferō*, with which it is cognate (as it is with English "bear" and "bring"); if we translated *epiphora* as "conferral," we would preserve the root they share and underscore that it is an act that we perform when we invent metaphors.

The word translated as "name" here is ὄνομα (*onoma*), which can also mean "noun." Our words "noun" and "name," in fact, come from the same root as *onoma*, one via French from Latin *nōmen*, the other from our Germanic heritage. Nouns, we say, *name* a person, place, or thing. This emphasis on names and nouns, as Ricoeur also points out, had lasting effects on the theory of rhetoric and of metaphor in particular, as if metaphors and other figures or tropes were affairs of words only and of nouns mainly, as opposed to whole sentences or utterances, to acts of conferring, referring, or transferring that might depend as much on verbs or adjectives or adverbs as on a switching of nouns.[3] As we will soon see, metaphors in poetry rely on changes of these other parts of speech more often than on changes of nouns.

Epiphora, in any case, is the more generic term, and metaphor is a kind of *epiphora*. Metaphor itself, in Aristotle, has a more generic meaning than we would give it today, however, and, since it is the only instance of *epiphora* Aristotle gives, the two terms seem effectually synonymous. They have the same verbal root, as we saw. The prefix *meta-* could mean any number of things, such as "among," "by means of," "back," "across," and "over." The verb *metapherō* could mean "carry over" or "transfer" (with the same root again) or "change." *Metaphora*, then, is a transferal or transference or translation; in fact, Latin *translatio* was used to translate *metaphora*. In modern Greek, *metaphora* also means "transport" or "transportation," and the Greek government has a Ministry of *Metaphora*. You can see trucks driving around Greece bearing the sign Μεταφορά, mobile metaphors themselves.

Aristotle identifies four types of metaphor, depending on what kind of "alien" name is applied. The first two types we would not call metaphor now, but rather synecdoche or metonymy, as we will see later. The application of genus onto species he illustrates by saying that the generic verb in "my ship stands here" (in English, we might prefer to say "my ship lies here") may substitute for the more specific verb in "my ship is moored here," because being moored is a species of standing (or we might say lying at anchor is a kind of lying). Of the opposite transfer, of species onto genus, he gives this example: in the sentence "Odysseus has performed ten thousand [myriad] noble deeds," the specific number replaces the generic "many." These two types, surely, are barely even figurative, let alone metaphorical, and not very interesting.

More to the point is the third type, species for species, where the transference comes from another semantic realm, a domain "alien" to the context. Aristotle gives two clauses as examples: (1) "draining away the life with bronze," where "life" (*psychē*) is treated as something liquid, such as blood, and (2) "cutting with the unyielding bronze," where "cutting" in Greek sometimes means "cutting off a stream of water," according to D. W. Lucas, and therefore could mean "draining" as well, as Aristotle goes on to say; the two clauses can substitute for each other.[4] This is certainly less than lucid. The first instance by itself would serve as an adequate example, for *psychē* is not normally thought of as a liquid (it has more to do with the breath); the word "draining" confers a liquid sense (the "alien" species) on a non-liquid species. The second example is less clear by itself (though perhaps clearer to Aristotle's original audience), and it is not necessary to give an example to show that another verb can mean what the first means and vice versa. Aristotle then confounds the matter by saying they are both instances of "taking away," as if together they are an example of the second type, the application of species onto genus. And it does not help matters that "bronze" in both expressions is a metonymy for "sword" or "spear," and that in one instance it has an epithet ("unyielding"). He is presumably quoting someone, perhaps Empedocles.[5]

I think this third type can be justified nonetheless, despite its distracting examples. According to Hedwig Konrad, when we transfer a word to make a metaphor, we must "forget" or eliminate quite a bit of the transferred meaning. When we say "Achilles is a lion," we must forget about certain features of a lion, such as its tail and mane, its four feet, and so on, and consider only its strength, speed, and ferocity. In other words, we are abstracting certain traits in

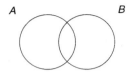

Figure 7.1 Simple Venn diagram

a lion shared by Achilles, and by the same token abstracting certain traits in
Achilles shared by lions. They are two species, then, of the genus of strong, fast,
and fierce creatures. Konrad writes, "The two terms of a metaphor behave like
two species joined by the representation of a genus."[6]

Or we could think of it through a Venn diagram. Where A is Achilles
and B is a generic or typical lion, the overlapping lozenge in the middle is
strength, speed, ferocity, and whatever else Achilles might plausibly share
with a lion; the middle is the locale of metaphor. The diagram suggests that
there might be degrees of metaphor, something Aristotle and most theorists since Aristotle seem not to have considered – or at least degrees of
aptness. Whether or not this is a sufficient account of metaphor in general,
it seems to make sense of Aristotle's third type (see Figure 7.1).

Things can get more complicated, of course, than "Achilles is a lion." In
the sentence "Achilles crouched, snarled, and pounced," the main com-
parator noun ("lion") is unspoken but implicit in the three verbs, which are
literal when governed by "lion." The metaphor succeeds, we might say,
because the three leonine verbs can stay in the middle space belonging to
both A and B. But in the sentence "Achilles crouched, his tail twitching,
then snarled and pounced," the metaphor evaporates. The twitching tail
cannot occupy the central lozenge, and we would have to conclude that we
are reading about a lion named Achilles.

If these three types of metaphor were the only ones Aristotle could come
up with, he might not be remembered as its prime explicator. It is his
fourth type, "analogy" (*to analogon*), that has impressed itself on all subsequent discussions of metaphor until recently, and still shows up in
handbooks of literary terms. In the *Rhetoric*, he does not even bother
with the first three but goes right to the fourth, with lots of examples
(1411a–b). In the *Poetics*, he explains analogy as "what may happen when of
four things the second stands in the same relationship to the first as the
fourth to the third; for then one may speak of the fourth instead of the
second, and the second instead of the fourth" (1457b14-19, translated by
Dorsch in *Classical Literary Criticism*). For example, a cup is to Dionysus as

a shield is to Ares, so we could call a cup "Dionysus' shield" and a shield "Ares' cup." To put it in a formula,

Literal or normal: 1 Dionysus : 2 cup :: 3 Ares : 4 shield→
Metaphorical: 1 Dionysus : 4 shield :: 3 Ares : 2 cup

This example is convincing enough, but rather decorative, even comical. More fundamental and fruitful is his next example: "old age is to life as evening is to day." We may switch either term with its analogous term and assert "he is in the evening of life" or "the day is entering old age." In the *Rhetoric*, Aristotle gives a variant of the same metaphor, with a life likened to a year rather than a day, by quoting Pericles as saying that the youth who perished in the war have disappeared from the state as if the year has lost its springtime. Many more examples follow, all from orators, whereas the *Poetics* only quotes poets.

For many centuries, discussions of figures or tropes stayed more or less within the Aristotelian paradigm and categorized all the figures as substitutions, with metaphor a substitution based on analogy or resemblance, usually of noun for noun. In the twentieth century, however, quite a few new theories emerged, such as Konrad's, based on logic, rhetoric, psychology, linguistics, or a combination of these disciplines (such as semantics and semiotics). They have brought greater depth and greater clarity to the theory of metaphor, though there is something irreducibly messy about the subject that no theory has fully tidied up.

Grammatical Forms

Before turning to some of these theories, we should note that the Aristotelian legacy of noun-substitution as definitive of metaphor imposed certain limits not only of understanding but even of recognizing metaphors in poetry. To help correct for this loss, Christine Brooke-Rose has demonstrated (in *Grammar of Metaphor*) in great and often subtle detail many of the grammatical forms a metaphor might take in poetry. In what follows, I offer my own categories and examples, prompted by her own.

[NP] is [NP]

The grammatical form "[NP] is [NP]," where both elements are nouns or noun phrases, would seem to be the most basic form, but it is less common than we might expect.

Life's but a walking shadow   (Shakespeare)

The Child is father of the Man   (Wordsworth)

L'Aigle, c'est le Génie! ("The Eagle, that's what
genius is")   (Hugo)

Der Tod das ist die kühle Nacht ("Death is the chilly
night")   (Heine)

La Nature est un temple ("Nature is a temple")   (Baudelaire)

A Sonnet is a moment's monument   (D. G. Rossetti)

> Old age is
> a flight of small
> cheeping birds
> skimming
> bare trees
> above a snow glaze   (William Carlos Williams)

Love is a universal migraine   (Graves)

Occasionally we see a negative version of this form:

> This life is not a circus where
> the shy performing dogs of love look on   (Ferlinghetti)

Or a combination of negative and positive:

> As this life is not a gate, but the horse plunging
> through it.   (Hirshfield)

I wonder whether anyone has made a study of such "negative" metaphors.
The results might be interesting, though they would probably overlap with
the technique of piling on metaphors (or similes), which we will look at
shortly, since it implies that they are all "negative" – or at least inadequate.

[NP], [NP]

A variant of "[NP] is [NP]" would be its implicit form, "[NP], [NP]":

The god of war, money-changer of dead bodies   (Aeschylus)

Invention, Nature's child   (Sidney)

that churl Death   (Shakespeare)

Busy old fool, unruly sun   (Donne)

O Wild West Wind, thou breath of autumn's being (Shelley)

Life the hound
Equivocal
Comes at a bound
Either to rend me
Or to
befriend me (Robert Francis)

My Life had stood—a Loaded Gun—
In Corners (Dickinson)

Not, I'll not, carrion comfort, Despair, not feast on thee (Hopkins)
this open book ... my open coffin (Robert Lowell)

On a larger scale, the "[NP], [NP]" form might occupy an entire brief poem, as in Ezra Pound's famous haiku called "In a Station of the Metro": "The apparition of these faces in the crowd; / Petals on a wet, black bough."

Several of these and those that follow are personifications – that is, attributions of human characteristics to something not human, and in particular not animate: Nature as a child, Death as a churl, the sun as a fool.[7]

[NP] of [NP]

There are many other forms. One prominent form follows Aristotle's example "the cup of Ares," where both terms are nouns or noun phrases:

Nel mezzo del cammin di nostra vita ("In the middle
of the path of our life") (Dante)

this bank and shoal of time (Shakespeare)

That liquefaction of her clothes (Herrick)

the opening eyelids of the morn (Milton)

my arrows of desire (Blake)

the silent sabbath of the grave (Charlotte Smith)

the grapes of wrath (Julia Ward Howe)

the foul rag-and-bone-shop of the heart (Yeats)

a cool web of language (Graves)

Gewitter der Rosen" ("storm of roses") (Ingeborg Bachmann)

the flute end of consequences   (William Stafford)

the heavy industry
of each other   (Mark Strand)

[NP]'s [NP]

Similar to "[NP] of [NP]" would be "[NP]'s [NP]":

the heart's forest   (Wyatt)

Time's fell hand   (Shakespeare)

love's sensual empery   (Chapman)

Spring's dewy hand   (Charlotte Smith)

Love's rubber armor   (Updike)

a housefly's panicked scribbling on the air   (Schnackenberg)

The Updike example might be a double metaphor: (1) "love's armor," a
commonplace image, going back at least to Renaissance love sonnets, in
the form "[NP]'s [NP]"; and (2) "rubber armor," in the form "[A][N],"
where [A] is an adjective and [N] a noun. There are many examples of the
latter, of course, such as these:

[A][N] (adjective–noun)

rhododaktulos Eos ("rose-fingered Dawn")   (Homer)

swift-footed Time   (Shakespeare)

the lazy leaden-stepping hours   (Milton)

the intruding sky   (Wordsworth)

the dying year   (Shelley)

A Quartz contentment   (Dickinson)

The shrill demented choirs of wailing
shells   (Owen) (i.e., artillery shells)

furnished souls   (Cummings)

the lilting house   (Dylan Thomas)

the green freedom of a cockatoo   (Stevens)

vulturous boredom   (Plath)

The example from Wilfred Owen is a complex case, for its larger structure is "A of B" ("choirs of shells"). Since the "choirs" have already been called "shrill" and "demented," the adjective "wailing" might seem superfluous, but it is effective enough, and to add a not strictly necessary adjective in this context (the sheer number of shells implied by "choirs") brings out a little the sheer repetitiveness of the bombardment.

[NP][V] (noun-phrase–verb)

Pale Death with impartial foot knocks at the doors of poor men's hovels and king's palaces.	(Horace)
Nor shall my Sword sleep in my hand	(Blake)
and a friendly tree fragrant with flowers solaces his ashes with soft shade	(Foscolo)
The sweet land laughs from sea to sea	(Swinburne)
The yellow fog that rubs its back upon the window-panes	(T. S. Eliot)
winds went begging at each door time flicks out	(Geoffrey Hill)
its tricky whip	(Ferlinghetti)
Even the bees had knocked off for the day	(Billy Collins)

Collins's example is interesting. The verbal phrase "knocked off" is a slang expression for "quit work" or "stopped working," and if we applied one of those, especially the latter, to bees in a hive, it might not seem a metaphor at all. But, of course, even the quasi-technical term "worker bee" and the common phrase "busy bee" are ultimately metaphors, since what bees do is not literally work or business, though it might seem so to our anthropomorphizing eyes. What Collins has done is revive this dead metaphor, and reveal it as a metaphor. This, as we will see, has been the goal of many poets, explicitly so in the modern era.

Sometimes the metaphor implicit in a noun–verb construction will be made explicit in a simile (with "like" or "as"):

Leningrad dangled like a useless pendant at the side of its prisons	(Anna Akhmatova)
the moon rattles like a fragment of angry candy	(Cummings)

[V][NP] (verb–noun-phrase)

Noun phrase and verb phrase can be in the opposite order:

I can Wade Grief	(Dickinson)
Some women marry houses	(Anne Sexton)
I have been eating poetry	(Mark Strand)

These are in the indicative mood, but sometimes we find the form in the imperative:

Weave, sweet harp, at once
In Lydian melody
This song also   (Pindar)

Awake, Aeolian lyre, awake!   (Gray)

Spin love just as a worm spins silk thread from inside   (Mickiewicz)

[Pp] [Prep] [NP] (participle–preposition–noun-phrase)

blasted with ecstasy	(Shakespeare)
suckled in a creed outworn	(Wordsworth)
appareled in celestial light	(Wordsworth)

[NP] has [NP]

I know death hath ten thousand several doors
For men to take their exits   (Webster)

Thou hast a voice, great Mountain   (Shelley)

The Brain has Corridors   (Dickinson)

O the mind, mind has mountains   (Hopkins)

The passage from Shelley, and the Donne and Shelley passages under "[NP], [NP]" earlier, are instances of personification through apostrophe, and that reminds us that some expressions, no matter what their grammatical form, may be metaphorical even if they have no metaphorical word, as long as they are addressed to an inanimate object or an abstraction. Had Shelley written just "O great Mountain" and left it at that, he would still have personified the mountain, attributing consciousness and understanding to it, simply by speaking to it. We shall return to apostrophe briefly in the section about tropes.

Metaphors can be even more implicit than this. In Denise Levertov's lines "After I had cut off my hands / and grown new ones," there is no metaphorical term at all, but we know we are not to take the lines literally, and not just because it would have been impossible for her to cut off her second hand. These are metaphorical hands, and a metaphorical cutting.

There are other possible forms, such as the adverbial construction "flowerly I die" (Dylan Thomas), and I hope the reader will find it as interesting to search for them as I have. Poets have never felt obliged to lay out their metaphors in "[NP] is [NP]" form or in any other form, and they often combine the forms presented in this section so that metaphor links with metaphor, as in Cummings's clause "a moon / scratches the skin of the organized hills." But now we shall turn to recent theories about how metaphor works.

Theories of Metaphor

Probably the most influential twentieth-century discussion of metaphor in English is the final pair of chapters in I. A. Richards's *The Philosophy of Rhetoric* (1936). Though he was renowned as a literary critic, Richards dismisses the idea that metaphor is the preserve of poets, or that it is a special and exceptional use of language; he goes so far as to say that "metaphor is the omnipresent principle of language," and it is difficult to eliminate even in science and philosophy, where we want our terms to be as precise and unequivocal as possible. He defines metaphor as "two thoughts of different things active together and supported by a single word, or phrase, whose meaning is a result of their interaction." His emphasis throughout his book is on the *activity* of words (and thoughts), on what he calls their "interinanimation."[8] That unusual word he took from a poem by John Donne, and it is not yet admitted into the *OED*,[9] but it captures his sense of the way words can animate or enliven each other by interacting in unusual contexts.

Richards has had better luck with two terms he proposes for the two parts of a metaphor – "tenor" and "vehicle" – in order to extricate the parts from the prevalent terminological confusion through which, for example, "metaphor" is applied sometimes to the whole expression and sometimes to one part of it. The tenor is "the underlying idea or principal subject which the vehicle or figure means." To enlist Eliot's line "The yellow fog that rubs its back upon the window-panes," we might say that the vehicle is an animal of some sort, maybe a cat, while the tenor, of course, is fog. But

Richards might have been more thorough and precise. On his own assumptions, he should not suggest that it is the vehicle that "means": if anything, it is the tenor that means, and the vehicle that bears the meaning, as the *means* to the meaning, perhaps. Better put, both tenor and vehicle contribute to the meaning; it emerges from their interaction or interinanimation.[10]

Though he emphasizes the omnipresence of metaphors in language, Richards analyzes several of them taken from poetry, largely to illustrate the failings of earlier treatments. Lord Kames, he says, quotes a line spoken by Othello – "Steep'd me in poverty to the very lips" – and finds it wanting, for "Poverty must here be conceived to be a fluid which it resembles not in any manner." Richard concedes Kames's point that poverty, the tenor, is a state of deprivation, while a vat or sea for steeping, the vehicle, is an instance of superfluity. He tries to rescue the line, however, by putting it back into context, a longish speech by Othello, where there are other metaphors involving liquids, and by noting Othello's mental derangement at the time he makes this speech. But we might question this rescue. It is surely right to look at the context, but it seems too easy to resort to Othello's state of mind to explain away an extreme or forced metaphor. And is it so extreme? Isn't there an interesting and persuasive sense in which a person can be steeped or soaked in poverty? To be impoverished through and through, with absolutely no hope of regaining any wealth – wouldn't that be well described as being steeped? One could be swimming in a sea of poverty, desperately seeking dry land. We do not find it odd to say a man is "up to his ears in debt," and if debt can be a liquid, why not poverty? (Recently, we have learned to say homeowners are "under water" when their mortgage debt is greater than the market value of their home.)[11] Perhaps, too, in the domain of the tenor, we can find connotations that are liquid enough, such as the likelihood that a man in abject poverty will lack a roof over his head and be frequently drenched with rain. Richards did much in his many writings to open readers' minds to the richness of metaphor, and, in taking his argument further here, I hope I am acting in his spirit.

In an important article of 1954, Max Black offered two new terms, and they divide the terrain of metaphor a little differently from Richards's terms.[12] He gives a simple example: "The chairman plowed through the discussion." The word "plowed" stands out as metaphorical, and Black calls it the "focus" of the metaphor. The rest of the sentence, which we take as literal, he calls the "frame," and he makes the useful point that if we change the frame, we might change the metaphor, or make it literal. After reviewing the "substitution" theory and the "comparison" theory, both of which he thinks might account for only certain metaphors, he sides with the "interaction" theory of Richards as the best so far, though he has some reservations about Richards's argument and terminology. Black offers a metaphor for metaphor – a filter – and suggests that the principal subject is "seen through" the metaphorical expression. In the example "Man is a wolf," we look at the subject "man" through the filter "wolf" (the focus): it is not a matter of substituting another word (as in "Man is vicious") but of mobilizing what he calls the "system of associated commonplaces" about wolves, what "everybody knows" about them, but filtered or organized so that only relevant wolf lore is brought to bear. In the end, this may be a kind of substitution after all, but a substitution of a system of meanings rather than a single word or meaning of a word. He is not far from Konrad's idea that we must forget certain things we know about wolves, though he perhaps dwells more on what things we might remember, so that "Man is a wolf" emerges as a richer and more interactive expression than it first may appear.

Black's term "focus" prompts the thought that a filter is like a lens. A lens might magnify, but it might also alter its subject in other ways, moving parts of it into and out of focus, distorting shapes, or adding colors. A telescope and a microscope give different perspectives on things, and "perspective" is the term Kenneth Burke chooses for the application of metaphor: "Metaphor is a device for seeing something in terms of something else. It brings out the thisness of a that, or the thatness of a this."[13] A lens is also like a light and, as Denis Donoghue has well said, a metaphor is seeing one thing "in the light of another."[14] Everything radiates its own distinctive light, and it may illuminate anything else brought within its range.

In his 1958 textbook, *Aesthetics*, Monroe Beardsley aligns himself more or less with Richards, though, like Black, he finds Richards vague and inconsistent with his terminology, and he claims Black's own discussion leaves out how we know that a phrase in a certain context is a metaphor in the first place and not literal. What feature or features alert us that we are not to take an assertion or attribution literally? Beardsley proposes a "Controversion Theory," which relies on the distinction between "designation," the primary or denotative sense of a word or phrase – the sort of thing found in dictionary definitions – and "connotation," the secondary senses, not all of which we may be aware of until a metaphor brings them to our attention, and which could never be listed in a dictionary (though maybe in a vast encyclopedia). He calls the tenor "the subject" and the vehicle "the modifier," terms borrowed from grammar. A metaphor, then, "is a significant attribution that is either indirectly self-contradictory or obviously false in its context, and in which the modifier connotes characteristics that can be attributed, truly or falsely, to the subject."[15]

"Connotes" is key. At the primary or designative level, for example, the attribution "metaphysical streets" (a phrase from Wallace Stevens) is obviously false, even absurd, but if we find it in a poem and therefore have reason to think it is seriously meant, we look for connotations in the modifier ("metaphysical") that render the attribution of it to the subject ("streets") significant, perhaps on the grounds that both metaphysics and streets are labyrinthine. This resort to connotations is much like Black's mobilization of the "system of associated commonplaces," but it adds the motive for doing so: self-contradiction or logical absurdity. Metaphor, then, is a way to resolve or reduce the literal conflict or collision.

Beardsley also makes explicit two rules that govern, or should govern, our reading of metaphors: "For a metaphor is a miniature poem, and the explica-tion of a metaphor is a model of all explication" (144). The Principle of Congruence states that the connotations must fit the subject, they must be relevant, so we must eliminate some (or "forget" them, as Konrad says), while the Principle of Plenitude states that "All the connotations that can be found to fit are to be attributed to the poem: it means all it *can* mean, so to speak" (144). Beardsley's theory of metaphor might be sufficient without the second principle, which is a program for deep and subtle reading, but if a connotation occurs to you (say, metaphysics has many intersections and so do most streets, or metaphysics leads nowhere and so do some streets) and you see no reason to rule it out as irrelevant or distracting, then by all means put it into play as you ponder the poem. Metaphors bring to light connotations of the subject ("streets") that we had not known before, and connotations of the attribution ("metaphysical") as well: they do not just transfer meaning but create it.[16] Or, as Denis Donoghue has said, "The force of a good metaphor is to give something a different life, a new life" (2), or "more abundant life" (71).

About Beardsley's connotations, we might ask: aren't they subjective? We might grant that a dictionary will list primary meanings that anyone who speaks the language must acknowledge are objectively "in the lan-guage," but as we get down to secondary meanings, and more and more subtle nuances, don't we leave objectivity behind and enter the realm of personal associations? In the sentence "The lion of the Greeks fell upon the hapless Trojans," we understand (1) that "lion" is substituting for "Achilles," and (2) certain leonine traits are attributed to Achilles, such as ferocity, strength, and speed, traits that anyone who knows English, or knows anything about lions, will recognize as embedded in the concept of a lion. But suppose you happen to find lions especially beautiful, or espe-cially ugly, or, having seen them only lying about in zoos, pretty much harmless. Some different connotations may be at work in your mind.

Suppose you have learned that it is the lionesses, not the lions, who do most of the hunting. What does that fact do to your understanding of the metaphor? Beardsley, as we saw in the preceding chapter, thinks interpretation is perfectly possible on the basis of objective features of a common language, so he would caution us to try to set aside any idiosyncratic associations we have accumulated and dwell instead on those connotations that are common, or easily available, to all adult speakers of the language.[17] We might need some historical research to find out, for example, whether the Greeks knew that the females do most of the hunting, or whether Greek lions were different from African lions in that respect. But by the time we went that far down the path of interpretation, we would have reached the point of diminishing returns. One of the skills needed to interpret metaphors is to know when to stop.

Neither Black nor Beardsley relies on the idea of resemblance or Aristotle's "analogy," and we might feel that they have thereby left out something essential to metaphor. Metaphor, after all, is akin to simile, and the very word "simile" points to similarity or resemblance. But it may be possible to bring resemblance into harmony with theories based on filters or controversion by noting that connotations or associated commonplaces, when shared by focus and frame, or subject and modifier, usually imply a similarity of some sort, whether a visual image or something more abstract. Because the words for them share a few connotations, metaphysics and streets – Wallace Stevens would have us believe – resemble each other in a few respects.

Beardsley's approach assumes that our normal expectation, whether we are reading a poem or conversing with friends, is that a statement will be literal or proper, and only if the literal meaning is absurd or in some other way defective will we fall back on plan B and assume it is metaphorical, or at least figurative. Many philosophers of language argue that ordinary human communication or conversation would be impossible or very slow and difficult if we did not obey several implicit conventions or "maxims" of cooperation, such as that our utterances will be truthful, relevant to the situation at hand, and unambiguous, among others. These are the default settings of what H. P. Grice calls "conversational implicature"; we might call it the principle of courtesy or charity. Metaphor, irony, and other modes violate these settings and thereby trigger in our minds a back-up strategy of figurative interpretation. This reaction may be what takes place in many cases, but, as Raymond Gibbs has argued, research on how people actually cope with metaphors has shown that they often do not go through this two-stage process but instantly grasp them.[18] Our minds (or brains) may be more attuned to metaphors than philosophers have thought, even to unusual metaphors, perhaps because we know unconsciously that they underlie most of our vocabulary and constantly extend it. In any case, we may be able to draw a new definition of poetry out of this debate: poetry is a realm of speech where the parameters of conversational implicature are reset so that literal meanings are no longer the default. Not as catchy as "spontaneous overflow of powerful feelings," to be sure, but a lot more useful. In daily conversation, if we met such a phrase as "metaphysical streets," we would stop and regroup; in poetry, when we meet even a perfectly literal and factual statement such as "Two roads diverged in a yellow wood," we also stop and sniff the air: something metaphorical, even metaphysical, may be lurking down one of the roads.

Poetry could not succeed in inviting us to alter the normal settings if it did not first invite us to take it seriously. Jonathan Culler has recently argued that Grice's principle of cooperation applies strongly to poems: we presume they are (or will be when we fully take them in) meaningful or interpretable or at least coherent, even if they seem obscure, nonsensical, or trivial at first.[19] We do so not because poems are speech-acts like those of daily life, or even representations of speech-acts by a poetic speaker or persona (though they may be), but because a poet and publisher, we assume, would not go to the trouble of putting a poem before us if they didn't think it was significant or worth our time. There are limits to this principle of cooperation or generosity, of course, because a poem may remain stubbornly impervious to our efforts, and life is too short to waste it on an irritating and unrewarding text. I have sometimes felt that certain "poets" have abused our welcoming, Gricean openness and published things called "poems" that really are senseless and trivial. If we rebuked them, they might appeal to the Zen-like idea that anything in the world can be appreciated as wonderful if it is meditated upon attentively, and any so-called poem might induce such an epiphany. If that is so, it is we who do the work, and we have the right, if only because there are already a billion poems in the world, to withdraw our charity and show such poems the door.

This may be the moment to consider Noam Chomsky's famous sentence "Colorless green ideas sleep furiously," which he offered in *Syntactic Structures* (1957) as one of two kinds of "nonsense." The sentence is perfectly grammatical or "well-formed" but it is nonsensical semantically, whereas "Furiously sleep ideas green colorless" is ungrammatical as well as nonsensical in meaning. The point is certainly well taken, but he was throwing red meat to the poets, quite a few of whom, such as John Hollander and Clive James, wrote poems that culminate quite meaningfully in Chomsky's first sentence. To put it in a poem, we might say, is to set loose the connotations or associations of all its words. Chomsky was concerned only with their primary meanings or denotations, but poets like to poke all around and everywhere beneath these first levels: "colorless" can mean "dull" or "stodgy," for instance, while "green" can mean "new" or "immature." Shelley's "Ode to the West Wind" had already come very close to saying that ideas sleep like seeds in the earth and even dream until they are awakened. To sleep furiously might mean to have furious dreams. And so on.[20] As far as that goes, the kinds of syntactic dislocations in poetry that we examined in chapter 5 might even let us rescue the ungrammatical version, if we may add two commas: "Furiously sleep ideas, green, colorless" is no more ungrammatical than "Silently enter Greeks, vengeful, enraged." Poets can be really annoying.

Tropes: Metaphor, Simile, Metonymy, Synecdoche, Apostrophe

Metaphor is akin to several other figures of speech or tropes (from Greek *tropos*, meaning "turn" or "twist"), of which the closest is simile. The standard definition of a simile is that it is a comparison with "like" or "as." It is also standard to add that it is an explicit metaphor, or that, as Aristotle states it, a simile "that lacks a word" (presumably the Greek equivalent of "like" or "as") is a metaphor (*Rhetoric* 1407a3).[21] Let's look at a few examples.

> Like as the waves make towards the pebbled shore,
> So do our minutes hasten to their end　　(Shakespeare)

> Here is your husband, like a mildew'd ear,
> Blasting his wholesome brother　　(Shakespeare)

> This City now doth like a garment wear
> The beauty of the morning　　(Wordsworth)

> How statue-like I see thee stand　　(Poe)

> Mais la tristesse en moi monte comme la mer ("But sadness in me rises like the sea")　　(Baudelaire)

> With beauty like a tightened bow　　(Yeats)

> And then she turned
> And, as the ray of sun on hanging flowers
> Fades when the wind hath lifted them aside,
> Went swiftly from me　　(Pound)

> When the evening is spread out against the sky
> Like a patient etherized upon a table　　(T. S. Eliot)

a flower
aloof
Flagrant as a flag   (William Carlos Williams)

Once my nose crawled like a snail on the glass   (Robert Lowell)

My black shoes stand on the floor
Like two open graves   (Robert Bly)

The nights snapped out of sight like a lizard's eyelid   (Plath)

A Canada goose rides up,
spread out like a grey suede shirt   (Anne Sexton)

I sit in my chair
as quietly as a fuse   (Margaret Atwood)

It is clear that similes such as these are a lot like metaphors, and in some instances they do indeed make explicit what is already metaphorical. If Hamlet had left out the mildewed ear and said only "Here is your husband, blasting his wholesome brother," his words would imply a plant disease no less, because of the meaning of "blast," and if Wordsworth had written "This City now doth wear the beauty of the morning," the line would imply clothing without including the garment. But "Like a patient etherized upon a table" is in no way even hinted at by "spread out against," which is barely metaphorical to begin with; the simile is forced and disturbing, and rightly famous. Perhaps Eliot could have written "When the evening is etherized upon the sky": would that have conveyed what we find in the original? I think not, for "patient" and "table" add telling detail to the scene we are to project onto the evening sky, or to the filter we are to see it through. In the same way "like a snail" adds quite a bit to "crawled . . . on the glass," and "as a fuse" entirely transforms, in fact almost reverses, what we would take "quietly" to mean by itself. In Cummings's example from the list of metaphors, "the moon rattles like a fragment of angry candy," we see a double addition to the original metaphor in "the moon rattles": (1) "like a fragment of candy" is a startling addition, though it is certainly consistent with the meaning of "rattles" (presumably the last piece left in a tin box); and (2) "angry candy" is a metaphor itself, apt enough within the simile (the candy wants to get out of solitary confinement, perhaps), but more jarring when applied back to the moon.

We should also note the acoustic space many of these similes occupy, for poets often unite the terms of a simile with similar sounds. Poe's "statue" and "stand"; Baudelaire's *moi, monte,* and *mer;* and Yeats's "beauty" and "bow" are obvious examples. Williams's "a flower / aloof / Flagrant as ∟ flag" is striking and strange, and perhaps a little flagrant. We would expect "fragrant" after "flower"; "flagrant" comes as a surprise, especially after "aloof," which seems opposite in meaning to it. As it stands, we have three alliterative clusters of fl- (not to mention the recurrent -g-) and the same consonants in reverse order in "aloof."

These similes seem to add a meaning, perhaps a meaning no one would have thought of when considering a spread-out evening or sitting quietly in a chair, but they also close the metaphor to all other possible meanings. The evening is spread out against the sky *not* like a dinner served upon a picnic blanket, *not* like a squadron of soldiers looking for the enemy, and *not* like numberless other things that might be spread out against something else, but just like a patient etherized upon a table. It is this limiting characteristic of simile, its assertion of resemblance or equivalence in such and such a respect, and not in other respects, that has led some theorists to deny that similes are explicit metaphors, or that metaphors are compressed or elliptical similes, as Aristotle, Quintilian, and many others have declared. Others have pointed out that similes are not metaphorical at all, explicitly or otherwise, for they are (or most of them are) literally true. It is literally true that Achilles is like a lion, in certain respects; it is false, and therefore metaphorical, that Achilles is a lion. Similes are like metaphors, in certain respects, according to this argument, but they are not metaphors.

Metaphor is often contrasted with metonymy, and the contrast may tell us something useful about metaphor. Unfortunately, there has been only loose agreement as to what metonymy is, and sometimes it is defined as a contrast to metaphor! In its earliest recorded use in Greek, μετωνυμία (*metōnymia*) is distinguished from metaphor but is not defined.[22] The word means "change of name" (*ōnyma* is a variant of *onoma*), too generic a definition to be helpful, rather like *epiphora* or "application." Quintilian also defines it very generally – "the substitution of one name for another" – but then gives some revealing examples of metonym types. "Neptune," he says, stands to "water," or "Vulcan" stands to "fire," as inventor to thing invented. In "a cup was drunk to the lees," a container stands for its contents. The possessor can be substituted for the possession, as when we say "a man was devoured" (meaning "his land") or "I am reading Virgil." Effect can replace cause, as in the phrase "pale Death" (death causes pallor). (We might also call that example a personification, of course, and hence a metaphor.) Several other kinds follow (*Institutes* 8.6.23–27). Long lists of these types have been offered during the many centuries since Quintilian, but what they have in common is association or contiguity: the item

substituted for another item is connected with it in some way, some
"literal" way, as cup holds wine, or man possesses land. When Hamlet
laments that his mother, so soon after his father's death, could "post / With
such dexterity to incestuous sheets" (1.2.156–57), he is not accusing the
bedsheets of strange metaphorical doings; it is a metonym for what his
mother is doing between those sheets. A metaphor, by contrast, involves a
transaction across two disconnected realms, such as metaphysics and city
plans, facial features and times of day ("the opening eyelids of the morn"),
and so on. This distinction seems very basic, and rich in implications, as we
will see, though there may be a gray area between them where it is hard to
discern whether a trope is one or the other or both.

Recent French analysts have deployed the terms *isotopie* and *allotopie* to
describe the two contexts or relationships a figurative term might have. If "cup"
is used to mean "wine," we may say the two words are isotopic – they belong to
the same *topie*, and one is an isotope of the other; if "cup" is used to mean
"shield," then the words are allotopic – they belong to different or disjunct
topies, and one is an allotope of the other. Contexts may change, of course. If
we're talking about, say, boxing, "The creampuff is waiting" is a metaphor:
"creampuff" comes from an allotopy (food types) that does not overlap with
strenuous human contact sports. But it can be an isotopic metonym to a
waitress who has forgotten the customer waiting for the tab for his dessert.[23]

Just as metaphors can die, as frequent repetition turns them into
common or literal terms, metonyms can also fade into literality. Perhaps
the best example of this process are the names of made things derived from
the places where they were originally made, such as "china," "cashmere,"
"canary," "hamburger," and "cheddar." There are hundreds of these in
English, some of them nearly invisible, such as "suede," which comes from
the French word for "Sweden," and "silk," which goes back to a Greek
word (*serikos*) for "Chinese," and "peach," which derives from the Latin
adjective for "Persian." Most of the fabrics we wear and half the food we eat
are metonyms of this kind. Even the Bible is a place-name metonym: it
comes from "little books" in Greek (*ta biblia*), itself a metonym from what
they are made of, "papyrus" (*biblos*), which was made in or exported from
the city of Byblos in Phoenicia.

But what about synecdoche, which often complicates discussions of
metonymy? Quintilian discusses it first (8.6.19–22), and defines it as
substituting a part for a whole, or a species for a genus; "roof," for
example, stands for "house," or "stern" for "ship." For a more interesting
example, he offers "the steers bring back the plow" as a metonymy for
"evening," since it is a part of evening's activities that draft animals return

to their yard or barn. He then says that metonymy is not very different from synecdoche.[24] Most scholars of rhetoric today consider synecdoche a kind of metonymy because it also involves exchanges within one semantic domain. But a group of structuralist rhetoricians in Belgium, under the name "Groupe μ" (the Greek μ for μεταφορά), has argued that synecdoche, which they define as "going from the particular to the general, from the part to the whole, from lesser to greater, from species to genus" is the most fundamental trope. A metaphor, on this assumption, "is the product of two synecdoches."[25] The idea seems to be that to get from "Achilles" to "lion," we first call Achilles "the ferocious," for example, thus singling out one of his prominent traits and placing him in a more general category of ferocious beings, and then we choose another instance of notably ferocious beings, the lion, which we could also call "the ferocious," in a synecdoche taken in reverse. Their meeting point is the equation of Achilles and lion.

Groupe μ uses the word "seme" for a minimal semantic feature, such as male vs. female, or young vs. old, and perhaps ferocious vs. gentle or tame, and "sememe" for a bundle of these semes in a word or concept, such as lion and Achilles, or metaphysics and street. The sememe corresponding to "metaphysics" might contain quite a lot of semes, such as "philosophical," "fundamental," "abstract," "difficult," "obscure," "labyrinthine," "pointless," and many more, no doubt highly debatable, while a sememe corresponding to "street" might include such semes as "on the ground," "in a city," "for vehicles," "with intersections," "paved," and maybe "labyrinthine" (at least in some cities). Synecdoches entail contractions or expansions of the number of semes. As we pass from the first sememe to the second via the seme "labyrinth," we contract and then expand the number of semes, first by leaving out every seme of "metaphysics" but "labyrinthine," then by singling out "labyrinthine" among the other semes of "street." In this case, the bridge connecting the sememes seems rather narrow, whereas in "Achilles is a lion" the bridge, or the lozenge made by the overlapping circles, seems larger.

It is hard to see how this exercise in structural semiotics improves much on earlier theories; the "reduction of semes," for example, is very like the forgetting of irrelevant associations or connotations. A metaphor, moreover, may be analyzable logically as the product of two synecdoches, but that does not describe what it is like to read one or invent one. Nor does this procedure rule out such possible products as "the lion is a tiger," which can pivot on semes shared by both cats: is it a metaphor? It's the pivot that matters, the turn or twist (the meaning of *tropos* in Greek) that can bring into consciousness an entirely new idea. Afterward, we can see that one or two semes have been herded through a gateway from one corral to another, but there is certainly no lexicon, conscious or unconscious, that could contain all semes (and maybe even sememes) in advance. Metaphors appear to *create* semes. And this theory, too, relies on something like the Controversion Theory, the notion of an initial "affront to (linguistic) reason," which triggers the reduction procedure – an affront which, in poetry at least, may not exist.[26]

To recur to a subject in Chapter 1, since the time of Saussure, whose major book was published posthumously in 1916, linguists have increasingly adopted his fundamental distinction between the "syntagmatic" and the "associative" aspects of language, though he dwelled mainly on the former, which he called the dimension of "combination."[27] Today, linguists usually deploy the term "paradigmatic" for "associative." Syntagmatic relations are grammatical relations of words within phrases, clauses, and sentences. So, in the noun phrase "the many pretty little red schoolhouses," there are quite a few syntagmatic rules that govern the order of these words. "The," for example, the definite article, must precede the other four modifiers. Definite articles belong to the set of "determiners," a set which also includes indefinite articles ("a" and "an"), demonstratives (such as "this") and quantifiers (such as "many" and "five"). Some quantifiers, called "predeterminers," must precede the definite article (as in "all the schoolhouses" or "both the schoolhouses") and some may not ("*many the schoolhouses"), but the latter might precede the indefinite article ("many a schoolhouse"). Determiners as a category precede adjectives, but some adjectives precede others: it is odd to say "the red little schoolhouse," though it would be permissible in certain narrow contexts; odder would be "the red little pretty schoolhouses." Native English speakers know that the six words in "the many pretty little red schoolhouses" must be in that order, though few speakers, indeed few linguists, can make the rules explicit. These are among the syntagmatic rules of English: they govern the grouping and ordering of words in a phrase and of phrases within a clause or sentence, or what we might call the horizontal dimension of language.

The other aspect or axis, which we might think of as vertical, is the paradigmatic, associative, selective, or substitutive pole. For example, "these" might be substituted for "the," "few" for "many," "ugly" for "pretty," "large" for "little," "black" for "red," and "factories" for "schoolhouses," giving us the analogous phrase "these few ugly large black factories." Above each word in our original phrase hover various options. Saussure says they are "in absentia," but they could be actualized and made present.[28] There are rules governing these operations, largely classificatory: an adjective of a certain type can replace another adjective of the same type, and so on. A large number of phrases of this kind are in paradigmatic relation to each other.

In a brilliant and influential article of 1956,[29] Roman Jakobson redefined the syntagmatic or combinatory level as metonymy and the paradigmatic or selective level as metaphor. Then he connected the two functions to two types of aphasia or speech disorders: (1) the "similarity disorder," in which patients can make syntactic connections and associate objects with contexts ("knife" may lead readily to "fork" or "bread") but cannot come up with the word for the thing when shown it; and (2) the "contiguity disorder," where patients lose command of grammatical words such as prepositions and articles as well as word-inflections, but hold on longer to lexical words or their roots. "Metaphor," Jakobson summarizes, "is alien to the similarity disorder, and metonymy to the contiguity disorder."

Jakobson's theory of aphasia, after stimulating some further research, seems to have lost its importance among neurologists and psychologists, and the minimal Saussurean notion of syntax as "combinatory" has been left behind by more powerful models of syntax proposed by Noam Chomsky and his followers, which show quite clearly that syntax is governed by rules that have little to do with contiguity in any but the vaguest sense. Moreover, to substitute "factory" for "schoolhouse" along the paradigmatic axis, or "black" for "red," seems less metaphorical than metonymical, since both factory and schoolhouse belong to the isotopy of building types, and black and red are both colors. To say "the schoolhouse is a factory" is certainly to create a metaphor, or so one hopes, but that does not imply that the two six-word phrases are metaphors for each other in any but, well, a metaphorical sense. Paradigmatic processes are not literally metaphorical processes. Still, Jakobson's identification of the syntagmatic axis with metonymy and the paradigmatic axis with metaphor has prompted a good deal of interesting work. In the aphasia article itself, he makes some sweeping generalizations about literature: that Romanticism privileges metaphor, for instance, while Realism privileges metonymy, and that within poetry lyric is metaphorical and epic metonymical. He thus lays out a program of research. Metaphor has always been the queen of tropes, receiving most of the attention of rhetoricians and literary critics for centuries, but in recent years metonymy has gained prestige and been made the subject of interesting studies in many fields. And, of course, poets use metonymy too.

We mentioned apostrophe earlier as a means of personification, and hence metaphor – even if no metaphorical term, focus, vehicle, modifier, or allotopic seme is explicitly stated – and we should expand a little on this function. Originally considered a gesture or figure an orator might use, apostrophe, from Greek ἀποστροφή, is a "turning away" from the audience to address someone or something absent. Quintilian gives it the briefest treatment (*Institutes* 9.2.38). His first example, "What was that sword of yours doing, Tubero, in the field of Pharsalia?" is not a metaphorical attribution, since Tubero is a person, but his other two examples – "For I call upon you, O Alban hills and groves" and "O Porcain laws! O Sempronian laws!" – might be considered minimally metaphorical because they attribute sentience to natural objects or social institutions. When hills and groves are "called upon," they are taken as human or personal, ready perhaps to be made into witnesses of the speaker's deeds or guarantors of his claims, but nothing more is attributed to them. In the same vein, Coleridge invokes "Ye clouds," "Ye Ocean-Waves," "Ye Woods," and "Thou rising Sun" to "Bear witness for me, wheresoe'er ye be, / With what deep worship I have still adored / The spirit of divinest Liberty" ("France: An Ode," first stanza), but as he names each witness, he adds particular human character-istics: the ocean waves, for instance, "Yield homage," like a medieval vassal, "only to eternal laws" (4). "Thou," the first word of Keats's "Ode on a Grecian Urn" already personifies the urn by implying it can hear him, and perhaps speak (as it does in the end), but with the rest of the line, "still unravished bride of quietness," we are deep into a metaphor, almost an allegory, whereby the urn is a young woman on her nuptial eve.

The Pervasiveness of Metaphor

In the spirit of I. A. Richards's contention that metaphors pervade com-mon speech, George Lakoff and Mark Johnson have drawn attention to what they call "metaphorical concepts" or "conceptual metaphors" in their books, especially *Metaphors We Live By* (1980), the title of which points to the non-literary domain of their subject, but which they then followed up with *More Than Cool Reason: A Field Guide to Poetic Metaphor* (1989). The metaphors they unearth in the earlier book range in generality from "Argument is war" (they state them as equations) and "Time is money" to such "ontological" metaphors as "Events are containers." When we say "He attacked every weak point in my argument" or "I shot down his argument," we are carrying the tenor of "argument," as Richards might say, on the vehicle of "warfare," and when we say we "spend time" or "lose time," or we live on "borrowed time," we are transferring money terms onto time. These cases need only be stated to reveal themselves as meta-phorical. More subtle and abstract are such expressions as "I went to the race" (an event is an entity) and "I dropped out of the race" (an event-entity is a container). In this and similar cases, which Lakoff and Johnson are very good at detecting, we seem to be at the borderland between metaphor and metonym, or even between metaphor and literality, because much depends on how literally an event, for example, can be said to "take place" and whether prepositions, such as "to" and "out of" in these expressions, can be said to be literal about space but metaphorical about time – indeed, whether spatial relations are the inevitable vehicle for temporal relations. These are deep waters, to use a familiar metaphor (perhaps "Thinking is sailing a ship"), and we will try to navigate them again shortly.

But we should say something about their second book, which is about poetry, and which all students of poetry will find interesting. They could do worse than begin at the back, with the "Index of Metaphors," where ninety metaphors are listed in propositional form: "Birth is arrival," "Death is a reaper," "Life is a flame," "Life is a journey," "People are plants," "Time is a thief." These categories are illustrated in passage after passage of English poetry as well as biblical, classical, and several other sorts of verse. "Life is a journey," for instance, is expressed in the opening line of Dante's *Inferno*, which we quoted earlier under the "[NP] of [NP]" form; in Jesus' admonition to enter in at the strait gate; in the entirety of Bunyan's *Pilgrim's Progress*; in Frost's "The Road Not Taken"; and in many other works. The categories, moreover, intersect and build large quasi-systems. "Life is a journey" belongs to the same domain as "Birth is arrival" and "Death is departure," as well as several others on the list. "People are plants" and "Death is a reaper" imply one another, as any reader of Shakespeare's sonnets will recall. "Life is a day" is another metaphor poets richly exploit, as Lakoff and Turner document, though it is an opportunity missed not to mention Aristotle's use of it in the founding treatment of their subject.

Lakoff and Turner deploy a different set of terms from those of Richards or Black, terms now widespread in analyses of metaphor. In the metaphor "Life is a journey," "journey" is the "source domain" and "life" is the "target domain." The target domain is the tenor or literal sense, while the source domain is the vehicle or focus, loosely speaking. "Target" and "source" are metaphors themselves, of course, though to make them match with each other and blend into one metaphor, "source" ought to be changed to "quiver" or "arsenal." The idea seems to be that we shoot various images at a target idea until we hit it. It is a good metaphor. Pindar used it several times for his own songs; for instance, "I hope / . . . to hit the mark head on, / shooting, like an archer, from my bow" (*Nemean* 6.27, translated by Race). To call the source and the target "domains" rather than "words" or "expressions" is important, ɔ, for it keeps us alert to the fact that "life" and "journey" and most other ɔrds, aside from technical terms in mathematics or science, are rich in connotations or semes, features that occupy the Venn circles. Lakoff and Johnson call them "slots," and speak of "mapping" slots from the source domain onto the target domain. "For example, to map the PATH slot of the JOURNEY schema onto the domain of LIFE means understanding the events of one's life as constituting the points of a path, which necessitates creating a COURSE OF LIFE slot in the LIFE domain."[30] Reaching a destination in the source domain maps onto fulfilling a purpose in the target domain, while going far along on the path, or crossing a border the path meets, might map onto the death slot: "Remember me when I am gone away," Christina Rossetti wrote, "Gone far away into the silent land" ("Remember").

Earlier, we noted that Beardsley, Donoghue, and others have insisted that metaphors produce meanings; they do not just bring out latent ones that we haven't noticed. They do not, in other words, just shuffle semes about that have already been recorded in some immense lexicon – they create them. In the terms Lakoff and Johnson have established, we could say that the target domain (say, "life") did not have the slots corresponding to the source domain ("journey") until it was structured by the source domain through the use of metaphors.[31]

Lakoff and Johnson are not interactionists or "interinanimationists" in their approach to conceptual metaphors, for they point out that many of them are not reversible.[32] Life may be a journey, but it would be odd to say that a journey is a life, taking life as the source domain and a journey as the target. Setting out on a trip would then be seen as being born, perhaps, and arriving at the destination as dying. Not very likely in ordinary speech, no doubt, but it would not be surprising to find a poet or novelist making that reversal somewhere.

From reading either of their books, you will come away much more attuned to the pervasive but largely subterranean ways of metaphor in everyday speech; and from *More Than Cool Reason,* more appreciative of the ways poets bring these ways to light. Though they do not mention him, both these projects go back at least as far as to the philosopher Friedrich Nietzsche (1844–1900), who constantly hammered away at the claim that nearly everyone, including philosophers, has forgotten that the "concepts" that they take as literally true, the "proper" meanings they rely on, are all originally metaphors, along with "concept" and "proper" themselves. What we take as truth is really "a mobile army of metaphors, metonymies, and anthropomorphisms" that long usage makes seem "fixed, canonical, and obligatory"; "truths are illusions about which one has forgotten that this is what they are; metaphors which are worn out and witho power."[33] Abstractions are concrete images whose life has drain former professor of philology, Nietzsche deploys the weapon of et) what he calls "genealogy" to reveal these dead metaphors for what is especially interested in moral and religious terms, and devotes : in *On the Genealogy of Morality* to showing how such words as "good," "bad," and "evil" were redefined when Christianity, the religion of the weak, unhealthy, life-denying but multitudinous herd of plebeians, more or less overthrew the strong, healthy, life-affirming values of the pagan aristocracy. The German word *schlecht* ("bad"), he says, is identical with *schlicht* ("plain, simple"), a clue to its origin as a term the nobility used for the common folk. (They are both related to English "slight.") The Greek word ἐσθλός (*esthlos*), which in Homer meant "good," "brave," or "noble," in its root sense means "one who is, who possesses reality, who is real, who is true," as opposed to the underlings who are liars; the root is *es-*, which is found in Greek *esti*, Latin *est*, German *ist*, English "is," and so on. *Malus*, Latin for "bad," he connects with Greek *melas* ("black"), which reveals that the early inhabitants of Italy were dark-skinned or dark-haired in contrast with their blond Aryan conquerors.[34]

Of these etymologies, only *schlecht* still seems sound. (Nietzsche might have noted that English "cretin," meaning a dwarfed and deformed idiot, comes from French *crétin*, which means "Christian"!) The origin of *esthlos* is obscure, and no historical linguist today connects *malus* with *melas*. It is somewhat embarrassing for Nietzsche's radical genealogy of morality that he gets several key words wrong, but the philological approach has proven very fruitful as our knowledge of historical linguistics has improved since his day. Take "concept" itself. The PIE root **kap-* meant "grasp." In Latin it evolved into *cāpio* ("take"), the participle of which (*cāptus*) led to English "capture" and "captive," and then into *concipio* ("take together"), the participle of which (*conceptus*) gives us "concept"; via French, we get "conceive." When we say we "grasp" a concept or "come to grips" with it, we repeat its etymology. The German word for "concept" is *Begriff*, which is akin to the verb *greifen* ("grasp, grip"). The word "comprehend" in English goes back through Latin to the PIE root **ghend-*, which also meant "grasp" or "seize"; the same root via Old Norse produced English "get." When we "get it" (such as a joke), we comprehend it: we seize it. Nietzsche does not spell all this out, but he does say that the history of such terms is a matter of suppression of metaphor by violence, not just absent-minded forgetting. Concepts themselves are seized.[35]

Nietzsche likens his own philosophizing to the work (or serious play) of an inventor or creative artist, such as a poet, who comes up with new metaphors to refresh or animate our sense of things, but does not let them congeal into "concepts" by insisting on them, or insisting on them alone. He wrote poetry of his own, as well as music, and his most popular work, *Thus Spake Zarathustra*, might be called a (very long) prose poem.[36]

The German philosopher Martin Heidegger (1889–1976), who wrote an immense study of Nietzsche, relies heavily on etymologies to establish how philosophers in the west have lost their awareness of "Being" since some time before Plato. Like Nietzsche's, quite a few of Heidegger's etymologies are mistaken, such as his claim that the Greek word for "it is necessary" is related to the word for "hand";[37] such errors are a greater problem for him than for Nietzsche because, whereas Nietzsche thinks everything is metaphor and flings metaphors about with cheerful abandon, Heidegger is trying to recover what he thinks is a fundamental non-metaphorical state of the world we inhabit.

In Heidegger's wake, Hans Blumenberg undertook an ambitious program of "Metaphorology," which was mainly a series of studies of metaphors used by philosophers, such as "Light as a Metaphor for Truth" – the title of one of his articles – and *Shipwreck with Spectator: Paradigm of a Metaphor for Existence*, a short book. He calls such metaphors "absolute" metaphors, for they founded basic philosophical concepts, but he does not think we can go back to something pre-metaphorical such as Heidegger's "Being." Metaphysics, he believes, is metaphorics taken literally, and it is time to investigate the metaphors as metaphors. Unlike Nietzsche and Heidegger, however, he does not make much use of etymologies, preferring to trace metaphors through philosophical, religious, and literary texts.

Much more etymological is Onians's 1951 study, *The Origins of European Thought*, in which with great erudition he tries to show that certain words for abstract ideas, such as αἰών (*aiōn*), usually translated "life" or "lifetime" (whence English "aeon" or "eon"), have very physical or concrete earlier meanings – in this case, something like "spinal marrow," a liquid that leaks out when we weep and especially when we die. He finds many examples of the ancient European notion that life, youth, and health are wet, while old age and sickness are dry. A striking example is "sapience," a word for "knowledge," which goes back to the Latin verb *sapere*, which meant "to have flavor" before it meant "to be wise" or "to think." The usual assumption was that the intermediate stage had to do with "taste" – a person with "taste" would be intelligent – but here too Onians connects intelligence with a liquid: *sapere* is akin to Latin *sapa* ("new wine"), English "sap," and German *Saft* ("juice"). He notes Old Icelandic *safi* ("sap") seems akin to *sefi* ("mind"); perhaps Greek *sophos* ("wise") is also related. In the eyes of our European forebears, to be savvy is to be sappy.

Interest in historical metaphorology remains high, and quite a few studies have appeared recently that focus on a single metaphor or related complex of metaphors. To give just one instance, Claudia Bergmann's *Childbirth as a Metaphor of Crisis* (2008) carefully examines hundreds of passages of the Hebrew Bible where, as her title indicates, personal or national crises are likened to a woman in labor. The formulaic simile "like a woman giving birth" for a people or nation fearing attack occurs once in the Psalms (48.7) and fifteen times in the prophets Isaiah, Jeremiah, and Micah. It is striking and strange. Bergmann does not take up the Greek New Testament, but surely this metaphor is resumed in Paul's letter to the Romans 8.22, where he says (in the King James version) "the whole creation groaneth and travaileth in pain together until now."

Bergmann cites passages from ancient Near Eastern texts that say that being born is to leave a dark place and see the light of the sun. We could find comparable passages from ancient Greek texts. In the *Odyssey*, Menelaus says he had no wish "to go on living or see the light of the sun" (4.540), while Tiresias in the realm of Hades (a name that probably means "unseen") asks Odysseus, "How is it you have left the light of the sun?" (11.93). The sun-god Helios plays a large role in the *Odyssey*, which is about a hero who has been away from home for nineteen years and has been unseen by the known world for nine of them. His return coincides with a festival of Apollo at or near the winter solstice, as if he stands in for the god of light when the sun and moon come back into alignment (the so-called Metonic cycle of nineteen years). So it is, perhaps, that an "absolute" or "ontological" metaphor inspired the structure of the great prototype of the quest-romance.

To see the light, to see by light, to be seen in the light seem to be inevitable basic metaphors. Blumenberg confines himself to philosophical texts in his study of light as truth, but we can find that metaphor lurking in dozens of common expressions. We say "I see" for "I know," for example, just as the Greeks said οἶδα (*oida*) for "I know" – the perfect aspect of **eidō* ("I see"), from **weidō*, akin to Latin *videō* and English "wit" and "wise." We say such things as "It dawned on me," "he brought to light an obscure case," "a bright student," "a brilliant idea," "an illuminating article," "lucid prose," "a model of clarity," and "a good illustration of her point." When we "elucidate" something, we "cast light" on it. We speak of the Age of Enlightenment and the benighted Dark Ages. Certain truths are "self-evident" – "evident" deriving from *videō*. When basic metaphors are inescapable, as I think this one is, then we are at the borderland of metaphor itself. Light may be more than a metaphor for truth; it is arguably close to a literal synonym of it, or at least its precondition. Jacques Derrida plays with the idea that the terms we use for both metaphor and truth are derived from light or its absence – that is, the rising and setting sun – so that all metaphors are "heliotropes."[38]

Do metaphors "go all the way down"? It may be that acts of metaphorizing created the bulk of the vocabulary of every language, and if we could roll time far enough backward we could give a concrete or physical etymology for every word, however abstract.

There is a process found in all languages that linguists call "grammaticalization," whereby words that were once "lexical" or meaningful undergo a semantic weakening or "bleaching" (a good metaphor, that) and devolve into functional or grammatical words or morphemes: prepositions, auxiliaries, inflections, and the like. Thus, the fully fledged verb "go" becomes the auxiliary verb for the future tense in many languages ("I'm going to eat," *Je vais manger*). The adverb and preposition "down," the opposite of "up," is derived from the noun "down," still in use in England to mean "hill" (it is related to "dune"). It is easily traced: the Old English word "adun" is a shortened form of "ofdun," which is in effect "off" + "dune" – that is, "from the hill," downward, into the valley. The adverbial and adjectival ending "-ly," as in "manly" or "happily," is akin to "like" (as in "man-like" or "happy-like"); they both go back to a word meaning "form, shape, body," and even "corpse." (A mortuary was called a "lich-house" until the nineteenth century; and "corpse" in German today is *Leiche*.) In an interesting contrast, the Romance languages make adverbs by attaching the word for "mind" to adjectives: in French, the adjective *heureux* ("happy") becomes the adverb *heureusement* ("happily"), the suffix deriving from Latin *mente*, the ablative case of *mens* ("mind"). The adverb originally meant something like "in a happy mind," whereas the equivalent in the Germanic languages meant something like "in a happy shape or body."[39]

These recruitments of concrete lexical words (for going, hill, shape, or mind) for mainly grammatical purposes are examples of metaphors drained of metaphoricity. It is hard to conceive, however, how language could get started by metaphor alone. Are proper names metaphors? What about basic deictic or pointing words, such as "this" and "that," "here" and "there"? Perhaps language started with those. We have no idea, and in speculating this way we are in danger of so stretching the idea of metaphor that it loses all meaning. Wallace Stevens, then, may be right that "There is no such thing as a metaphor of a metaphor. One does not progress through metaphors. Thus reality is the indispensable element of each metaphor."[40] Or, we might say, the concept of metaphor depends on a concept of its opposite, the normal or literal against which metaphor stands out as metaphor. If metaphor is a deviation or departure from ordinary usage, there must be a "zero degree" of language for metaphor to deviate from. It may be that all we can do is postulate such a language, and approximate it to varying degrees (in scientific prose, perhaps, or symbolic logic); it may be impossible to find it or construct it in pure form. And it keeps changing. Metaphors die; they become relexicalized – that is, given new definitions that become literal or current – and given enough time their etymologies may be lost. They may be grammaticalized and lose all independent meaning. New metaphors invade the language, and not just metaphors but the great host of figures and tropes that are also thought to be deviations from the norm: metonymy, synecdoche, litotes (understatement), hyperbole (overstatement), paronomasia (punning), and so on – all of them with hard-to-remember Greek names.[41] Can we imagine even the simplest description of an everyday event that would have no recourse to any of these?

Another reason it may be impossible to get behind, or beneath, metaphors is that the very concept of metaphor is metaphorical. Not only is its etymology based on a physical act, a "carrying across" or "transporting," but the distinction between metaphorical and literal (or proper) rests on certain philosophical distinctions, such as that between material and mental, that themselves rest on metaphorical acts. Jacques Derrida investigates this circularity or paradox in detail in "White Mythology." As Paul Ricoeur sums up the matter, "The paradox is this: there is no discourse on metaphor that is not stated within a metaphorically engendered conceptual network. There is no nonmetaphorical standpoint from which to perceive the order and the demarcation of the metaphorical field. Metaphor is metaphorically stated."[42] We might as well relax, then, and enjoy the endlessly creative process of metaphorization and demetaphorization without trying to "get to the bottom of it" – to deploy, of course, another metaphor.

Metaphor and Defamiliarization

It seems sensible to say, then, that words and sentences pass into and out of metaphoricity. Or that the metaphor–literal distinction itself floats over the language, and alights now here, now there, to sort out what is what, like an angel of linguistic change. We say a table has legs, a chair has arms, a stairway has a head and a foot. These were certainly metaphors once, but now they are "dead metaphors," and dead metaphors are no longer metaphors but have become literal or "proper" expressions. "Dead metaphor" itself illustrates the point: is it still a metaphor, or is it a dead metaphor? In any case, if we say, prompted by the angel, that our table is a quadruped, we revive the dead metaphor (it was only asleep) as we evoke image of our table deciding to stretch its legs, or sit down on two of m, or walk out the front door. For a moment we have an enlivened picture of the table: we see it with new eyes.

And this is where poets come in. They must take the language as they find it, where most of its metaphors are dead: nearly everything is literal, proper, normal, current, familiar. Their job is to waken the dead, pour new wine out of old bottles, or, as Ezra Pound said, "make it new." This task has been explicitly taken up by poets since the Romantic era, though many earlier poets felt the duty to state familiar truths in fresh ways. Coleridge wrote in retrospect of his and Wordsworth's joint project, the *Lyrical Ballads* (1798), that Wordsworth

> was to propose to himself as his object, to give the charm of novelty to things of every day, and to excite a feeling analogous to the supernatural, by awakening the mind's attention from the lethargy of custom, and directing it to the loveliness and the wonders of the world before us; an inexhaustible treasure, but for which in consequence of the film of familiarity and selfish solicitude we have eyes, yet see not, ears that hear not, and hearts that neither feel nor understand. (Coleridge, *Biographia Literaria*, Ch. 14 [2:6–7])

Shelley repeats Coleridge's telling phrase in his *Defence of Poetry*: "Poetry ... purges from our inward sight the film of familiarity which obscures from us the wonder of our being."

The Russian Formalist movement of the early twentieth century theorized about the devices with which writers estranged or distanced the familiar world. Victor Shklovsky in his essay "Art as Technique" (1917) worked out the idea of *ostranenie* or "defamiliarization": "The technique of art is to make objects 'unfamiliar,' to make forms difficult, to increase the difficulty and length of perception because the process of perception is an aesthetic end in itself and must be prolonged." There are many devices besides metaphor by which this might be accomplished, and Shklovsky mentions, for example, Tolstoy's choice of a horse for the narrator of one of his stories. We might think too of Cervantes's novella "The Dogs' Colloquy" (1613) or Gulliver's encounter with the horse-people called Houyhnhnms (1726). The German playwright Bertolt Brecht came up with several "alienation effects" (*Verfremdungseffekte*) to break the dramatic illusion, hinder the audience's emotional identification with the characters, and encourage critical thinking: devices such as deliberately bad acting, captions on placards, commentary by a narrator, interpolated songs, and direct addresses by actors to the audience.

But for poets the main such device will be metaphor. The language of poets, Shelley says:

is vitally metaphorical; that is, it marks the before unapprehended relations of things and perpetuates their apprehension, until the words which represent them, become, through time, signs for portions or classes of thoughts instead of pictures of integral thoughts; and then if no new poets should arise to create afresh the associations which have been thus disorganized [i.e., no longer integral], language will be dead to all the nobler purposes of human intercourse.

This subsidence and disorganization of metaphor over time has been well described by John Wright as "semantic entropy" (*Shelley's Myth of Metaphor*, 31), a good metaphor itself that borrows a term from physics. But fresh contingents of new poets keep entering the workforce, bringing with them new metaphors, similes, metonyms, and other tricky tools, scrubbing off the creeping film of familiarity and banality from our windows and eyeglasses, and staving off the second law of semantic thermodynamics by "organizing" new energetic poems. "Reality is a cliché from which we escape by metaphor," says Wallace Stevens.[43] How long can this go on? Billy Collins imagines the end of it all in "The Trouble with Poetry" when

> the day finally arrives
> when we have compared everything in the world
> to everything else in the world,
> and there is nothing left to do
> but quietly close our notebooks
> and sit with our hands folded on our desks.

If entropy doesn't wear us down, the completion of the great collective poetic project might simply silence us. But that day seems far off.

There was a little trend in English poetry not long ago called "Martian Poetry," which might be taken as a sign of desperation – Have we indeed run out of metaphors? – but which produced some delightful new ones nonetheless. Craig Raine's celebrated poem "A Martian Sends a Postcard Home" (1977), which started the vogue, begins this way:

> Caxtons are mechanical birds with many wings
> and some are treasured for their markings –
>
> they cause the eyes to melt
> or the body to shriek without pain.
>
> I have never seen one fly, but
> sometimes they perch on the hand.

It is like a riddle, but because it is not very hard to find the answer we can enjoy the witty details lurking under the pretense that a naïve tourist is confronting this mechanical device for the first time. The pretense is broken briefly at the outset with the term "Caxtons," for the Martian tourist would not have heard any earthling calling the things by that name, but it is charming in itself, and provokes the thought that Martians in their own language name things after their inventors or discoverers, as physicists on this planet do, with their ohms, volts, amperes, newtons, and curies. (Caxton was the first English printer.) It is one of Quintilian's types of metonym. I hope my reader will stop for a moment and take a new look at what he or she is holding, unless it is an eBook, in which case this would be a good opportunity to type in a new defamiliarization effect.

Though he is not usually grouped with the Martians, Charles Simic's little poem "Fork" will make you hesitate to use one for a while. Among other things, "It resembles a bird's foot / Worn around the cannibal's neck." (He has also done "Knife" and "Spoon.")

Though there may be no shortage of good new metaphors, some poets have made clear their frustration with all metaphors – and similes, of course – or at least their inadequacy before certain experiences or sensations, whether it is of the divine, the sublime, the evanescence of insight, or the raw physical thisness of the world. Shelley seems to have taken very seriously the role of the poet as he describes it in the *Defence* – to reveal "the before unapprehended relations of things" and to "create afresh" what has been lost or filmed over – and at the same time seems to have despaired over his own power, or the power of the language, to do so. The result was his characteristic tendency to pile on metaphors or similes, something we might call "overkill" if his purpose were not the opposite of killing. To describe a beautiful woman in "Epipsychidion," he tries these five extravagant metaphors (112–19):

> See where she stands! a mortal shape indued
> With love and life and light and deity,
> And motion which may change but cannot die;
> An image of some bright Eternity;
> A shadow of some golden dream; a Splendour
> Leaving the third sphere pilotless; a tender
> Reflection of the eternal Moon of Love
> Under whose motions life's dull billows move[.]

And then, as if suddenly self-conscious about his strenuous effort, he calls her a metaphor!

> A Metaphor of Spring and Youth and Morning;
> A Vision like incarnate April, warning,
> With smiles and tears, Frost the Anatomy
> Into his summer grave.   (120–23)

He does something similar with similes in "Hymn to Intellectual Beauty," the subject of which is abstract and elusive, to be sure. The first stanza has six similes:

> The awful shadow of some unseen Power
>> Floats though unseen among us; visiting
>> This various world with as inconstant wing
> As summer winds that creep from flower to flower;
> Like moonbeams that behind some piny mountain shower,
>> It visits with inconstant glance
>> Each human heart and countenance;
> Like hues and harmonies of evening,
>> Like clouds in starlight widely spread,
>> Like memory of music fled,
>> Like aught that for its grace may be
> Dear, and yet dearer for its mystery.

The last simile, "Like aught," is a kind of algebraic *x*, a place-holder for all the other similes that might be inserted, like the "Metaphor" in "Epipsychidion." The sheer number of metaphors and similes that Shelley typically musters prompts the thought that the most important things in the real world, as well as our deepest experiences, all transcend verbal description. Each analogy may capture something of them, and several of them together may approach an adequate account, but it can only approach it — and even that may not be true, as the recourse to the aught-simile suggests. These passages glory in their inventiveness, and at the same time despair over the inadequacy of what they invent.

Wallace Stevens seems to have had more to say about metaphor, and to say it in his poems, than any other modern poet writing in English. Several of his poems have "metaphor" in their titles, such as "The Motive for Metaphor." In that poem, addressed to "you" (his readers? himself?), he first describes the state of mind that "you prefer": autumn or spring, the seasons of change, of obscure moonlight cast on "things that would never be quite expressed" (like Shelley's themes), a realm of never-ending metaphors with "the exhilaration of changes" they bring. You would rather float in this crepuscular poetic world of "intimations" than face the noonday sun, "The ABC of being," that elementary reality that precedes all words about it, "the hammer / Of red and blue, the hard sound," or, as the brilliant final line states it, "The vital, arrogant, fatal, dominant X." This X is a sort of negative variant of the *x* that I suggested for Shelley's "aught" place-holder, the beautiful thing that

eeps inspiring more metaphors in order to get closer to it; here it is the
raw element, not even as specific as A or B or C, from whose glare you
shrink, fleeing to metaphors in order to escape its inhospitable terrain.
And yet how is this X described here if not metaphorically? Aren't
"ABC" and "X" themselves metaphors for this "literal" reality? They
are almost also puns on "literal," since the literal meaning of "literal" is
"made of letters" (Latin *litera* means "letter of the alphabet").[44] Letters,
too, were sometimes called "elements" in English (*QED* "element" IV.14.
a) after Latin usage of *elementa*.[45] We can imagine Wallace Stevens
sitting at his typewriter, noting the hard sound of its hammers, and
thinking that, though poems are made of words, when we type them
they are made of something elemental, something we cannot hear when
a poem is recited and barely notice when we read it. In any case, not
only is "X" itself a metaphor, but it is made into something alive
("vital"), even human ("arrogant") to boot. There is no escaping it.
When we retreat into the realm of metaphors, we are really retreating
into a realm of *different* metaphors from those in the realm we are
leaving.[46]

   Stevens made another intriguing effort to point to non-metaphorical
reality in "The Man on the Dump," a funny and sarcastic poem about the
endless supply of poems, "the janitor's poems / Of every day," that end up
on the dump, full of boring old images and metaphors. "The freshness of
night has been fresh a long time," he says, in a lovely self-refuting line. Even
worse are the images of flowers and dew: "dew, dew dresses, stones and
chains of dew, heads / Of the floweriest flowers dewed with the dewiest
dew." These are only tolerable in old poetry because they were fresh once:
"One grows to hate these things except on the dump." But the poem does
more than "reject the trash," if "trash" means clichés like flowers and dew:
it also rejects all attempts at images or comparisons. At moments, free of
similes, "the moon comes up as the moon." For the most part, however, we
sit on the dump and beat an old tin can, making more poems, more images,
trying to get nearer to something we believe in, whatever it is. But we come
no closer to reality. In the final two words of the final line, Stevens
wrenches the language to the breaking point, and I think he does so to
escape the tentacular grip of all metaphor, of all trash: "Where was it one
first heard of the truth? The the." At first, these last two words look like a
stammer, but they are closed by a period, and I think the second "the" is
not a definite article but a noun. They are not a hesitant continuation of
the question, but either a radical restatement of it (correcting "truth" to
"the") or a blunt answer to it, more likely the latter. It is like "the . . . X" but

goes farther down the road to sheer pointing. "The the" would be a radical restatement of "the truth" because even "truth" trails a little cloud of imagery. Any noun would do so, as even "X" did. By forcing the article into nounness, Stevens at the same time evacuates that category of everything, everything but "the," the little word we use to make our nouns "definite," make them refer to something really there. This mere definiteness is one reason I think the last two-word sentence answers the where-question. "The" is a locale of sorts, a place of direct encounter with truth, not mediated by words.

Is it a metaphor? It is certainly a startling deviation from normal usage, all the more so because in the rest of the poem, and in virtually all of his other poems, Stevens, unlike E. E. Cummings, is conservative in his syntax. He has invented a new word, "the" as a noun, and uses it not the way I have been using it here, as the word itself (and in quotation marks), but as a sign of a real thing or state of affairs, the theness of things. In the end I think it is literally a metaphor, a metaphor to end all metaphors, but then, in the end, it doesn't matter much. That final jolt, a little like being slapped by a Zen master, is meant to snap us out of our immersion in language, if only for a moment, but in that disconcerting moment, as Stevens says, "one feels the purifying change."

Other poets have periodically sworn off metaphor. To take a last example, the young Sylvia Plath enlists the *Alice in Wonderland* books as a continual reference in her sonnet "A Sorcerer Bids Farewell to Seem." It begins: "I'm through with this grand looking-glass hotel / where adjectives play croquet with flamingo nouns." As metaphors themselves, these may not bear much looking into, but then that might be part of the point, as one playful analogy after another takes up a prop from *Alice*. Let's pause on the croquet allusion. Suppose Plath had written "adjectives play croquet with nouns," leaving out the flamingo, and we had no other reason to think of the game Alice tries to play. That would be an interesting metaphor: we would probably take the adjectives as corresponding to people and the nouns to balls, or to the ball-slot in the source-domain, and so we might think of how real adjectives send real nouns flying about, perhaps colliding with other nouns, and so on. A little theory of grammar might emerge, somewhat like the old suggestion that inflections are inflictions – that is, endings on nouns are bruises or scars inflicted by verbs. But with "flamingo" in play, the nouns become mallets, and quite unreliable ones, unable to strike balls, which were frisky hedgehogs in any case. Does this suggest that nouns are unreliable, and even the most skillful speakers (players) cannot reach their communicative goal with them? Maybe, but probably not; the parallels are not sustainable for long, and in any case more analogies come along about white rabbits and mad hatters, so any effort to ponder the implications of one of them is dispatched by the cheery arrival of the next. At the end, the speaker announces: "it's time to vanish like the cheshire cat / alone to that authentic island where / cabbages are cabbages; kings: kings." It is the dream of the perfect, "authentic" language of univocal correspondence between name and thing, perhaps Adam's ideally onomatopoeic language, where every word is the right word for its referent. But this could hardly be a language for poets to use, let alone sorcerers, and Sylvia Plath was soon to become known for her vivid, sometimes frightening, metaphors, such as when she calls her poems stillborn fetuses, well-formed but dead (in the poem called "Stillborn").

Afterword: A Metaphor for Poetry Itself

In Wallace Stevens's notebook are several metaphors for poetry or a poem. "A Poem is a meteor." "Poetry is a pheasant disappearing in the brush." "A poem is a café."[47] Any of these might have led to poems themselves, and they are intriguing and fun to think about. But there has been one premier metaphor since ancient days: a poem is a flower, and poetry or a set of poems is a garland or bouquet. It is pretty much dead today, though Stevens himself revived it briefly in "The Man on the Dump" by showing how dead it is, but it was the first resort of poets from the Greeks to at least the nineteenth century.

Sappho, whose poems are full of literal flowers, at least once implies they stand for poems when she scolds an uncultivated woman for neglecting "the roses of Pieria," Pieria being the birthplace of the Muses.[48] Pindar was more explicit, speaking of "my hymns' pleasing flowers" in one ode and "the blossoms of hymns" in another, while "I cultivate the choice garden of the Graces."[49] By the Hellenistic era, it had become routine to consider poems as flowers woven into a garland. Meleager (first century BCE) compiled a set of verse epigrams he called *Stephanos* ("Garland"), and likened each poet to a flower; another *Stephanos* was compiled by Philip in the first century CE. The word *anthologia*, first found in Lucian's satire *The Fisherman*, where it referred to a collection of words and passages culled from Plato, is literally a "gathering of flowers" or "bouquet." The *Greek Anthology* is the major collection of short poems that has survived from antiquity, and now any collection of writings of any kind is called an

+  florilegium

anthology in English. The Latin equivalent, *florilegium*, was used while in English, but is now extinct; in French, *florilège* still seems almost as common as *anthologie*.

Nicholas Udall made a collection called *Flovres for Latyne Spekynge, selected and gathered oute of Terence* (1533). George Gascoigne made one with a more extravagant title: *A Hundredth Sundry Flowres bound up in one small Poesie. Gathered partly (by translation) in the fyne outlandish Gardens of Euripides, Ovid, Petrarch, Aristotle and others; and partly by Invention out of our owne fruitfull Orchardes in Englande* (1573). Robert Allen in 1600 published *Englands Parnassus, or, The Choysest Flowers of our Modern Poets*; Abraham Cowley's first published poems were called *Poetical Blossoms* (1636); a book called *Flowers Strowed by the Muses* appeared in 1662; and so on and on, up to Robert Louis Stevenson's still popular *A Child's Garden of Verses* (1885), and beyond. The same tradition in French is found in such titles as *Les Fleurs de Poésie Françoyse* (1534), and it lies behind Baudelaire's shocking title *Les Fleurs du Mal* ("The Flowers of Evil") (1857). (Swinburne called Baudelaire a "gardener of strange flowers" in *Ave atque Vale*.) In Russia, the poets Pushkin and Delvig organized an annual anthology called *Northern Flowers* (1825–32).

Our word "poesy" has a pertinent offspring. "Poesy" is older than "poetry," but is now quaint or archaic. In the fifteenth century, it could mean "motto" (in verse) and then "bouquet" or "bunch of flowers" of poetry; we still occasionally use the word "posy" for "bouquet" or "nosegay," and forget its connection with "poesy." We see this use in Gascoigne's title, and Phillip Sidney plays on it when he addresses his fellow poets who "every flower . . . into your poesy wring" (*Astrophel and Stella*, Sonnet 15).

Hölderlin calls language itself "the flower of the mouth" ("Germania" st. 5). In Chapter 5, we quoted Keats, who is "wreathing / a flowery band to bind us to the earth" ("Endymion" 1.6–7). In his "Valedictory Sonnet" (1838), Wordsworth rehearses the metaphor with a minor variation: the sonnets in this group are "cultured Flowerets" that were culled from here and there, one at a time or in "scattered knots," and then arranged "in several beds of one parterre." After nursing that image for the whole octave, he begins the sestet by saying, "But metaphor dismissed," and bids farewell to the reader.

What can we make out of this wilted, dried-out metaphor for poetry? Is it possible to recapture something freshly picked and springlike in it? Can we defamiliarize it? I am not suggesting poets might exploit it further these

days: I think it will remain on the dump, but the dump is full of images that
were fresh once, and it is our first duty as readers of old poetry to try to feel
our way into it with as few prejudices as possible, with generosity of spirit,
and with historical imagination. What must underlie the metaphor "a
poem is a flower," first of all, is surely beauty: they are both beautiful –
they delight the ear or eye. The problem for some of us today, then, is that
flowers themselves seem merely pretty or decorative and not very enchant-
ing. We can see them, if we look, in grocery stores year-round even in
northern climates. So we can clean off this film of familiarity and get closer
to the force of the metaphor if we come to appreciate how beautiful, how
striking, flowers are, or once were, even in the warm Mediterranean
climate; there were not so many of them, or so many kinds, and they
were not always available.

Flowers, too, live brief lives, especially roses, which became symbols for
the evanescence of girls' beauty. Are poems also fleeting? The metaphor
surely arose before writing added a second means, after people's memories,
of preserving them. A poem was usually a song, a performance, very often
with dancers and musicians; perhaps the knowledge that a beautiful hour
listening to Sappho would remain only in our minds, and only for a while,
made flowers seem more apt a likeness.

Flowers are also symbolic in most western cultures, though the symbolism has varied a good deal; flowers send messages; they are already poetic.
They were scattered on newlyweds and winners of games, and they were
placed on people who had died, and by their gravestones; poems too were
sung at weddings, victory celebrations, and funerals, and sung with the
intent to preserve the names of those who shone during their day on earth.
Not all metaphors are reversible, but "a poem is a flower" is: a flower is a
poem, too. It is earth's way of bursting into song.

We might note, too, that just about when serious poets began to give up
on the idea that poems were flowers, they also began to give up making
them beautiful – at least in any traditional sense, with meter, rhyme,
alliteration, and so on. "The Waste Land" is not a beautiful poem, and
could hardly be called a flower, though there are flowers in it. Meanwhile,
"serious" music grew more and more dissonant, or abandoned tonality
altogether so that dissonance could no longer be resolved, and the visual
arts turned toward "realism" and then "expressivism" and "surrealism" and
a rapid series of new modes, most of which frankly embraced the ugly.
Perhaps beauty in a more abstract sense still seems appropriate to these
works in the eyes of their admirers, but they could not be called flowers, or
a flowering of their art.

By now, however, we have gone far beyond our subject. Metaphor dismissed.

Notes

1. Ricoeur, *Rule of Metaphor*, 17.
2. Valéry, *Art of Poetry*, 176.
3. Ricoeur, *Rule of Metaphor*, 14–16.
4. Aristotle, *Poetics*, ed. Lucas, 204–05.
5. Aristotle, *Poetics*, ed. Lucas, 204.
6. I am relying on Ricoeur's account of Konrad's theory (Ricoeur, *Rule of Metaphor*, 104–10).
7. Denis Donoghue (*Metaphor*) contrasts metaphor with personification (6) but gives no reason. Lakoff and Johnson (*More than Cool Reason*) assume that personification is a kind of metaphor (72ff.); I agree with them.
8. I. A. Richards, *Philosophy of Rhetoric*, 92, 93, 52.
9. A shortened variant in Donne, "interanimates," and its adoption by Richards in an earlier book as "interanimation," may both be found in the *OED*.
10. Richards, *Philosophy of Rhetoric*, 97. "Vehicle" is itself an interesting metaphor for metaphor, or part of metaphor: I like to think of the vehicles driving around Athens with *Metaphora* painted on their sides. The tenor would be the word *Metaphora*, the vehicle would be the vehicle.
11. The metaphor is old. A character in Fielding's *Joseph Andrews* (1742) says, "If I can hold my head above water, it is all I can. I have injured myself by purchasing. I have been too liberal of my money" (3.13). The *OED* cites an instance from 1604.
12. Reprinted in Black, *Models and Metaphors*, 25–47.
13. Burke, "Four Master Tropes."
14. Donoghue, *Metaphor*, 84.
15. Beardsley, *Aesthetics*, 142.
16. Ricoeur has good discussions of Black (83–90) and of Beardsley (90–99). In a later article ("More about Metaphor"), Black replies to Beardsley that there is no single reliable diagnostic criterion for identifying metaphors; they do not have to be contradictory or absurd.
17. He and Wimsatt wrote an essay to this effect called "The Affective Fallacy."
18. Gibbs, "Process and Product," 254–58; he discusses Grice's "implicature" here.
19. Culler, *Theory of the Lyric*, 260, 282–83.
20. For more on Chomsky's sentences, see Jahn, "Colorless Green Ideas."
21. The Greek is ambiguous; this translation makes the most sense.
22. Dionysius of Halicarnassus, *De Demosthene* Ch. 5.
23. See Botet, *Petit traité*, 35–38.
24. The meaning of the word *synekdokhē* in Greek is not much help: it meant something like "receiving one thing with another," and then "taking one sense

with another" and thus "interpretation." Some rhetoricians would distinguish between two kinds of synecdoche: part for whole, and species for genus.

25. Group μ, *General Rhetoric*, 102, 107.

26. Group μ, *General Rhetoric*, 107. For a searching discussion of Groupe μ, see Ricoeur, *Rule of Metaphor*, 157–72. Culler, *Structuralist Poetics*, 75–95, has a lucid account of A. J. Greimas, a predecessor of Groupe μ.

27. Saussure, *Course in General Linguistics*, 123–24.

28. Saussure, *Course in General Linguistics*, 123.

29. "Two Aspects of Language and Two Types of Aphasic Disturbances," reprinted in Jakobson, *On Language*.

30. Lakoff and Turner, *More than Cool Reason*, 63.

31. On this, see also Kövecses, *Metaphor*, 9.

32. A point made by Botet, *Petit traité*, 20–21.

33. "On Truth and Lie in an Extra-Moral Sense," in Nietzsche, *Portable Nietzsche*, ed. Kaufmann, 46–47.

34. *Genealogy*, 12–13.

35. Colin McGinn has recently argued that mental "grasping" is not a metaphorical extension of manual grasping but a literal kind of "prehension" (*Prehension*, 82–85).

36. For a thorough and interesting study of Nietzsche's theory of, and use of, metaphor, see Kofman, *Nietzsche and Metaphor*. Nietzsche had precedents in Carlyle, who said language is all metaphors except for a few primitive elements (*Sartor Resartus* [1834] 1.11), and in Emerson, who said "Every word which is used to express a moral or intellectual fact, if traced to its root, is found to be borrowed from some material appearance" ("Language" [1841]), and farther back in Leibniz, Vico, and Hegel.

37. Heidegger, *What is Called Thinking?* 186–87.

38. Derrida, "White Mythology." See also Ricoeur, *Rule of Metaphor*, 288–89.

39. Students of French and other Romance languages often wonder why the adverb is based on the feminine form of the adjective. The reason is that the noun *mens* in Latin is feminine.

40. *Opus Posthumous*, 179.

41. An exhaustive list of such terms may be found in Lanham's *Handlist*.

42. Ricoeur, *Rule of Metaphor*, 287.

43. *Opus Posthumous*, 179.

44. This may be the place to note that "literal" and "literally," which I have used three dozen times in this chapter, are questionable terms for the opposite of "metaphor" and "metaphorically," but we need some such terms, and I trust their meanings in context are clear enough. For some time, "literally" has been used in obviously metaphorical contexts to mean "really," as in the famous opening sentence of Joyce's "The Dead": "Lily, the caretaker's daughter, was literally run off her feet." For a good discussion of the impossibility of "literal translation," see Bellos, *Is That a Fish?* Ch. 10.

45. There is an attractive theory that Latin *elementum* comes from the three successive letters LMN. Just as we speak of the ABCs, or use an abecedarium

(an alphabet or alphabetical list of things), the Romans may have also referred to their alphabet as their LMNs. "Alphabet" itself, of course, comes from Greek AB (alpha beta).

46. Ricoeur, in *Rule of Metaphor*, quotes part of this poem (99) but he does not discuss it. Donoghue discusses it at some length, alongside other Stevens poems (185–207); my own approach to it is quite different from his.

47. From *Opus Posthumous*, 158, 173, 170.

48. Campbell, ed., *Sappho and Alcaeus*, 99.

49. *Olympian* 6.105; 9.48, 27 (Race, *Pindar I*).

CHAPTER EIGHT

Translating Poetry

The Latin word for "metaphor" is *translatio*, which is also the source of our word "translation." A metaphor might be seen, then, as a kind of translation from one semantic domain to another, but within the same language. We mainly use "translation," of course, to refer to the carrying over of a work or text from one language to another, what Jakobson calls "interlingual translation,"[1] and metaphors within such a text are often quite readily translatable: *Akhilleus leōn esti* is the same metaphor as "Achilles is a lion." Whether it makes sense to say, for example, that an English version of a French sonnet is a metaphor for the original sonnet would be an interesting topic to pursue, but our focus in this chapter will be on the challenges of making such versions in the first place, and to what extent linguistics can shed light on them.

At the outset, we need to face the usual objection. Robert Frost reputedly said, "Poetry is what gets lost in translation."[2] Or, as John Denham wrote in 1656, "Poesie is of so subtile a spirit, that of pouring out of one Language into another, it will all evaporate."[3] Since it is obvious that quite a few things in poems need not evaporate or get lost in translation – such things as plot, argument, stanzaic structure, and metaphors – this objection rests on the notion that "poetry" is something like a wine that doesn't travel well, or a gas that escapes as soon as you unbottle it. It must be something having to do with subtleties of connotation, nuance, and style, as well as an effect arising from the sounds peculiar to its language, especially metered and rhymed, which together embed the poem in an intricate complex of semantic and sonic associations that only a native speaker could fully appreciate.

Surely this objection is both self-evident and futile. It is right as far as it goes, though it goes farther or less far in different poems, and in different pairs of languages. It is also perfectly obvious, for what poetry-lover who understands two languages ever doubted that exact equivalences are impossible to find? And it is also pointless, for what are we to do: give up translating poetry? That seems to be the implication. We would then have to remain ignorant of all the world's poetry except what is found in the one language, or perhaps two or three, that we know well.

In any case, translators keep translating poetry, and many of them are fine poets themselves, well aware of how much must get lost, but well aware too of what might be gained, not by improving on the original (though even that might be possible in some cases) but by making a good new poem, one that is accurate or faithful enough to count as a version of the source but that also "works" as a poem in its new language. Poetry gets lost, and poetry gets found.

Poetry translation has everything to do with linguistics – not so much with theory or with the systematic concepts we have been examining in this book, but with detailed knowledge of the two languages involved ("source" language and "target" language, as they are often called), and with generalizations not far beyond or above those languages. By the latter, I mean the sort of patterns that differentiate specific languages from each other, such as the fact that the major Romance languages, and many other European languages, use the definite article more than English does, notably for abstract nouns: "Love isn't everything" is "L'amour n'est pas tout" in French (literally "The love isn't everything"). Or that French and German, among other languages, no longer distinguish between the simple past tense and the present perfect, as English still does, a fact that came across recently when an English-speaking German who survived a train crash told a BBC reporter, "I have heard a loud sound and then I have felt the car stop suddenly." Knowledge of these comparative facts, and hundreds more like them, is the prerequisite of good translation. Abstract generalizations and theories about translating, on the other hand, strike me as only occasionally interesting and helpful. Many theories dwell on the trade-offs between accuracy and beauty, as Frost's remark implicitly does, but it is difficult to say anything thought-provoking on this topic at a general level. Some theories are more about the social and political purposes of translations, or the ideological assumptions behind them, than about linguistic principles. Some studies are historical. Pascale Casanova, for example, explains with many interesting details how it was that French became *La langue mondiale* (her title) in the sixteenth century and remained so until the late twentieth, in large part through serving as the intermediary language of translations. Shakespeare, for instance, was first translated into Spanish, Italian, and Portuguese via French. But only an occasional comment tells us anything about French itself, or how to go from English to French, or French to Portuguese.

Some linguists and cognitive scientists recently, such as Noam Chomsky, Jerry Fodor, Daniel Dennett, and Steven Pinker, have debated the possibility that there is a universal human "mentalese" or a "language of thought" that underlies all natural languages. Such an innate language might contain dozens of fundamental concepts (such as body parts, colors, kinds of movement, or causality), or it might, as Fodor believes, contain thousands of concepts that are much more specific. If it turns out that there is such a mental language, translators might feel heartened, but the debate continues, and in any case none of its advocates, I believe, has argued that there could be mentalese poetry, or that proof of a universal semantic substrate would make it any easier to translate poetry from one language to another.

I think most translators are only mildly interested in translation theories, many of which have little to do with linguistics. This chapter, then, will mainly deal with particular cases, where the devil is in the details (and the angel, too), though I will mention a few ideas from the theorists.

Causley and Rimbaud

I will begin with one of the most celebrated sonnets of Arthur Rimbaud and its translation by the English poet Charles Causley:[4]

Le Dormeur du val	Sleeper in a Valley
C'est un trou de verdure où chante une rivière	Couched in a hollow, where a humming stream
Accrochant follement aux herbes des haillons	Hooks, absently, sun-fragments, silver-white,
D'argent; où le soleil, de la montagne fière,	And from the proud hill-top beam falls on beam
Luit: c'est un petit val qui mousse de rayons.	Laving the valley in a foam of light,
Un soldat jeune, bouche ouverte, tête nue,	A soldier sleeps, lips parted, bare his head,
Et la nuque baignant dans le frais cresson bleu,	His young neck pillowed where blue cresses drown;
Dort; il est étendu dans l'herbe, sous la nue,	He sprawls under a cloud, his truckle-bed
Pâle dans son lit vert où la lumière pleut.	A spread of grass where the gold sky drips down.
Les pieds dans les glaïeuls, il dort. Souriant comme	His feet drift among reeds. He sleeps alone,
Souriait un enfant malade, il fait un somme:	Smiling the pale smile that sick children wear.
Nature, berce-le chaudement: il a froid.	Earth, nurse him fiercely! He is cold as stone, And stilled his senses to the flowering air.
Les parfums ne font pas frisonner sa narine;	
Il dort dans le soleil, la main sur sa poitrine	Hand on his breast, awash in the sun's tide
Tranquille. Il a deux trous rouges au côté droit.	Calmly he sleeps; two red holes in his side.

Rimbaud's sonnet, heir to the centuries of sonnets that this preternaturally gifted boy of 16 had swiftly devoured and mastered, wears its "sonnetness" on its sleeve, as indeed many sonnets before it had done; it is self-consciously a sonnet, displaying its perfect knowledge of the rules while at several points breaking them, or at least stretching them, with a hint of cheekiness. Its alexandrines (twelve-syllable lines) are correct, and the rhymes are alternately feminine and masculine, as the tradition prescribes: octave fmfm fmfm, sestet ffm ffm. All but one pair of rhymes are "rich" in the best French manner – that is, they are *rimes riches* as opposed to the *rimes suffisantes* that prevail in English. So *rivière* and *fière* rhyme not only on the final vowel and consonant, which would be *suffisante*, but also on the glide vowel -*i*- that precedes them; *narine* and *poitrine* rhyme richly by including the -*r*- before the -*ine*. Only *comme* and *somme* are merely sufficient rhymes. Yet Rimbaud enriches his rhymes beyond *rime riche* in three of the four pairs in the octave: *haillons* and *rayons* rhyme on two syllables; *rivière* and *fière* share a labio-dental sound, the first voiced (v), the second voiceless (f); and *bleu* and *pleut* share a labial, again the first voiced (b), the second voiceless (p). There are certainly precedents for these superrich rhymes, but it strikes me as unusual to have so many of them in one sonnet; in any case, the effect seems not only to enhance the musicality of the poem but to call attention to its technique: Look what I can do! I suspect that Causley was impressed by these sound patterns, and gave to his translation not only a strong set of rhymes but other interesting musical effects, such as alliteration, though without quite the same sort of conspicuous display.

The classical alexandrine required a caesura in the middle, a pause between phrases each with six syllables. (Rimbaud's first two lines are classical in this respect.) With the Romantics, especially Hugo, the alexandrine was often redivided, notably into "ternary" form – that is, into three four-syllable phrases (as in line 5), but sometimes into many other proportions, such as the 2+6+4 of the final line. I think it is strange and striking, however, to indicate a caesura after just one syllable, as Rimbaud does in lines 4 and 7, reinforcing it with strong punctuation marks both times. *Luit* ("shines") stands out sharply, and seems to shine through the remainder of the line, making it froth or foam with rays, while the grammatically parallel *Dort* ("sleeps') is thrust on us with equal force, almost so as to bully us into believing it, as if the speaker either cannot face the truth himself or wants to hide it from us (we continue to feel badgered by the repetitions of *il dort* in the sestet).

The enjambments, too, are striking, and would have offended a tradi-
tionalist. The phrase *haillons / D'argent* straddles a line-break, but line 2 is
grammatically complete without the adjectival phrase on line 3 so the effect
is that of an afterthought, or a fact withheld: rags . . . of silver! It heightens
the incongruity, and thereby brings out the brightness of the scene: even
these "rags" shine! More likely to offend are lines 9 and 10: *Souriant comme
/ Souriait un enfant malade* ("Smiling as / A sick child would smile"). Line 9
is glaringly incomplete syntactically, and seems clumsy, with *comme*, which
is tightly bound to its complement, pressing up against the line-break as if
it were – as it is – an artificial barrier to natural movement. So the line-
break itself stands out, as does the following verb *Souriait*, underlining the
"fact" that it is a smile we are seeing (though that of a sick child), rather
than the rictus of death.

This foregrounding of form and technique, as if the sonnet is preening
itself as a sonnet, sits uneasily with its seemingly heartfelt, even naïve,
content: its realistic scene-painting, its appeal to nature to intervene as if it
were a pastoral elegy, and its understated but carefully prepared shock at the
end, seemingly designed to elicit grief and protest at the waste of war. The
sonnet's popularity must be due largely to its "argument," to its staging of a
forgotten tragedy emblematic of many thousands: a young man, likened to a
child, killed for some reason of state or other, and to its appeal to commonplace but noble emotions. The brevity and clarity enforced by the form of a
sonnet must be a factor, too, but the distinctive little tricks Rimbaud inserts,
though they may not be noticed on a first reading, are a little distracting,
even disquieting, on re-readings. (I wonder, however, if this sonnet can ever
really be re-read. Rimbaud might have counted on so capturing his reader's
curiosity on a first reading that he or she would be unconscious of the
artifices; as for second-readers, Rimbaud may have thought they would
include only a few fellow poets who would admire his skill.)

I may be out of my depth here, as my ear for French is not good enough
to pick up all the nuances of tone or connotation that may be in play, but
my object is to consider the way an Englishman who was not a native
speaker of French coped with the sonnet, and perhaps my abilities and
disabilities are comparable to his.

Let me begin with what was doubtless the first problem Causley con-
fronted. The sonnet opens with a "hole" and ends with "two holes."

> C'est un trou de verdure . . .
>
> . . . .
>
> . . . Il a deux trous rouges au côté droit.

Does a first-reader notice the recurrence of *trou*? I don't know, but there it is, and once you notice it, the artfulness of the sonnet forbids you to dismiss it as an accident of no importance. Everything in this sonnet seems important. *Trou* seems just a little strange in the first line, and thus calls attention to itself. It is not, I think, an idiomatic usage for a hollow or a valley. It might connote a "nook" or "nest," from a self-deprecating usage (like "my hole-in-the-wall"), but it is still a hole. More than in English, too, it suggests "grave": to bury someone is to put him *dans le trou*, to be dead is *être dans le trou*. If that connotation is summoned up here, it is certainly to the point, but it subtly undermines the ostensible strategy of withholding any hint that the sleeping soldier is dead until near the end; yet, since he is not even mentioned in the first quatrain, the first *trou* might not reveal the ending until the end, as it were, when the subliminal vibrations it sets off are amplified by the pair of *trous*.

The holes are brought into each other's orbit, moreover, by being colored: "a hole of greenery" and "two red holes." Even if we keep "grave" out of our minds, we notice the obvious symbolism of green youthful life yielding to red death, and since colors are so salient throughout – silver (line 3), blue (6), green again (8) – along with the shining light (4, 8, 13), we are led to suspect some mysterious significance in the fact that the young soldier has found a place to die that resembles what killed him. And then we may wonder: why *two* holes in his side? Wouldn't it have been more symmetrical, more poetically just, if there were one red hole in his side? And why his *right* side? Is that significant? We are soon lost in speculation, and out of touch with the simple story.

A translator, of course, does not have to worry about the number or location of the bullet holes, as they are givens, but he or she must make a difficult decision about the first *trou*. Causley decides to leave it out. By calling it a "hollow," I think, he domesticates the slightly weird French, removing a distraction from a naturalistic reading. "Hollow," of course, sounds a little like "hole," to which it is akin etymologically, and that may be enough to set off the vague vibration, which in turn supplies a mainly sonic rondure to the poem without the metaphysical or allegorical elbow in the ribs. When Robert Lowell translated the sonnet in *Imitations* (1962), he opted for the strangeness of "hole" and made the most of it, placing it at the end of the line to rhyme with "whole" (3) – a rather French *rime riche*, in fact – and then placed "two red holes" at the end of his final line, rhyming with "rolls" (13), which in turn echoes "rolled," which ended line 9.

The swollen river sang through the green hole,
and madly hooked white tatters on the grass.
Light escaladed the hot hills. The whole
valley bubbled with sunbeams like a beer-glass.

The conscript was open-mouthed; his bare head
and neck swam in the bluish water cress.
He slept. The mid-day soothed his heaviness,
sunlight was raining into his green bed,

and baked the bruises from his body, rolled
as a sick child might hug itself asleep . . .
Oh Nature, rock him warmly, he is cold.

The flowers no longer make his hot eyes weep.
The river sucks his hair. His blue eye rolls.
He sleeps. In his right side are two red holes.

He thereby make the holes chime even more strongly than they do in the French, where neither instance ends a line. One commentator thinks Lowell's first "hole" reveals him as "too close to his dictionary for comfort" (Little, "A Study in Comparative Translation," 195), but I would argue that he is more forthrightly Rimbaudian in doing this, even ultra-Rimbaudian, whereas Causley is more cautious, more concerned, perhaps, to create a plausible or digestible poem in English. Even in Lowell's revised translation, which he published in *History* (1973), and where he drops rhymes to allow greater accuracy, removes the needless "swollen," and restores the whole poem to the present tense of the original, he stays with "hole":

The river sings and cuts a hole in the meadow,
madly hooking white tatters on the rushes.
Light escalades the strong hills. The small
valley bubbles with sunbeams like a beerglass.

Since he keeps his distracting "beerglass," which seems to owe its existence in the first version to the need to rhyme with "grass" (and it is not even a true rhyme, because the stress is off), it is clear that literal fidelity was not his only motive for retaining "hole" as well; on reflection, though he reduces its clangor, "hole" is still what he wants.

What we might call Causley's tact, his omission of little semantic stumbling blocks, seems to have led him to leave out the sonnet's final word: *droit*. No doubt, having decided to expand *dans le soleil* to "awash in the sun's tide" (for reasons we will return to), he felt cramped in the final line; something had to go, and the apparently unmotivated detail of *droit* seemed expendable. Is it? Rimbaud chose to place it in the climactic position of the poem, completing the shocking revelation, and of course rhyming with *froid* in the preceding tercet. Causley implies it does not matter which side the soldier was wounded on, though it matters that there are two wounds. Perhaps he thought Rimbaud gave us these details, along with all the others, mainly to convey a sense of a neutral photographic record, and that none of them is symbolic, so to retain one of them ("two" but not "right") is sufficient to sustain Rimbaud's effect. He may have doubted that "right" had any symbolic meaning, anatomical, religious, political, or otherwise; he may have thought it was motivated solely by how it sounded, not only rhyming with *froid* but echoing nicely the sounds of *deux trous rouges au côté*. To end it with *gauche* would not have sounded so good, and it would have been a feminine rhyme, a problem for the strict pattern of the poem, even if he had a rich rhyme for it earlier. If these were Causley's thoughts, they seem reasonable, but it is not so clear that Rimbaud is as reasonable as Causley. To drop that detail is to remove a striking if enigmatic peculiarity that, with a little effort, ought to have been preserved.

It might, after all, suggest the wound that Christ received on the cross from the soldier's spear. The Gospel of John (19.34) does not tell us which side was pierced, but the pictorial tradition almost invariably makes it the right. Causley somewhat muffles the possible allusion, but at least he does not reverse the wounded side, as Lowell does in his second version, which ends: "He has two red holes in his left side." I cannot imagine what led Lowell to do so.

Another odd touch deserves a comment. The soldier's feet are *dans les glaïeuls* (9). What flowers are these? The word seems to derive from *gladiolus*, which means "sword-shaped," appropriate enough for a soldier in Rimbaud's world of vaguely symbolic resonances, but "gladiolas," the cultivated garden flowers, may be a poor choice botanically. "Sword grass" would over-translate it, and the botanically more probable "flags" would distract the reader by being too appropriate for a soldier! (See Little, "A Study in Comparative Translation," 196.) The real source of *glaïeul* may be Old French *glai*, "joyous tumult," from a Frankish word related to English "glad." That a French reader would know this I rather doubt, though it would add to the false happiness of the locale. In any case, Causley settles for "reeds," with its hint of Christ's Passion – he was fed vinegar in a sponge on the end of a reed (Matthew 27.48) – while Lowell in both his versions leaves out the whole line. "Reeds," at least, offers no obstacle, and some reeds do have sharp-edged leaves.

This discussion of the vagaries of *trou* and *droit* and *glaïeuls* illustrates the general tendency of Causley's translation toward a greater restraint of form and chastity of diction. It has no enjambments, nothing remotely as unclassical as Rimbaud's *comme*. It generalizes *narine* ("nostril") to "senses" (12). And it removes the informal phrasing in the opening – *C'est un trou de verdure* (1), and *c'est un petit val* (4) ("It's a hole of greenery" and "it's a little valley") – which must have sounded too casual and choppy. Rimbaud's syntax is more coordinate than subordinate in structure, with its first independent clause complete by the first caesura, with two dependent clauses beginning with *où* both complete by line 4, and then another complete independent clause, all in the first quatrain. By contrast, Causley's first quatrain is one long dependent clause, gracefully distributed into couplets, the first about the stream, the second about the sunbeams, all poised to bring out the main clause, "A soldier sleeps," at the opening of the following quatrain. It is artful and effective rhetoric, but it is a different thing from the short, restless clauses and downscale register of the original.

In at least one respect Causley goes beyond Rimbaud at several points, rather in Rimbaud's spirit, but of course with inevitable sacrifices. Water pervades the original octave: a river sings, flecks of foam ("rags") hook on the grass, the valley froths or bubbles with light rays, the soldier's neck bathes in the cresses (*water*cresses in English!), and the light "rains." All this liquid suggests the water of life in the valley around the dead youth; in retrospect, or on a second reading, the blood implicitly flowing from the two red holes seems the same thing, the life-blood, now joining the water in the valley-hole. Part of the shock of the ending, indeed, may arise from the feeling that we should not have been shocked by it: we should have seen it coming. Causley understood the importance of the water imagery, and extended it beyond the octave. "Laving the valley in a foam of light" is a fine line, though it adds "laving" to what Rimbaud gives us. Instead of bathing the soldier's neck, Causley pillows it, but then makes the cresses "drown," preserving the water image but prematurely projecting a sinister note. The soldier's feet "drift" among the reeds, as if he is afloat. And indeed, in the penultimate line Causley adds the striking phrase "awash in the sun's tide," echoing the *mousse de rayons* (4) and *la lumière pleut* (8), but going far beyond Rimbaud's simple "in the sun." The implicit image is that the soldier has drowned.

Not only water but color and light pervade the original poem. They convey the sense that all of nature is bursting with life, life so brilliant and energetic and beautiful that for the soldier to be snatched from it seems all the more terrible. Or perhaps we are meant to see the scene as full of youth, green and warm and full of motion, an emblem of the soldier himself as he was a few hours ago. In any case, a translator should retain as much of the color and light as possible, especially the green of *verdure* (1) and *vert* (8); much depends on it. It is hard to understand, then, why Causley abandons both greens. He does preserve the silver foam, the blue cresses, and of course the red holes; he adds a gold sky (8), not inappropriately for the *lumière* raining down; he keeps *pâle* (8), though he transfers it to the smile (10); but the hollow is colorless and the bed is only implicitly green from the grass. A translation cannot do everything, but in considering what he must sacrifice Causley ought not to have chosen the color most symbolic of life, and most opposite to red. He also detracts once from the light as well, where he translates *sous la nue* as "under a cloud" without, apparently, feeling troubled by the fact the *lumière* nonetheless pours down onto the bed. I would have made the same mistake myself, since the dictionary gives "cloud" as the primary sense, but in poetry *nue* (and especially *la nue*) means "sky." It is exactly like the obsolete English word "welkin," which once meant "cloud" (like the cognate German *Wolke*), and then came to mean "sky" or "firmament"; "sky" itself once meant "cloud" (as in Chaucer's *House of Fame* 3.1600), having been borrowed from Old Norse *sky* ("cloud").

Causley must also have given thought to whether, and when, Rimbaud betrays the surprise ending. He drops one of Rimbaud's lines, *il fait un somme*, "he is taking a nap," but preserves the insistent repetition of *dort* (7, 9, 13), the bed, and of course the title. He may have thought the game was up with the simile in lines 9 and 10, "smiling as a sick child would smile," so to add "he is taking a nap," as a sick child would do, may have struck him as overly manipulative or coy, not to mention too casual in diction. In any case, Causley seems to leave little doubt by line 11: "Earth, nurse him fiercely! He is cold as stone[.]" To turn *Nature* into "Earth" is to move from life to death: Latin *natura* comes from the root meaning "birth," while earth, though it is our mother, is where we are buried (in a hole) when we die. "Fiercely" is a possible translation for *chaudement*, but it seems odd and excessive with "nurse" (as it would with *berce*, "cradle" or "rock"), and loses the contrast with *froid* (*chaudement* means "warmly"). "He is cold as stone," of course, implies death. That clause, in fact, strikes me as a mistranslation of *il a froid*, not so much because of the addition of the stone but because Causley takes it as *il est froid*, which might indeed be followed by *comme une pierre*. The English is ambiguous, the French is not: when you say of someone *il a froid* you mean he feels cold (to himself), and he has to be alive to feel it. Anyone who is as cold as stone must be dead. And where Rimbaud has "the scents do not make his nostril tremble," Causley has the much less ambiguous "And stilled his senses to the flowering air" (12). A sleeper's nose might not twitch, but he is dead if his senses are "stilled." In sum, Causley's earlier and more gradual revelation of the truth is of a piece with the decorum and tact we noted earlier, as if he felt that Rimbaud's postponement of the truth to the very last line is too abrupt and clever – too much like the trickery of a detective novel.

Both Causley and Lowell turn Rimbaud's sonnet, which is loosely Petrarchan, into a Shakespearean sonnet, by reorganizing the sestet, which rhymes eef ggf, into a third quatrain and a final couplet, rhyming efef gg. Lowell conceals this transformation by arranging the last six lines as two tercets, while Causley is more forthrightly Shakespearean in his typography. Is this the right thing to do to Rimbaud? Certainly a case can be made for it. Rimbaud himself loosened the tight rhyming requirements of the Petrarchan sonnet, as well as the French sonnet, by introducing two new rhymes in the second quatrain; that is a step toward the Shakespearean pattern. More to the point, the overall movement or argument of the poem – an assertion sustained through thirteen lines and then reversed, though implicitly, in the final line – well suits the frequent Shakespearean practice of postponing the "turn" or *volta* until the final couplet.

Causley has written a fine Shakespearean sonnet that, all things considered, preserves about as much of the original as such a translation can; only an unrhymed and unmetrical "trot" might have captured more semantic detail, but it would have jettisoned much of what makes the original a poem. He adds a few things, but nothing as gratuitous or tasteless as Lowell's beer-glass, baking bruises, and weeping hot eyes (surely Rimbaud's scene is sunny and warm, but not hot). He has fine lines and phrases and a satisfying musical pattern throughout, with a good deal of alliteration and assonance. He leaves out a few things and makes a few mistakes, but I think a reader not closely familiar with the original would not feel uncomfortable or confused. It is a good English poem, with something of Causley's characteristic sincerity, clarity, and firmness of structure. Gone, however, whether for better or for worse, are the very French, rather surrealist, sometimes baffling little touches that the frighteningly precocious poet of 16 liberally sprinkled throughout his seemingly heartfelt anti-war poem.

Longfellow and Goethe

Probably the best-known and most loved lyric poem in German is Goethe's "Wandrers Nachtlied II" (1780). Here it is, alongside a word-for-word "gloss":

Über allen Gipfeln	Over all summits
Ist Ruh,	Is rest;
In allen Wipfeln	In all treetops
Spürest du	Feelest thou
Kaum einen Hauch;	Scarcely a breath;
Die Vögelein schweigen im Walde.	The little birds are silent in the woods.
Warte nur, balde	Only wait, soon
Ruhest du auch.	Restest thou too.

It is a delicate and subtle little poem, addressed to *du*, the intimate singular form of "you," which I have given as "thou" here so as not to suggest the indefinite "you" of English, which means "one." "Thou," of course, and the -est verb-endings, are no longer in use now, and were growing archaic in 1780 (though they lingered in poetry); in German, then and now, there is nothing archaic about the corresponding forms. A translator today must use "you," but that is already to sacrifice an important tone or feeling: the original is spoken to *thee*, alone, as if whispered to a friend or beloved, or maybe to a child.

The second problem a translator faces is due to the rhymes. They cannot be sacrificed. In this short poem, with only one line longer than six syllables, twelve of its thirty-eight syllables are rhymes, nearly a third of them, and some of them echo other words by assonance (*Kaum* and *Hauch*) or alliteration and consonance (*Walde* and *Warte*). Most of this music must be retained somehow, or the translation is not serious. The trouble is that line 5, which rhymes with the final line, ends with *Hauch*, and *Hauch*, alas, means "breath." All translators know that if they end a rhymed line with "breath," they are committed to "death" sometime soon, and vice versa. But *Tod* is not looming at the end of Goethe's poem. Or is it? Although *ruhest*, like the earlier noun *Ruh* (line 2), means "rest" (as well as "silence" and "peace"), "rest" has connoted "death" in English for many centuries (as in "rest in peace"). So has *ruhen*: "rest in peace" is *Ruhe in Frieden*, and "Here lies X" is *Hier ruht X*. To contrive to end line 8 with "death," then, as most readers would expect, is a temptation.

And yet, on the face of it, the poem is about sleep. It is the night-song of a wanderer, who might be seeking an inn, or at least a safe place outdoors,

)r the night. The birds are silent because they are asleep, surely. But then, "only wait." Surely, too, your brief wandering on earth will end soon. Death seems to hover, gently, with no urgency, over the rest you seek.

So what is a translator to do? Henry Wadsworth Longfellow in 1845 offered this version:

> O'er all the hill-tops
> Is quiet now,
> In all the tree-tops
> Hearest thou
> Hardly a breath;
> The birds are asleep in the trees:
> Wait, soon like these
> Thou, too, shalt rest.

He has preserved the rhyme-scheme, and all the rhymes are perfect[5] but the last: "breath" rhymes with "rest." He avoids the noun "rest" in line 2, corresponding to *Ruh*, so the verb "rest" at the end seems a little more striking. To keep the "too," however, which is the final word of the original (*auch*), he needs something parallel to "rest," and he makes it by translating *schweigen* ("are silent") as if it were *schlafen* ("are sleeping"). Goethe certainly implies the birds are sleeping, but he does not quite say so. In the original, "rest" prevails over the whole scene, explicitly over all the hill-tops, and implicitly in the tree-tops, so when "thou too" find rest you will be joining the whole of nature and not just the birds.

By ending line 5 with "breath," which would have been very difficult to avoid, Longfellow arouses in his readers the expectation of "death," but to actually write "death" ("Thou, too, shalt find death," for example) would have been too blunt, almost absurdly discordant with the gently welcoming spirit of the poem. In settling on "rest," he lets "death," the inevitable partner of "breath," float above the ending without touching down on it. He may have found the only adequate solution to the problem.[6]

Foreignization

These two examples provide us with plenty of examples of the choices translators must make among competing demands. If there are rhymes in the original, we want rhymes in the translation, but words of similar meaning seldom rhyme in both source and target languages, so if we insist on a complete rhyme scheme, we may well force the poem into a Procrustean bed and distort its pattern of meanings. Enjambments often translate readily, but the shock of unusual enjambment may be much less in the target language. Primary senses of words may be captured – indeed, must be captured – but secondary connotations may be lost and new ones inserted. Among secondary meanings may be allusions to the Bible or the classics, and they may depend on precise wording. And, as we noted with Causley's Rimbaud, it is hard to resist smoothing or domesticating the weird or spiky bits of the original, or even to notice we are doing so. Even if we avoid doing so, we will probably lose another sort of allusion in Rimbaud's case: the implicit reference to the tradition of French sonnets. Just the opposite effect may be in play in Goethe's poem, which is much freer in form; its very freedom may allude to the rigidities of contemporary French-influenced German verse, evoking a little shiver of intimacy and sincerity and surprise. These intra-literary touches may elude translation altogether.

Some translators have argued for preserving something of the original alienness or otherness of the source text. "Good translation is demystifying," Lawrence Venuti writes: "it manifests in its own language the foreignness of the foreign text." He cautions against the "illusory effect of transparency" that "fluent" translations convey.[7] Of course, as he concedes, translations that preserve much of the exotic character of the original are unlikely to find many readers, but his argument is a good one to consider from time to time in translating poetry. A few touches of "foreignization" will not only remind readers that it is indeed a foreign text they are reading, but may add interesting resonances to the overall meaning.

In his many translations, Ezra Pound seems to have been a foreignizer before the theory existed, though some of his phrasings are difficult to distinguish from archaizing, or making something seem old within the same literary tradition, something he did even to his own poetry. To give just one brief example, in his version of "The River-Merchant's Wife: A Letter" by the eighth-century Chinese poet Li Po (or Li Bai), Pound creates a charmingly exotic little expression for the polite, indeed deferential, form of the second-person singular pronoun. Here are the first seven lines:

> While my hair was still cut straight across my forehead
> I played about the front gate, pulling flowers.
> You came by on bamboo stilts, playing horse,
> You walked about my seat, playing with blue plums.
> And we went on living in the village of Chokan:
> Two small people, without dislike or suspicion.
>
> At fourteen I married My Lord you.

Two earlier lines begin with "you," though the original Chinese lacks them. When the status of the two small people changes, and she becomes his wife, the original has an honorific pronoun (君, *jūn* in modern Mandarin, but perhaps quite different in Li Po's own language), which can also mean "master" or "sovereign." English has no honorific pronouns, so Pound created one. Note how different the effect would be if it were put in normal English: "At fourteen I married you, My Lord." Whether or not Pound has caught the nuance right (he knew only a little Chinese and was working off other translations), he has produced "a flavor of Chinese," which nicely illustrates the idea of "foreignizing."[8]

A striking example of foreignizing, but one that cannot readily be imitated in translating other poems, is John Felstiner's version of Paul Celan's *Todesfuge* ("Death-Fugue") from German into English. This celebrated poem is incantatory and repetitive, structured a little like a fugue with interweaving voices or themes, and Felstiner takes advantage of the repetitions to insinuate bits of German into the English in a manner intelligible to a reader with no knowledge of German. Only *Deutschland* is never rendered "Germany," but "your golden hair Margareta / Your ashen hair Shulamith" is transformed first as "your goldenes Haar Margareta / your aschenes Haar Shulamith" (twice) and then, in the final pair of lines: "dein goldenes Haar Margarete / dein aschenes Haar Sulamith." Meanwhile "Death is a master from Deutschland" becomes "Death is a master aus Deutschland," then "Death is ein Meister aus Deutschland," and finally, just before the couplet about the two women, "Der Tod ist ein Meister aus Deutschland." Felstiner thereby delivers the poem back into German, where it belongs, and takes the reader on a harrowing journey into the death camp, where it is set.

Two Haiku

Translation between kindred languages is difficult enough, beset as it is by apparent equivalences that conceal subtle but crucial differences, but at least such languages may share cultural and historical associations and even a common poetic ancestry – in the case of European poetry, going back to the Greek and Roman classics. To bring a poem across a major linguistic and cultural divide will involve greater difficulties and greater losses. And yet the very size of the divide makes it even more important to try to do so. I will sketch some of the challenges a couple of Japanese haiku would pose to a translator. Though I lived in Japan for a year I learned only a little of the language, but I think my beginner's grasp of it is enough for singling out a few interesting points on which translatability pivots.

The popular female poet Chiyo (1703–75) composed this haiku:

> Yami no yo ga
> Darkness's night but
> mimi ni tsuki no yo
> in ear(s) moon's night
> hototogisu.
> cuckoo.

This verbless little poem is so condensed it resembles a telegram from the skies, which is more or less what it is about. Two contrasting noun phrases about two different kinds of night (*yo*) lead to a solitary noun, the name of a bird; the bird would seem to stand for, or be described by, or to have brought about, the second kind of night. But before we go any further, we had better note a few things about Japanese grammar. Japanese nouns are uninflected – they do not take endings that indicate case or number – but there are some particles that follow nouns that do indicate case, though not number. One of these is the possessive particle *no*, which is something like the reverse of "of," close to the -s ending of the genitive case in English. We might want to say "night of darkness," but the Japanese order is the opposite: "darkness's night," and then "moon's night"; *yami* and *tsuki* are contrasting nouns. The other particle here is *ni*, the preposition "in" (or "at" or "to" or "for," all possible here), following *mimi* ("ear"), making it a "postposition" rather than a "preposition," to be exact; it functions like the dative inflection of some European languages. Japanese also lacks articles, both definite and indefinite, like Latin. It cannot say "the moon," just "moon" – though, if it had to, it could say "that moon" (or, more likely, "yon moon," as it has three "deictic" positions).[9] It also lacks a plural marker, and makes no distinction between mass-nouns such as "darkness" and count-nouns such as "ear," so without an explicit indicator we can only guess whether one or both ears of the speaker are involved, or, for that matter, whether many ears are implied, because there is no "I" in the poem: it could be "our ears" or "one's ears" or just "the ear" or "an ear." We can assume that "darkness," "night," and "moon" are singular, but we can be less sure about "cuckoo"; though it is more plausible to think of a single cuckoo calling out at night, we cannot rule out the possibility that there are two or three of them. It may not matter much, and indeed the very distinction between one and many, which a translator must cope with, are of no concern to the original poem. The poem is not deliberately vague, in other words, though it is more condensed than prose; it is dealing, we might say, with the essence of night and moon and cuckoo.

Then there is the cuckoo problem. What struck European poets about the European cuckoo (*Cuculus canorus*) were: (1) its haunting two-note song (*canorus* means "melodious"), whence the name "cuckoo"; (2) its early return in the spring; and (3) its habit of laying its eggs in the nests of other species, whence its association with cuckoldry, a word derived from "cuckoo." The Asian or lesser cuckoo (*Cuculus poliocephalus*), widespread in Japan, has a very different call, described on one avian website as a "loud, husky chattering song, 'eat your chóky pepper'" (*Handbook of the Birds of the World*). It must be a striking call, especially during a quiet night, and there is a long tradition of Japanese (and Chinese) poetry that celebrates it. I suspect that the charming Japanese word for the bird, *hototogisu*, which fills the final line of this and many other haikus, is onomatopoeic in origin, like "cuckoo" and similar words in every language of Europe. Though this bird also lays its eggs in other birds' nests, that disagreeable fact seems absent from the Asian poetic tradition – at least I haven't come across it in reading through several volumes of Japanese and Chinese poetry in English – and it would be interesting to know why it has escaped notice. This bird does not notably stand for the return of spring, either – in fact, rather the opposite: it often has associations with melancholy, homesickness, or longing for absent friends and family, perhaps because the bird's migration in the fall was more striking than its return.

So what is a translator to do? To use "cuckoo" in the last line is to risk evoking what the European cuckoo has meant in western literature, and the last thing we want here is a hint of sexual infidelity. It might be better to leave it as *hototogisu*, but then a footnote will be necessary, and a translation that requires footnotes would not be considered a translation at all by many readers of poetry. When so much is lost even around a bird name, however, we can make a case that the best we can do, and the truest to the "otherness" of this other culture, is to provide a transcription of the sounds of a poem, a word-by-word gloss, and a lot of notes, as I have done here.

Something else that must evaporate in translation, though it might also be missed by Japanese readers today, is the long tradition of *hototogisu* poems. In some of them, the bird's call at night is a kind of light, just as it is in Chiyo's haiku. A five-line poem by Ki Tsurayuki (884–946) has been translated this way: "Summer night— / I close my eyes / And the cuckoo / With its one cry / Marks the dawn."[10] I think this means that the cuckoo's cry brings a kind of light to the mind of the speaker even though it is still night – perhaps a kind of revelation, as when we say "it dawned on me." A later poem by Fujiwara Sanesada (1139–91) has been rendered: "The cuckoo called: / I looked towards the sound, / But only the moon / Of the dawn was there."[11] This is presumably the real moon, a crescent rising just ahead of the sun, but the linking of call and light is still decisive. To one who knows the long history of poetry, Chiyo's poem will echo and evoke and allude to it in rich but very light touches of "intertextuality."

What can a translator do about the 5–7–5 form of haiku? As we noted in Chapter 2, the Japanese syllable is defined differently from the way linguists define it – that is, all syllables have one mora (there are no diphthongs or long vowels, no consonant clusters, no codas) and what looks like a coda in a final -*n* is counted as another syllable (in ancient Japanese it was probably -*nu*). But to count English syllables is close enough. Can they be distributed among the three lines in effective phrases and sounds? Even if we decide we can live with "cuckoo," we have to pad out the final line with three more syllables. "I hear the cuckoo" would be too crude, and redundant, since "ear(s)" would have already been named in line 2, and it is night, after all: one isn't going to *see* the cuckoo. And putting "I" in there is a little too self-assertive for this impersonal observation. Probably the best we can do is "It is the cuckoo," with three useless but fairly harmless little words. We should remember, too, that there was probably an understood pause of three morae at the end of the first line and a pause of one mora at the end of the second. (See page 49 above.) The three-beat pause makes "but" a little less satisfactory as a rendering of *ga*, since "but" leans forward while *ga* leans back. The first line seals itself off a little, as if it meant something like "yes, it is darkness's night," and we might punctuate it with a dash, but something like "but" seems essential to any English rendition of line 2. That line, with its shorter pause at the end, might be punctuated with a colon, to both lead into, and delay for a beat, the cuckoo.

It is surely essential to capture the contrast between the two kinds of night – we might almost say the two possessors of night, *yami* and *tsuki* – so we might try "Night of darkness, but / in my ears a night of moon." But "night of moon" doesn't sound like English, so we might try "in my ears a moonlit night." That sounds all right, though it loses the parallel construction of the original. Is there a way to pick up something of the similarity between *yami* and *mimi*, which begin the lines they are in? I don't think we can find appropriate synonyms for "darkness" or "ear" that sound like each other, but we might try to bring out a hint that darkness and ear can each *contain* a kind of night. So perhaps: "In the darkness, night, / But in the ear, moonlit night: / It is the cuckoo!" I invite my readers to keep trying different phrases until something shines in their ear.

There is no stumbling block like "cuckoo" in the other haiku I will discuss, but it has some subtle features difficult to capture in English. It is by a younger contemporary of Chiyo, the eminent poet Buson (1715–83):

> Yuku ware ni
> Going for me
> todomaru nare ni
> staying for you
> aki futatsu.
> autumns two.

The two verb forms *yuku* and *todomaru* are not really gerunds, as the English gloss suggests. We might be tempted to offer "It's for me to go / it's for you to stay," but the Japanese words are not infinitives either, which the language lacks. They are basic finite forms in the present tense, but like all Japanese verbs they are unmarked for person, so to use gerunds or infinitives in a translation does not seem misleading. Like the Chiyo poem, the phrases are contained nicely in their three lines, and the first two are parallel, even with a kind of rhyme on the two pronouns, *ware* and *nare*. But if the two friends rhyme, they must now part, and autumn is coming. We can take autumn as the literal season that, now come round, demands the parting of the friends, as the speaker must end his summer visit, or we can take it as a metaphorical autumn, a kind of dying, that the parting itself, whatever caused it, will bring about. There is no need to choose between these readings, and other resonances are possible, readily enough translated because autumn and parting have melancholic meanings in virtually all cultures. What is harder to capture is the last line. To someone reading or hearing the original poem slowly, *aki* would certainly be taken as singular for a moment, perhaps as leading to something like "divides us" or "will be harsh." So it is a little surprising to find *futatsu* as its modifier. "Two" might have come earlier, but the simple placing of the contrasting fates of the friends in separate lines is twoness enough. The poem implies that such is the union of souls between these two friends that, when they part, something metaphysical happens: autumn itself splits into two. That in turn might suggest that the friends will experience their autumns very differently, but I think we might take it as hinting that the two autumns may well be very much alike, sad and lonely for each friend as he longs for the other, but they will be too far apart to even consider trying to share their autumns, which will remain two. And there may also be a hint, if I am not imagining things, that their autumns apart will each seem like two autumns, either in length or in intensity of autumnness. Many of these nuances will be carried across by the inevitable English rendering of "two autumns" (padded out to "there are two autumns," perhaps), but not that little shiver of uncertainty that Japanese word order and the lack of plural markers provide.

The The

I would like to conclude these reflections by considering the peculiar ending of Wallace Stevens's poem "The Man on the Dump," which was discussed in Chapter 7. The last line is "Where was it one first heard of the truth? The the." As I was trying to understand what this poem tells us about metaphors, I got to wondering how on earth this line could be translated into a language with genders – that is, into virtually any other European language, where definite articles, along with some pronouns and all nouns, adjectives, and other determiners, fall into masculine or feminine categories, or, if there are three genders, into masculine, feminine, or neuter. If the last two words are a stammer, as a few of my colleagues have suggested, then there is a simple answer: use the gender of the article preceding "truth." I have found two translations that seem to have that idea in mind. An on-line Italian version, by Giuseppe Genna, offers this: *Dove fu che qualcuno menzionò la verità? La la* ("Where was it that someone mentioned the truth? The the"). *Verità* is feminine, so the article, *la*, is repeated. A German version by Rainer Schmidt reads: *Wo hörte man denn zuerst von der Wahrheit? Der der* ("Where did one first hear of the truth? The the"). Here *Wahrheit* is feminine, so the article, *der*, is repeated. German marks articles for case (and number) as well as gender, so the form *der*, which we might at first take as the masculine nominative singular, is in fact the feminine dative singular here, following the preposition *von*. A more exact rendering of the German back into English, then, would be "Where did one hear of the truth? Of the of the."

But surely the last two words are not a stammer, not a hesitant continuation of the question, but, as the punctuation alone implies, it is either: (1) a substitution of "the" for "truth," as if to restate the question more definitively ("Where was it one first heard of the the?"), implying that "the" is truth in a sense that is truer than the word "truth" can convey; or (2) an answer to the question posed, as if "the" is the location where one first heard of the truth. I lean toward the second of these, but the expression is so strange that it might mean the former, or something else altogether. At any rate, it seems certain that the second "the" is a noun. It is a noun in Stevens's line "There was that difference between the and an" in "Extracts from Addresses to the Academy of fine Ideas" (4.10), though both "the" and "an" might have been enclosed in quotation marks without a severe change in meaning, whereas if you put them around the second "the" in "The the" (making it "The 'the'") you will turn what seems a fundamental statement about reality, something ontological, into a statement about words. Of course, some linguistic determinists might say there is no difference, because language constitutes our world, but I don't believe that, and I don't think Stevens did.

Taking the second "the" as a noun, then, how should it be translated into a gendered language? A French translation by Gilles Mourier, posted on-line, reads: *Où donc entendit-on parler / Pour la première fois de vérité? Le le* ("Where then did one hear [someone] speak for the first time of truth? The the"). Mourier seems to agree that the article is not tied to the word "truth," though it is interesting that he leaves out the feminine article (*la*) that would normally precede *vérité*, unlike the Italian translator, who has *la verità*, perhaps because Mourier does not want to give the impression that he is simply "correcting" the gender of the article. In a two-gendered language, such as French and Italian, the masculine form would be the default or unmarked form, while in a three-gendered language, such as German, the unmarked form would be masculine or perhaps neuter. On the noun-based interpretation of the poem, the German might read *Der der*, or even *Der Der*, since nouns in German are capitalized, but, because this nominative form is identical to the dative feminine, to use it would import a distracting ambiguity. *Das das*, the neuter form, nominative case, or *Das Das*, would seem a better solution. It may sound strange to German ears, evoking Dada irrelevantly, but "the the" certainly sounds strange to English ears.[12] Mourier has it right with his *Le le*. Spanish has two genders, but it also has a neuter definite article (*lo*) used with adjectives to make them abstract nouns (as in *lo bueno* ["the good"]). A colleague who teaches Spanish has suggested *Lo el* for "The the": *el*, the article used as a noun, is masculine, the default form, but because it is akin to an adjective, the article that this article-noun takes is neuter.

Most modern European languages have definite articles, but suppose we want to translate Stevens's poem into Japanese, which lacks them. What could we do? The closest thing at hand would be the demonstrative determiners corresponding to "this" and "that." With them, we could not come very close, I think, to the effect of the original. There are three such terms, moreover, with three deictic positions: *kono* ("this" – near me), *sono* ("that" – near you), and *ano* ("that" – over there); we would have to choose one. We would have the same problem if we wanted, for some reason, to put the poem into Latin, which also lacked articles: we would have to use *hic, iste*, or *ille*. The case seems hopeless, for "this this" and "that that," whatever they might mean, don't mean "the the," whatever *that* means.

The sort of things we think of when we think of what gets lost in translation might be such words as French *esprit*, which means "wit" as well as "mind" and "spirit," or German *gemütlich*, which means "cosy," "comfortable," and something else ineffably German. Or we might think of idioms, registers, sound-effects, and distinctive word order. But here, at least in some languages, what gets lost is "the," and thus the poem as a whole, the very thing, the the.

Notes

1. As opposed to *intralingual* translation, or rewording, and *intersemiotic* translation, or transmutation into nonverbal signs. See Jakobson, "On Linguistic Aspects of Translation." David Bellos rightly objects to some of the extended meanings of "translation," such as turning a novel into a movie (*Is That a Fish?* Ch. 29).
2. What Frost actually said was a little less quotable: "I like to say, guardedly, that I could define poetry this way: it is that which is lost out of both prose and verse in translation" (Brooks and Warren, *Conversations*, 7). Poetry, then, is something other than verse or prose but may inhabit either one, but only in their original language.
3. Preface to Denham's translation of *The Destruction of Troy*, quoted in Bassnett-McGuire, *Translation Studies*, 59.
4. Arthur Rimbaud, *Poésies / Une saison en enfer / Illuminations*, 70; Charles Causley, *Sleeper in a Valley*.
5. Well, "hill-tops" and "tree-tops" rhyme on the slightly less stressed syllable of these compounds.
6. A solution replicated by Rita Dove in her translation, in *The New Yorker*, 13 November 2017, p. 63.
7. Venuti, *Scandal of Translation*, 11, 12. For some skeptical comments about foreignization, see Bellos, *Is That a Fish?* Ch. 5.
8. The phrase "a flavor of Chinese" is Robert Frost's description of Pound's translations: Brooks and Warren, *Conversations*, 10.
9. "Deictic" words, as we noted in Chapter 4, are dependent on the positions of speaker and addressee, such as "I" and "you," "here" and "there," "now" and "then." English used to distinguish among three positions with "this," "that," and "yon."
10. Translated by Geoffrey Bownas and Anthony Thwaite in *Penguin Book of Japanese Verse*, 83.
11. Bownas and Thwaite, *Penguin Book of Japanese Verse*, 101.
12. I am grateful to Rainer Schmidt for his personal communications about his choice of *Der der*.

APPENDIX

Quantity and Pitch in Greek Verse

In Chapter 2, I suggested that, even though the basis of Greek meter is the length of time a syllable occupies, the pitch accent of spoken Greek might sometimes be recruited for special effects. In everyday Greek, we think, the voice rose about a musical fifth on some syllables (marked acute in written texts), and rose to a fifth and then fell on other syllables, always long (marked circumflex); if the acute fell at the end of a word, it was probably raised a little less, perhaps a third (marked grave), unless the following word was an "enclitic," a little unaccented word that attached to the preceding word (with a meaning such as "some" or "my"). All words have only one pitch accent unless, again, an enclitic induces an acute on the final syllable of a polysyllabic word whose normal accent comes early.[1] No doubt a pitched syllable was often louder, and it is probable that there were secondary stresses of a sort on some unaccented syllables. But neither pitch nor stress was the basis of Greek (or Latin) meter, and in spoken Greek the accent was just as likely to fall on a light syllable as a heavy one. The question naturally arises: was the pitch accent ever taken into consideration by poets? The demands of quantitative meter were so rigorous, one might think, that poets could hardly have made the effort to do something interesting with pitch as well. Still, here and there, some striking patterns are evident.

The opening two lines of the *Odyssey*, for example:

ἄνδρα μοι ἔννεπε, μοῦσα, πολύτροπον, ὃς μάλα πολλὰ
andra moi ennepe, mousa, polytropon, hos mala polla
man me tell, Muse, much-turning, who (was) very much

πλάγχθη, ἐπεὶ Τροίης ἱερὸν πτολίεθρον ἔπερσε:
plank^h^t^h^ē, epei Troiēs hieron ptoliet^h^ron eperse.
driven about, after Troy's holy citadel he sacked.

The first line is all dactyls, and the pitch accent falls on the heavy (downbeat) syllable of the first four *metra*; the circumflex[2] on μοῦσα would sound like an acute on the first mora of the diphthong (ou, probably pronounced like English oo). But then, just when we are told that Odysseus was buffeted about, the accent also hops about before it settles down with a repeated syncopation on the second light syllable before each of the last two *metra*.

— U U —UU — U U — UU — UU — X
ἄνδρα μοι | ἔννεπε, | μοῦσα, πο|λύτροπον,| ὃς μάλα | πολλὰ
andra moi ennepe, mousa, polytropon,   hos mala polla

— U U— —— UU— UU —U U— X
πλάγχθη, ἐ|πεὶ Τροί|ης ἱε|ρὸν πτολί|εθρον ἔ|περσε:
plank^h^t^h^ē, epei Troiēs hieron   ptoliet^h^ron eperse.

For another example, here are the opening lines of the *parodos* (the entry of the chorus) of Aeschylus' *Agamemnon*:

U U— U U—U U— UU—
δέκατον | μὲν ἔτος |τόδ' ἐπεὶ | Πριάμου
dekaton   men etos tod' epei Priamou
(It is the) tenth year now since Priam's

U U —UU—
μέγας ἀν|τίδικος,
megas antidikos,
great   adversary

UU—UU— — UU ——
Μενέλα|ος ἄναξ |ἠδ' Ἀγα|μέμνων,
Menelaos anax ēd' Agamemnōn
Menelaos lord   and Agamemnon

U U— UU———— — —
διθρόνου | Διόθεν |καὶ δισ|κήπτρου
dit^h^ronou Diot^h^en kai diskēptrou
of double-throned from Zeus and double-sceptred . . .

Until halfway through the third line it is all regular anapests, and if you note the acute accents you see a striking pattern. The first line falls into two halves identical in pitch pattern: U U — U U — (twice) where the boldface shorts are accented. The second line has two identical *metra* like the first *metron* of each pair in the first line: U U —. The third line begins with two identical *metra* like the second *metron* of the first line: U U —. Then the third line pivots its meter dramatically to dactyls, to bring out the doomed hero of the play, and perhaps to allude to Homer's meter; there is no accent on the first of these two dactyls but the second has an acute on the downbeat. The fourth line, with its repetition of *di-*, reverts to anapests, and again the first two *metra* are accentually alike: ∪ ∪ —. And then the final two *metra*, which we might call dactyls too, echo the final pair of the third line: no accent in the first of these (not counting the grave) but an acute on the downbeat of the second.

Is this sort of pattern a fanciful illusion? Is it merely the result of chance? We might not expect an oral bard such as Homer, who had to improvise his performance, to be capable of such a thing, but even he would have had a lifetime to revise his lines and think up some good new ones. Aeschylus certainly sat down and wrote his plays, and may have revised them during rehearsals. (In Chapter 3, we saw a passage from Euripides that is also remarkable for its placement of pitches.) We would need to look at a lot of verse, and establish some statistical controls, but I would not rule out the likelihood that, at least for brief passages, Greek poets were capable of building an intricate interplay between meter and pitch.[3]

Notes

1. On evidence for the pitch accent, see Allen, *Vox Graeca*, 116–30, and Stanford, *Sound of Greek*.

2. In the typeface used here the tilde (~) substitutes for the circumflex (^).

3. One factor militating against making much out of pitch patterns is that, in choral odes, there is little correspondence between strophe and antistrophe in accents, while there is – as there must be – exact correspondence between (quantitative) meters.

    When I was a student at Swarthmore College in 1965, I heard W. B. Stanford lecture on Greek pitch accents, and I taught myself to chant them according to his theory, which he published in 1967 as *The Sound of Greek*. Shortly after his visit, I noticed the pattern in the *Agamemnon*, and sent my findings to him. He sent a kind reply encouraging me to pursue the subject, but I did not go on in Classics and I let it go.

Works Cited

Abrams, M. H. *The Mirror and the Lamp: Romantic Theory and the Critical Tradition.* Oxford University Press, 1953.

Abrams, M. H., and Geoffrey Galt Harpham. *A Glossary of Literary Terms*, 9th edn. Boston: Wadsworth Cengage, 2009.

Aeschylus. *The Frogs.* Ed. W. B. Stanford. London: Macmillan, 1958.

Alkire, Ti, and Carol Rosen. *Romance Languages: A Historical Introduction.* Cambridge University Press, 2010.

Allen, W. Sidney. *Vox Graeca: The Pronunciation of Classical Greek*, 3rd edn. Cambridge University Press, 1987.

Anderson, Earl R. *A Grammar of Iconism.* Cranbury, N.J.: Associated University Presses, 1998. Especially Chs. 3, "Empirical Foundations," and 5, "Onomatopoeia."

Aristotle. *Poetics.* Ed. and commentary D. W. Lucas. Oxford University Press, 1968.

Auden, W. H. *The English Auden: Poems, Essays, and Dramatic writings, 1927–1939.* Ed. Edward Mendelson. New York: Random House, 1977.

Austin, J. L. *How to Do Things with Words.* Cambridge, MA: Harvard University Press, 1962.

Bakker, Egbert J. "Homeric Discourse and Enjambement: A Cognitive Approach." *Transactions of the American Philological Association* 120 (1990): 1–21.

Bassnett-McGuire, Susan. *Translation Studies.* London: Methuen, 1980.

Beardsley, Monroe C. *Aesthetics: Problems in the Philosophy of Criticism.* New York: Harcourt, Brace, 1958.

The Possibility of Criticism. Detroit: Wayne State University Press, 1970.

Behler, Ernst. *German Romantic Literary Theory.* Cambridge University Press, 1993.

Bellos, David. *Is That a Fish in Your Ear? Translation and the Meaning of Everything.* New York: Faber and Faber, 2011.

Benjamin, Walter. *Illuminations.* Trans. Harry Zohn. New York: Schocken, 1969.

Bergmann, Claudia. *Childbirth as a Metaphor of Crisis.* Berlin: De Gruyter, 2008.

Berthon, H. E., ed. *Nine French Poets: 1820–1880.* London: Macmillan, 1957.

Black, Max. *Models and Metaphors.* Ithaca, NY: Cornell University Press, 1962.

"More about Metaphor." In Andrew Ortony, ed. *Metaphor and Thought* (1979). 2nd edn. Cambridge University Press, 1993.

Blumenberg, Hans. "Light as a Metaphor for Truth" (1957). Trans. Joel Anderson. In David Michael Levin, ed. *Modernity and the Hegemony of Vision*. Berkeley: University of California Press, 1993.

Shipwreck with Spectator: Paradigm of a Metaphor for Existence (1979). Trans. Stephen Rendell. Cambridge, MA: MIT Press, 1997.

Bök, Christian. *Eunoia*. Toronto: Coach House Books, 2009.

Botet, Serge. *Petit traité de la Métaphore*. Presses Universitaires de Strasbourg, 2008.

Bownas, Geoffrey, and Anthony Thwaite, eds. and trans. *The Penguin Book of Japanese Verse*. London: Penguin, 1998.

Bradford, Richard. *A Linguistic History of English Poetry*. London: Routledge, 1993.

Bredin, Hugh. "Onomatopoeia as a Figure and a Linguistic Principle." *New Literary History* 27:3 (Summer 1996): 555–69.

Brooke-Rose, Christine. *A Grammar of Metaphor*. London: Secker and Warburg, 1958.

Brooks, Cleanth, and Robert Penn Warren. *Conversations on the Craft of Poetry*. New York: Holt Rinehart, 1961.

Burke, Kenneth. "Four Master Tropes." In *A Grammar of Motives*. New York: Prentice-Hall, 1945.

"On Musicality in Verse" (1940). In *The Philosophy of Literary Form*. New York: Random House, 1941.

Byron, Lord. *Byron's Letters and Journals*. 13 volumes. Ed. Leslie Marchand. Cambridge, MA: Belknap Press (Harvard), 1973–94.

Campbell, D. A., ed. and trans. *Sappho and Alcaeus*. Cambridge, MA: Harvard University Press (Loeb Classical Library), 1982.

Carper, Thomas, and Derek Attridge. *Meter and Meaning: An Introduction to Meter in Poetry*. New York: Routledge, 2003.

Casanova, Pascale. *La langue mondiale: Traduction et domination*. Paris: Seuil, 2015.

Causley, Charles. *Sleeper in a Valley* ("limited edition broadsheet"). St. Saviour, Jersey: Robert Tilling, 1979.

Chomsky, Noam. *Syntactic Structures*. 's-Gravenhage: Mouton, 1957.

Clark, John, Colin Yallop, and Janet Fletcher. *An Introduction to Phonetics and Phonology*, 3rd edn. Malden, MA: Blackwell, 2007.

Cole, Deborah, and Mizuki Miyashita. "The Function of Pauses in Metrical Studies: Acoustic Evidence from Japanese Verse." In B. Elan Dresher and Nila Friedberg, eds. *Formal Approaches to Poetry*. Berlin: De Gruyter Mouton, 2006.

Culler, Jonathan. *Structuralist Poetics*. Ithaca, NY: Cornell University Press, 1975.

Theory of the Lyric. Cambridge, MA: Harvard University Press, 2015.

Curme, George O. *English Grammar*. New York: Harper and Row, 1947.

Dane, Joseph A. *The Long and the Short of It: A Practical Guide to European Versification Systems*. University of Notre Dame Press, 2010.

Darwin, Charles. *The Descent of Man*. (1871). In James D. Watson, ed. *Darwin: The Indelible Stamp*. Philadelphia: Running Press, 2005.

David, A. P. *The Dance of the Muses: Choral Theory and Ancient Greek Poetics.* Oxford University Press, 2006.

Derrida, Jacques. "White Mythology: Metaphor in the Text of Philosophy" (1971). Trans. Alan Bass. *New Literary History* 6:1 (Autumn 1974): 5–74. Rpt. in *Margins of Philosophy.* University of Chicago Press, 1982.

Donoghue, Denis. *Metaphor.* Cambridge, MA: Harvard University Press, 2014.

Dorsch, T. S., ed. and trans. *Classical Literary Criticism: Aristotle, Horace, Longinus.* Harmondsworth: Penguin, 1965.

Drosdowski, Günther. *Duden: Das Herkunftswörterbuch.* Mannheim: Duden Verlag, 1997.

Eagleton, Terry. *How to Read a Poem.* London: Blackwell, 2007.

Ellmann, Richard. *Ulysses on the Liffey.* New York: Oxford University Press, 1972.

Fabb, Nigel. *Linguistics and Literature.* Malden, MA: Blackwell, 1997.
  What is Poetry? Cambridge University Press, 2015.

Fabb, Nigel, and Morris Halle. *Meter in Poetry: A New Theory.* Cambridge University Press, 2008.
  "Pairs and Triplets: A Theory of Metrical Verse." In Jean-Louis Aroui and Andy Arleo, eds. *Towards a Typology of Poetic Forms.* Amsterdam: John Benjamins, 2009.

Fenollosa, Ernest. *The Chinese Written Character as a Medium for Poetry.* Ed. Ezra Pound (1918). New York: Fordham University Press, 2008.

Flescher, Jacqueline. "French." In W. K. Wimsatt, Jr., ed. *Versification: Major Language Types.* New York University Press, 1972.

Gardner, Thomas. "The Old English Kenning: A Characteristic Feature of Germanic Poetical Diction?" *Modern Philology* 67:2 (1969): 109–17.

Gibbs, Raymond W., Jr. "Process and Product in Making Sense of Tropes." In Andrew Ortony, ed. *Metaphor and Thought* (1979), 2nd edn. Cambridge University Press, 1993.

Gilman, Margaret. *The Idea of Poetry in France.* Cambridge, MA: Harvard University Press, 1958.

Group μ. *A General Rhetoric.* Trans. Paul B. Burrell and Edgar Slotkin. Baltimore, MD: Johns Hopkins University Press, 1981.

Greene, Roland, ed. *The Princeton Encyclopedia of Poetry and Poetics,* 4th edn. Princeton University Press, 2012.

Hall, T. Alan, ed. *Distinctive Feature Theory.* Berlin: Mouton de Gruyter, 2001.

Heidegger, Martin. *What is Called Thinking?* [*Was Heißt Denken?* 1954]. Trans. J. Glenn Gray. New York: Harper and Row, 1968.

Henderson, Harold G. *An Introduction to Haiku.* Garden City, NY: Doubleday, 1958.

Hirsch, E. D., Jr. *Validity in Interpretation.* New Haven: Yale University Press, 1967.

Huntington, Cynthia, Heather McHugh, Paul Muldoon, and Charles Simic. "How to Peel a Poem: Five Poets Dine Out on Verse." *Harper's* (September 1999).

Jahn, Manfred. "'Colorless Green Ideas Sleep Furiously': A Linguistic Test Case and its Appropriations." In Marion Gymnich, Ansgar Nünning, and Vera

Nünning, eds. *Literature and Linguistics: Approaches, Models and Applications.* Trier: Wissenschaftlicher Verlag Trier, 2002.

Jakobson, Roman. *Language in Literature.* Cambridge, MA: Harvard University Press, 1987.

    On Language. Ed. Linda R. Waugh and Monique Monville-Burston. Cambridge, MA: Harvard University Press, 1990.

    "On Linguistic Aspects of Translation" (1959). In Lawrence Venuti, ed. *The Translation Studies Reader.* London and New York: Routledge, 2000.

Jakobson, Roman, and Linda R. Waugh. *The Sound Shape of Language*, 3rd edn. Berlin: Mouton de Gruyter, 2002. Especially Ch. 4, "The Spell of Speech Sounds."

Jameson, Fredric. *The Prison-House of Language.* Princeton University Press, 1972.

Jespersen, Otto. *Growth and Structure of the English Language* (1905), 9th edn. New York: Doubleday Anchor, 1956.

    Language: Its Nature, Development, and Origin (1922). Rpt. New York: Norton, 1964. Especially Ch. 22, "Sound Symbolism."

    "Symbolic Value of the Vowel I" (1933). In *Selected Writings*. London: Allen and Unwin, 1960.

Joyce, James. *A Portrait of the Artist as a Young Man* (1916). Rpt. New York: Penguin, 1992.

Kenner, Hugh. *The Pound Era.* Berkeley: University of California Press, 1971.

Kofman, Sarah. *Nietzsche and Metaphor.* Trans. Duncan Large. Stanford University Press, 1993.

Kövecses, Zoltan. *Metaphor: A Practical Introduction.* 2nd edn. New York: Oxford University Press, 2010.

Lakoff, George, and Mark Johnson. *Metaphors We Live By.* University of Chicago Press, 1980.

    More than Cool Reason: A Field Guide to Poetic Metaphor. University of Chicago Press, 1989.

Lambrecht, Knud. *Information Structure and Sentence Form.* Cambridge University Press, 1994.

Lanham, Richard A. *A Handlist of Rhetorical Terms.* Berkeley: University of California Press, 1969.

Lass, Roger. *Old English: A Historical Linguistic Companion.* Cambridge University Press, 1994.

    Phonology: An Introduction to Basic Concepts. Cambridge University Press, 1984.

Leach, Edmund. *Lévi-Strauss.* London: Fontana/Collins, 1970.

Leech, Geoffrey N. *A Linguistic Guide to English Poetry.* London: Longman, 1969.

Lévi-Strauss, Claude. "The Structural Study of Myth." *Journal of American Folklore* 78:270 (Oct.–Dec. 1955): 428–44. Rpt. in *Structural Anthropology.* New York: Basic Books, 1963.

Lieber, Rochelle. *Introducing Morphology*, 2nd edn. Cambridge University Press, 2016.

Little, Roger. "A Study in Comparative Translation: Rimbaud's *Le Dormeur du val.*" In Sergio Sacchi, ed. *Rimbaud: Le poème en prose et la traduction poétique.* Tübingen: Gunter Narr Verlag, 1988.

Lonsdale, Roger, ed. *The Poems of Gray, Collins and Goldsmith*. London: Longman, 1969.

Lowell, Robert. *History*. New York: Farrar, Straus, 1973.

Imitations. New York: Farrar, Straus, 1962.

Mallarmé, Stéphane. *Divagations* (1897). Trans. Barbara Johnson. Cambridge, MA: Harvard University Press, 2007.

McGinn, Colin. *Prehension: The Hand and the Emergence of Humanity*. Cambridge, MA: MIT Press, 2015.

McKie, Michael. "Semantic Rhyme: A Reappraisal." *Essays in Criticism* 46:4 (1996): 340–58.

Miller, G. A. "The Magical Number Seven, Plus or Minus Two: Some Limits on Our Capacity for Processing Information." *Psychological Review* 63:2 (1956): 81–97.

Nietzsche, Friedrich. *On the Genealogy of Morality* (1887). Ed. and trans. Maudemarie Clark and Alan J. Swensen. Indianapolis: Hackett, 1998.

The Portable Nietzsche. Ed. and trans. Walter Kaufmann. New York: Viking, 1954.

Odden, David. *Introducing Phonology*, 2nd edn. Cambridge University Press, 2013.

Olson, Charles. *Selected Writings*. Ed. Robert Creeley. New York: New Directions, 1966.

The Maximus Poems. New York: Jargon / Corinth Books, 1960.

Onians, Richard Broxton. *The Origins of European Thought: About the Body, the Mind, the Soul, the World, Time, and Fate*. Cambridge University Press, 1959.

Ortony, Andrew, ed. *Metaphor and Thought*, 2nd edn. Cambridge University Press, 1993. (1st edn. 1979).

Ovid. *Heroides and Amores*. Trans. Grant Showerman. Cambridge, MA: Harvard University Press (Loeb Classical Library), 1914.

Petrey, Sandy. *Speech Acts and Literary Theory*. New York: Routledge, 1990.

Picoche, Jacqueline. *Le Robert dictionnaire étymologique du français*. Paris: Robert, 1994.

Plato. *Symposium*. Trans. Alexander Nehamas and Paul Woodruff. Indianapolis: Hackett, 1989.

The Collected Dialogues of Plato. Ed. Edith Hamilton and Huntington Cairns. Bollingen Series of Princeton University Press, 1961.

Pope, J. C. *The Rhythm of Beowulf*. New Haven: Yale University Press, 1942.

Powell, Barry P. *Homer and the Origin of the Greek Alphabet*. Cambridge University Press, 1991.

Putnam, Hilary. "The Meaning of 'Meaning'" In *Mind, Language and Reality*. Cambridge University Press, 1975.

Race, William H. *Pindar I: Olympian Odes, Pythian Odes*. Cambridge, MA: Harvard University Press (Loeb Classical Library), 1997.

Reece, Steve. *Homer's Winged Words*. Leiden: Brill, 2009.

Richards, I. A. *The Philosophy of Rhetoric*. Oxford University Press, 1936.

Richards, Robert J. *The Romantic Conception of Life: Science and Philosophy in the Age of Goethe*. University of Chicago Press, 2002.

Ricoeur, Paul. *The Rule of Metaphor* [*La Métaphore vive*, 1975]. Trans. Robert Czerny with Kathleen McLaughlin and John Costello. University of Toronto Press, 1977.

Rimbaud, Arthur. *Poésies / Une saison en enfer / Illuminations*. Paris: Gallimard, 1999.

Ringe, Don, and Ann Taylor. *The Development of Old English*. Oxford University Press, 2014.

Robb, Graham. *Victor Hugo*. New York: Norton, 1997.

Roca, Iggy, and Wyn Johnson. *A Course in Phonology*. Malden, MA: Blackwell, 1999.

Rosen, Charles. *The Romantic Generation*. Cambridge, MA: Harvard University Press, 1995.

Russom, Geoffrey. *Beowulf and Old English Metre*. Cambridge University Press, 1998.

Sadler, J. D. "Onomatopoeia." *Classical Journal* 67:2 (Dec. 1971 – Jan. 1972): 174–77.

Saeed, John I. *Semantics*, 3rd edn. Malden, MA: Wiley-Blackwell, 2009.

Sampson, Geoffrey. *Writing Systems*. Stanford University Press, 1986.

Saussure, Ferdinand de. *Course in General Linguistics* (1916). Trans. Wade Baskin. New York: Philosophical Library, 1959.

Shaw, Robert B. *Blank Verse: A Guide to its History and Use*. Athens, OH: Ohio University Press, 2007.

Shelley, Percy Bysshe. *Letters*. 2 volumes. Ed. Frederick L. Jones. Oxford: Clarendon, 1964.

Sherbo, Arthur. *English Poetic Diction from Chaucer to Wordsworth*. East Lansing: Michigan State University Press, 1975.

Sipe, Thomas. *Beethoven: Eroica Symphony*. Cambridge University Press, 1998.

Sprinker, Michael. "Gerard Manley Hopkins on the Origin of Language." *Journal of the History of Ideas* 41:1 (Jan.–Mar. 1980): 113–28.

Stanford, W. B. *The Sound of Greek*. Berkeley: University of California Press, 1967.

Steele, Timothy. *All the Fun's in How You Say a Thing: An Explanation of Meter and Versification*. Athens, OH: Ohio University Press, 1999.

Stevens, Wallace. *Opus Posthumous*. London: Faber and Faber, 1957.

Stockwell, Robert P. "On Recent Theories of Metrics and Rhythm in 'Beowulf.'" In C. B. McCully and J. J. Anderson, eds. *English Historical Metrics*. Cambridge University Press, 1996.

Valéry, Paul. *The Art of Poetry*. Trans. Denise Folliot. New York: Vintage, 1961.

Vanasco, Jeannie. "Emily's Lists." *TLS* (13 May 2011): 11.

Vendler, Helen. *Dickinson: Selected Poems and Commentaries*. Cambridge, MA: Harvard University Press, 2010.

Venuti, Lawrence. *The Scandal of Translation*. London: Routledge, 1998.

Wachtel, Michael. *The Development of Russian Verse*. Cambridge University Press, 1998.

Watkins, Calvert. *The American Heritage Dictionary of Indo-European Roots*, 3rd edn. Boston: Houghton Mifflin, 2011.

Wesling, Donald. *The Chances of Rhyme: Device and Modernity.* Berkeley: University of California Press, 1980.

Wiese, Richard. "The Phonology of /r/." In T. Alan Hall, ed. *Distinctive Feature Theory.* Berlin: Mouton de Gruyter, 2001.

Wimsatt, W. K., Jr. "One Relation of Rhyme to Reason." *Modern Language Quarterly* 5 (Sept 1944): 323–38. Rpt. in Wimsatt. *The Verbal Icon.* Lexington: University of Kentucky Press, 1954.

The Prose Style of Samuel Johnson. New Haven: Yale University Press, 1941.

The Verbal Icon. Lexington: University of Kentucky Press, 1954.

ed. *Versification: Major Language Types.* New York University Press, 1972.

Wimsatt, W. K., Jr., and Monroe C. Beardsley. "The Affective Fallacy." *Sewanee Review* 57 (Winter 1949): 458–88.

Rpt. in Wimsatt, *The Verbal Icon.* Lexington: University of Kentucky Press, 1954.

"The Intentional Fallacy." *Sewanee Review* 54 (Summer 1946): 468–88.

Rpt. in Wimsatt, *The Verbal Icon.* Lexington: University of Kentucky Press, 1954.

Wright, George T. "The Lyric Present: Simple Present Verbs in English Lyric Poems." *PMLA* 89:3 (May 1974): 563–79.

Wright, John W. *Shelley's Myth of Metaphor.* Athens, GA: University of Georgia Press, 1970.

Index